ACTIVITY AND AGING

OTHER RECENT VOLUMES IN THE SAGE FOCUS EDITIONS

ACTIVITY AND AGING

Staying Involved in Later Life

John R. Kelly
editor

SAGE PUBLICATIONS
International Educational and Professional Publisher
Newbury Park   London   New Delhi

For information address:

SAGE Publications, Inc.
2455 Teller Road
Newbury Park, California 91320

SAGE Publications Ltd.
6 Bonhill Street
London EC2A 4PU
United Kingdom

SAGE Publications India Pvt. Ltd.
M-32 Market
Greater Kailash I
New Delhi 110 048 India

Printed in the United States of America

Library of Congress Cataloging-in-Publication Data

Main entry under title:

Activity and aging : staying involved in later life / edited by John
  R. Kelly.
      p. cm.—(Sage focus editions : 161)
    Includes bibliographical references and index.
    ISBN 0-8039-5273-2 (cl.).—ISBN 0-8039-5274-0 (pbk.)
      1. Aged—United States. 2. Leisure—Social aspects—United
  States. 3. Leisure—United States—Psychological aspects.
  I. Kelly, John R. (John Robert), 1930-   .
  HQ1064.U5A629 1993
  306.4'812'0846—dc20   93-2582

93 94 95 96 97 10 9 8 7 6 5 4 3 2 1

Sage Production Editor: Astrid Virding

Contents

Introduction

There seems to be little if any disagreement that the engagement in activity by older people is an important element in their quality of life. One approach to satisfactory aging designates two factors as "prerequisites." They are functional health and a viable level of financial support. Without both, every other aspect of life is limited, truncated, and even rendered impossible. For those who have the prerequisites or are able to cope adequately with their limitations, some combination of two other dimensions of life are critical: the quality of relationships, especially close ties with important others, and regular engagement in activity. The two are usually associated when activity is the context of the relationships and communication and sharing with others are a central component of the meaning of the activity. Physical and social activity are consistently associated in longitudinal study not only with higher life satisfaction (Palmore, 1979) but also with better health, longer life, and lower rates of institutionalization (Steinbach, 1991).

In this book, *activity* refers nontechnically to what people do. The focus is for the most part on activity other than employment and necessary maintenance. We are not limited to any set-apart or segregated realm. Rather, activity includes being alone and involved with others, engaged and disengaged, challenged and at ease, spontaneous and organized. Despite the agreement on the importance of activity, the issue has been given little relatively direct research attention. We tend to describe older people who are doing well as "active," "involved," "engaged," and even "busy." We express concern about isolation, dropping out, and inactivity as problems for older persons. We praise programs that engage older persons in regular, exciting, learning, and even demanding activity. We develop a new category of the "active old" to counter the stereotypes of age-related withdrawal. Theoretical formulations offer critiques and alternatives to "disengagement," at least for those who are not "frail" in health or ability. Yet, references to activity tend to be embedded in studies with other foci. We study relationships without identifying what it is that family and friends actually *do* together. We limit studies to particular kinds of programs without finding how they fit into the overall activity patterns of those we study. We even theorize about disengagement without finding out the meanings of engagement.

In 1961 a landmark collection edited by Robert Kleemeier, *Aging and Leisure*, was published that drew attention to the significance of activity in the lives of older persons. Several chapters were based on the Kansas City study of adult life in which a variety of activity engagements were found to be articulated with changing roles and orientations. Attention was given to the varied meanings of activity embedded in their community and family contexts. Now, more than 30 years later, the purpose of this book is to renew our understanding of the activity of older persons based on several lines of research on leisure and aging. It deals with theoretical frameworks for approaching what older people do and what their activity means to them. It ranges into several areas of social gerontology to seek connections between activity and issues such as relationships, resources, organizations, values, gender roles, settings, and developmental orientations. The aim is to bring together theoretical approaches, relevant research, and implications from a novel variety of sources. Several of the authors are social gerontologists who focus on aspects of aging related to activity. Others have focused on activity but usually in ways limited to specific types of activity, settings, or resources. Together the offerings should provide a new, if somewhat complex, agenda for a fuller explanation of what older people do and do not do. Analysis of what we do know should also provide a basis for lines of research into what is not known.

A number of issues will be addressed:

- What is the place and significance of activity in later life?
- What are the varieties of such activity?
- How do these activities articulate with the personal meanings and social contexts of later life?
- What are the common continuities and changes of activity in the later life course?

In selecting authors as well as issues, the editor has drawn on colleagues both in social gerontology and in leisure studies. Each perspective has developed theory and research that complements the other. With some exceptions, however, the two groups of scholars have not been in communication. This volume may help to improve that situation. Social gerontologists have learned a great deal about relationships in later life as well as about certain age-designated environments and programs. Those studying leisure have learned a great deal about the forms and meanings of a wide range of activity but have seldom tied that knowledge to the realities of aging. Cursory references to disengagement and "activity theory" have prefaced too many studies as though that is all that those studying aging have learned in the past 35 years.

This book is not a program book on "how to be happy though old," how to develop catchy programs for old folks, or even how to keep people active. There are some rather direct suggestions, however, about programs, factors in active engagement, and what is really important in the lives of later life adults. As a basis for the reconstitution of many programs, the book offers perspectives rather different from many programmatic presentations and identifies a number of misguided premises for many traditional age-designated offerings.

The book may be the basis for a number of conversations and revised agendas—about research and programs, hopes and problems, and even budgets and policies. Together the chapters offer some new ways of thinking about activity for the aging, new ways of relating formerly unconnected issues, and a new basis for launching further into this significant area of life and study.

References

Kleemeier, R. W. (Ed.). (1961). *Aging and leisure*. New York: Oxford University Press.
Palmore, E. (1979). Predictors of successful aging. *The Gerontologist, 19,* 427-431.
Steinbach, U. (1991). Social networks, institutionalization, and mortality among elderly people in the United States. *Journal of Gerontology, 47*(4), S181-S190.

PART I

Theory and Issues

There is no magical transformation that persons undergo at some standard age, certainly not at 65. There are transitions in later life that have powerful impacts on resources, opportunities, expectations, and relationships. Retirement does remove determinative obligations and schedules for those who have been employed. Being widowed does alter the most immediate context of life. Life does change for older adults in both sudden and incremental ways. Activities may also change. Sometimes cost is a factor; in other cases there are losses of common companions, physical abilities, or opportunities. The scheduled freedom of retirement may be countered by other changes that limit anticipated activity.

Yet, those who live through such transitional life events are still essentially the same persons who approached later life. They are still interested in much the same activities as before. They are still bonded to most of the same intimates, family and friends. They view life in much the same ways. Their life-styles remain relatively consistent, conventional or unconventional. If, as is the case for most adults in this culture, they tended to value their families highest in comparison with work or leisure, that commitment remains largely unimpaired. They reformulate their timetables, revise their budgets, and even adjust some associations. But they are still much the same persons. Their strategies for coping with the requirements and opportunities of life remain generally consistent. As a consequence, activity is like other aspects of later life in being characterized by a high degree of *continuity*.

1

Robert Atchley, in the opening chapter, applies his "continuity theory" to the area of activity. He does not claim that life does not change or that individuals do not reform their lives. Rather, how they go about living generally, how they define themselves, and how they comprehend the world change in evolutionary rather than cataclysmic ways in later life. There tends to be a "core self" of identity that is built up consistently through the life course. We come to evaluate our competence and ability in a continuous personal history. We usually go with what has gotten us to where we are now when faced with change. Nonwork activities may become more salient after retirement, but we build on previous experience. Later life selection and refocusing tend to be choice consistent with past learning rather than some sort of age-based "disengagement." Atchley suggests that Baltes's model of selective optimization with compensation offers one way of analyzing how social actors make decisions in regard to activity commitment and engagement. Older persons are still social actors who develop lines of action, not determined digits in the computer of life. They take significant action in both engagement and withdrawal, usually to achieve a balance of life that expresses a variety of themes and meanings.

Sharon Kaufman, in Chapter 2, extends her concept of the "ageless self" by analyzing the values expressed in later life activity commitment. The later life course continues to be a symbolic and active process in which persons develop and shape their lives. Activity orientation is more than "doing something"; it expresses central values. Those who have had a central self-concept of being productive, even of achievement, are likely to continue that orientation in freely chosen activity engagement. Many older persons express the continuity of self by wanting to do something of worth to others, by continuing to be productive in some way. The form of that expression is most often consistent with previous activity patterns, with former investments in skill and associations. The self-defined self as active and worthwhile continues to be a central element in choices. Age and retirement do not transform able selves into an image of the incompetent old. The arenas of effective action are infinitely varied—caregiving and teaching, sport and the arts, gardening and volunteering, organizations and writing, rebuilding cars and designing quilts, environmental activism and creative grandparenting. Identities of ability and worth do not suddenly dissipate when one no longer has to be at work five mornings a week.

It would be a mistake, however, to stereotype all activity by one meaning or dimension, whether productivity or withdrawal. Powell

Lawton, in Chapter 3, draws on several lines of research in demonstrating the multiple meanings of activity. Older persons continue to be complex in their orientations, relationships, and identities. As a consequence, their activity engagements tend to be multidimensional. There is involvement and relaxation, communication and solitude, creativity and entertainment. Older persons, still actively engaged in what Mary Catherine Bateson calls "composing a life" (Bateson, 1990), develop composites or "balances" (Kelly, 1987) of activity appropriate to their self-defined abilities, interests, and opportunities. The experience within the activity itself, "intrinsic" meaning, is important but may be related to developmental and social meanings as well. Factors in such selections include cohort and contemporary norms along with personal continuities and discontinuities. In later years, there may be a "miniaturization" of activity range in a process of constriction. This process, however, may be interpreted as selection and even streamlining for efficiency rather than simple withdrawal. The older person may be seen as retaining important meanings of engagement through compensation and constriction even when activities are altered or even discarded. Activity reflects both ageless values and orientations as well as age-related capabilities and expectations.

The emphasis on continuity should not obscure that there is also significant change in the lives of older people. Chapter 4 by David Chiriboga and Robert Pierce uses a unique longitudinal data set to trace age-related patterns of activity. Even through stressful events there is considerable continuity in activity investments. Despite wide differences in the types of activity, there is more stability than change even through stressful events. Further, their typology of activity styles ties activity patterns into more general life-styles. In the context of the life journey, leisure is not just a shopping list of activities but a pattern articulated with values and role sequences.

There is always the danger in North America that we focus entirely on our own research and forget that there are other cultures and social systems. In Chapter 5 Walter Tokarski reviews research in Europe that also addresses the activity patterns and meanings of older persons. The results may not be startlingly different but do illustrate that cultural values and opportunity structures are significant factors in activity engagement. Further, in contrast to the political fragmentation of interest in leisure activity in the United States, European countries are developing policies of "activation" as a response to the recognized significance of activity for older persons.

The themes of continuity in identities, values, and life strategies suggest that activity selections may express persistence in meanings even when forms and contexts of activity change. The multiple meanings of activity are both existential and social. That is, they express what the actor is and is becoming through action that creates as well as expresses the self. Activity, however, is also social in its relational aims as well as being based in the culture and opportunity structures of a particular social system and historical context. Who we have become and who we are becoming are both elements in what we choose to do as social actors.

References

Bateson, M. (1990). *Composing a life*. New York: Penguin.
Kelly, J. (1987). *Peoria winter: Styles and resources in later life*. Lexington, MA: Lexington, Free Press.

1

Continuity Theory and the Evolution of Activity in Later Adulthood

ROBERT C. ATCHLEY

If we are to understand how activities evolve in later adulthood, we need solid concepts to enable us to think clearly about activities and theories of adult development to help us explain how activities fit into personal evolution in later adulthood. This chapter is about *continuity theory* (Atchley, 1989), a theory of adult development, which proposes that in making adaptive choices middle-aged and older adults attempt to preserve and maintain existing psychological and social patterns by applying familiar knowledge, skills, and strategies. Applied to activities, continuity theory maintains that adults gradually develop stable patterns of activity and that, in adapting to aging, adults engage in thought and take action designed to preserve and maintain these patterns in their general form.

Perspectives Used in Continuity Theory

Continuity theory is *evolutionary*. It assumes that the patterns of ideas and skills, which people use to adapt and act, develop and persist over time; that a course of developmental direction can usually be identified; and that the individual's orientation is not to remain personally unchanged but rather consistent with the individual's past, to influence the direction and degree of change in accordance with the individual's goals. Thus individuals are presumed to play an active part in their own development.

Continuity theory is *constructionist*. It assumes that people, in response to their life experiences, actively develop individualized personal constructs (Kelly, 1955), ideas of what is going on in the world and why. Some of our most important personal constructs concern our concepts of self and our personal life-styles. Continuity theory also acknowledges that our personal constructs are greatly influenced by the social constructions of reality that we learn from those around us and from mass media.

Continuity theory is about *adaptation*. It assumes that individual choices are made not only to achieve goals but to adapt to constantly changing circumstances. Accordingly, continuity theory deals with the development and maintenance of adaptive capacity, particularly in the latter part of adulthood. One of the main ideas in continuity theory is that, in adapting to aging, people attempt to preserve and maintain long-standing patterns of thought and behavior that they believe constitute important and potent adaptive skills and arrangements. In other words, when faced with adaptive challenges, people tend to rely on what they see as their established adaptive strengths.

Continuity theory is about *selective investment*. It presumes that people make decisions, based on feedback from experience, about where it is best to focus their efforts to develop skills and knowledge. People select and develop ideas, relationships, environments, and activities based on their personal concepts of desired developmental direction and of available opportunity.

Continuity theory is *not* a theory of successful aging. Unlike activity theory and disengagement theory, which gave opposing prescriptions for successful aging (Havighurst, 1963), continuity theory predicts that in their choices people will show a bias toward what they perceive to be continuity. Success may indeed be the result of these choices, but in some cases it will not (Atchley, 1989). Continuity theory presumes that continuity and change are both present and that people prefer more continuity than change, all other things being equal. A rigid overemphasis on continuity, however, might well interfere with successful adaptation to aging.

A General Outline of Continuity Theory

In discussing continuity, it is important to understand the relationship between continuity and change. *Continuity is not an absence of change.* Continuity refers to a coherence or consistency of patterns over time. Specific changes tend to be given significance in relation to a general notion of a relatively continuous whole. Individual change and evolution are usually perceived as occurring against a backdrop of considerable continuity. Continuity in adult development is paradoxical; there is both similarity over time and obvious change—one can be identifiably similar in comparison with a past self and still have changed considerably.

Continuity is emphasized more than change based on observations by many investigators that aging people use continuity much more than change in describing their own development (e.g., Fiske & Chiriboga, 1990; Kaufman, 1987). People are apparently motivated not only to perceive themselves as characters exhibiting continuity over time but also to *act* to extend that continuity into the future as well (Markus & Herzog, 1991). Continuity theory thus contends that middle-aged and older adults are both predisposed and motivated toward inner psychological continuity as well as outward continuity of social behavior and circumstances.

Internal Continuity

Internal continuity is the persistence over time of psychological patterns of various kinds: temperament, affect, experiences, preferences, skills, dispositions, attitudes, values, beliefs, and worldviews. To have a sense of internal continuity, the individual must have the capacity to see inner change as connected or linked to his or her past and to see that past as sustaining and supporting and justifying the new self.

Self and identity are two important inner mental structures that persist over time. *Self* refers to what we think and feel when we focus attention specifically on ourselves. *Self-concept* is what we think we are like: our appearance, abilities, preferences, emotionality, personal goals, level of performance, attitudes, roles, and so on; the *ideal self* is what we think we ought to be like; and *self-esteem* is how much we like or dislike what we see. Self-esteem is a sum of the relative weights given to both *valued* and *disvalued* aspects of the self-concept (Bengtson, Reedy, & Gordon, 1985). Both the self-concept and the ideal self are often linked to the social roles we play and to social characteristics such as gender, age, race, and social class.

Identity refers to those aspects of self that the individual sees as remaining with him or her regardless of the social situation (Whitbourne, 1986). Some aspects of the self are situational, such as ambition at work, whereas others tend to be with us across a wide variety of social situations. Identity is a core self that stays with us throughout most of the settings in which we find ourselves. Identity also serves as the basis for dealing with new information about the self. Subjectively important changes occur mainly within identity, and changes seen as not affecting identity tend to be discounted as trivial. Identity also serves as the basis for the perception of both continuity and integrity. Identity is not an either/or construct. Identity is a holistic concept that tolerates contradictions.

From middle age on, there is considerable evidence of continuity in the *global* aspects of self. At the same time, there is also considerable evidence of change in *specific* aspects of self. Thus the global assessments and attributions that people make concerning themselves persist despite substantial changes in the details of everyday life (Atchley, 1991). Once formed, identity tends to be resilient, and the components of identity can apparently contain many contradictions and conflicting details without causing the individual to doubt the validity of the global assessment.

Individuals have strong motivation toward internal continuity. Continuity of ideas, especially about the self and identity, acts as an important foundation for everyday decision making. Internal continuity increases our sense of security by providing an element of predictability for actions we take. Indeed, without internal continuity we would be hopelessly confused. Individual competence requires continuity of both knowledge and skills.

The continuity principle within the self contains the ideas used as the basis of self-esteem, which is a function of the relation between one's perceived level of success and one's ideal expectations of self. Self-esteem can be raised either by increasing successes or by lowering ideal expectations. Of course, if ideal expectations of self increase and level of success remains the same, then self-esteem would decrease. Although in the short run people's feelings about themselves can fluctuate a great deal, self-esteem is a more global construct that incorporates data about successes in relation to ideals over a longer time span. For this long-range perspective to develop, there must be a concept of continuity operating in the definition of both success and expectations. It then follows that it is impossible to have durable self-esteem without reference to some notion of continuity.

Despite constant changes within persons and the world around them, achieving internal continuity is not especially difficult. Throughout adulthood, people accumulate an enormous body of data about themselves. In the development and maintenance of identity and self, ideal and actual selves influence one another. For example, a teenager may have an ideal self and identity centered on being an excellent tennis player. If success matches the ideal, then that aspect of identity may remain strong and perhaps even be turned into a vocation. But if the youngster lacks the talent or self-discipline or coaching necessary for success or has an unlucky injury, then reality will usually dampen that particular ideal self and it may even be dropped altogether. Early in adulthood, visions of hoped-for selves and dreaded selves drive motivation (Markus & Nurius, 1986). The results of behavior provide the feedback necessary to gradually identify areas of predictable success. People tend to develop most in areas where they reliably meet success. By middle age, most have identified preferences and competencies that predictably lead to satisfying results and have incorporated them into their identities. It is not difficult to maintain motivation toward inner continuity in the presence of proven patterns for producing a sense of inner well-being.

Mentally healthy adults thus have solid concepts of identity and self that persist over time. This continuity does not refer to an obsessive clinging to the past.

Instead . . . adult identity is like a stage play in which old sets are embellished and sometimes remodeled and new sets sometimes created to add new scenes to familiar acts. Familiar characters get new twists, some characters die or leave, and new characters get added although they are often superficial. However, the self, the perceiver, has absolutely no doubts about who is playing the title role. (Atchley, 1989, p. 187)

Inner continuity is thus a gradual evolution in which new directions are closely linked to and elaborate upon already existing identity.

Internal Continuity and Activities

As we look at how the concept of internal continuity might be applied to the study of activities, concepts such as orientation toward activity domains, activity competence, and activity preference refer to important inner dimensions that could be tracked over time. It is also important to consider the position that activities occupy in identity and self.

Activity domains are general settings for activity such as workplaces, community organizations, families, households, and recreational programs. People do not value these various domains equally; they tend to set different priorities on them and to invest time and energy in mastering these domains accordingly. For example, many people have jobs that are easily mastered and that offer little opportunity for development. Such people tend to downplay the importance of this activity domain in terms of developmental investment even though they understand that satisfactory job performance is an economic essential. By contrast, others have jobs that both require and offer opportunities for constant growth and development. Such people tend to invest large amounts of time and energy in developing and maintaining their job knowledge and skills.

Some people are focused in their orientation to activity domains. They tend to put most of their psychic investment, time, and energy into one activity domain. The workaholic, the person who is involved in a multitude of community organizations, the obsessive artist, the woman completely consumed in being a housewife are all examples of people who are quite focused in their orientation toward activity domains, perhaps overly so. They tend to let other domains slide.

Others take a balanced orientation toward activities and are invested in taking the time and having the knowledge and skills necessary to engage satisfyingly in a wide range of activity domains. Such people are accomplished at their jobs, involved in community organizations, devoted to their families, and skilled at a number of individual activities.

By the time people reach middle age, most have developed a clearly identifiable orientation toward activity domains. Indeed, the construct we call *life-style* is fundamentally influenced by the values contained in the person's orientation toward activity domains. Once fully formed, such orientations tend to persist over time.

Activity competence refers to the knowledge and skills needed to engage in a particular activity. Young people experiment with an enormous range of activities: games, crafts, music, art, dance, sports, fitness activities, outdoor activities, gardening, caring for animals, enjoying fine arts, household maintenance, cooking, reading, helping others, participating in a variety of organizations, and so on and on. Each of these areas of activity requires different knowledge and skills, which must be learned. Very early, most young people realize that it is impossible to be knowledgeable and skillful at everything. They use their experiences to identify those activity areas that both are interesting and seem to have development potential for them. By middle age, most people have spent more than 40 years selecting, refining, and developing their areas of activity competence. These areas of competence are a tremendous personal resource as well as a significant personal investment. It would be surprising if people did *not* continue to use this knowledge and these skills on into later life.

Activity preferences are the activities we value, and these preferences allow us to arrange our preferences into a rough hierarchy. Individual preferences are influenced both by social norms about the appropriateness and desirability of various types of activity and by the levels of satisfaction associated with our experiences of activities. One effect that aging can have on activity preferences is to relax the influence of social norms and increase the weight of personal experience. For example, launching one's children and retirement both are role changes that dramatically free the individual from social demands to put child rearing and employment ahead of other preferences. As a result, many people find that other areas of preferred activity blossom in later adulthood. But this new development is not usually *de nouveau*; instead, development is most likely to occur in activities that are already preferred and in which the individual already has some knowledge and competence.

Individuals vary in the extent to which their identities are based on activities and the position of activities as part of identity may change over time. Fiske and Chiriboga (1990), for example, characterized the types of statements people made about themselves as follows:

- biosocial givens—gender, eye or hair color, nationality
- roles and memberships—worker, housewife, lodge member
- abstract—a person, a human being
- ideological—Republican, Christian
- interests and activities—skier, sailor, theater buff
- physical self—strong, healthy, deaf

- sense of self—outgoing, happy-go-lucky
- interpersonal characteristics—sensitive, aggressive
- personal characteristics—mood states, thinking states

Fiske and Chiriboga found that the self statements of young adults tended to focus on intrapersonal and interpersonal characteristics. These people were trying to establish what they were like, and this had a higher priority than their activities. They described themselves in terms of personal qualities such as being enterprising, intelligent, knowledgeable, uncertain, or somewhat egotistical. They tended not to see themselves in terms of roles or activities. By contrast, empty-nesters tended to focus on interests, activities, roles, and memberships in their statements of self. The retired respondents were similar to the empty-nesters but had added a heightened concern with spirituality.

Fiske and Chiriboga (1990, p. 68) concluded that this evolution of identity seemed completely appropriate.

For people who are still struggling with who they are and where they are going, for example, a focus on inner concerns and self-descriptors seems quite fitting. Similarly, as the years stretch on and the self becomes established, it can now be characterized by givens: the activities and interests that have stabilized and now define the person. An interest in cars or music may not appear to be particularly descriptive of a twenty-year-old, for example, but to a sixty-year-old with a forty-year history of interest in cars or music, this interest may now represent a central theme in life.

Thus young adults often have a rich array of activities but do not know yet whether they want to define themselves in terms of activities and, if so, which ones. By middle age, most people have selected an array of activities and roles on which they are willing to bet their identities. This is why activities may seem more important to middle-aged and older people in comparison with young adults, who tend to take activities for granted and to be preoccupied with other aspects of self. Once people begin to stake their identities on activities, their motivation for continuity in activities is probably heightened.

External Continuity

External continuity is defined in terms of a remembered structure of physical and social environments, role relationships, and activities.

Perceptions of external continuity stem from being and doing in familiar environments, pursuing familiar interests, practicing familiar skills, and interacting with familiar people. External continuity is thus the persistence of a structure of relationships and overt behaviors.

A large number of research studies have documented that there is considerable continuity in skills, activities, and relationships in the lives of adults in their fifties and older.

> Again, this continuity is not a boring sameness for most but rather a comforting routine and familiar sense of direction. No doubt part of the impetus for external continuity is related to restricted opportunity structures resulting from ageism and societal disengagement, but probably a majority of it results from the satisfactions people get from exercising mastery and the value of experience in preventing and minimizing the deleterious effects of physical and psychological aging. (Atchley, 1989, p. 188)

Experience and practice are powerful preventive and compensatory mechanisms for minimizing the negative effects of aging on ability. Both require continuity of activities. Practice has been shown to maintain functioning and minimize declines in several areas of cognition and in physical capacity. Thus external continuity is not only a preference for the familiar but also a way of compensating for the effects of aging.

When adults feel the need for stimulation, they look first to domains in which they have proficiency and for which they have a preference. The specific activity a person selects may be new, but the domain usually is not. For example, people who see themselves as being good at one type of art, sports, or scholarship tend to see themselves as having the capacity to be good at other specific areas within the same general domain. Thus people can try new activities and exhibit continuity at the same time!

People are motivated toward external continuity by a combination of factors. First, people are expected by others to present themselves and behave in ways that are obviously tied to and connected with their past role performances. We want others to be predictable to some extent, so we expect them to display continuity. If we want social support from others, we may have to accommodate their desire that we show continuity. External continuity also increases the predictability of the feedback we get from others. And, as mentioned, external continuity is a way to cope with the physical and mental changes that accompany aging. People are also motivated toward external continuity because continuity reduces ambiguity. If we know that we want to preserve external continuity, then there are far-reaching implications for our choices of activities. Planning and decision making become easier. Especially in a postmodern world, where widely accepted life-style scenarios are hard to come by, continuity is an attractive way to cut through what sometimes seem to be endless numbers of activity choices. But by far the most important factor predisposing people toward external continuity is the success of the patterns. Our past and current activities are what have gotten us to where we are now; and to most people in later life, they seem to be the best bets for the future too.

External Continuity, Aging, and Activities

Continuity theory leads us to expect that, in adjusting their activities to adapt to aging, people would use their concepts of continuity in making decisions. Aging often brings a gradual reduction in the number of activities a person engages in and the amount of time allocated to them. However, Carstensen (1991) posited that this decline was not a result of disengagement but was instead the result of a lifelong process of gradual selection. For example, when she looked at longitudinal data on interpersonal interaction, Carstensen found that contact with acquaintances began to decline early in adulthood and continued to go down throughout middle age. By contrast, contact with close friends increased during the same time frame. She took these data to be more indicative of social selection than social withdrawal. These same data could also be taken as evidence that external continuity is more likely in the inner circle of social relationships than on the periphery.

Baltes and Baltes (1990) held that adaptation to physical, mental, and social changes (often decrements) associated with disability (often associated with advanced aging) was facilitated by a process they called *selective optimization with compensation*. Selection is required by the need to focus on high-priority activities in the face of environmental and physical constraints. Priorities are established by preexisting knowledge, skills, and motivations. *Optimization* refers to behavior by individuals to enhance and enrich their capacity to engage in the activities selected. The idea here is that by focusing energy and resources on selected activities one can still achieve satisfying results, but only if other activities are dropped. *Compensation* is the final element, and it refers to the use of both psychological compensations such as mnemonics to aid memory and technological compensations such as hearing or mobility aids. The point here is that people do not simply accept decrement. They tend to try to compensate for the change so that their level of functioning remains as intact as possible. Baltes, Wahl, and Reichert (1991) contended that this model of selective optimization with compensation could be used to maintain satisfying activity even among those who are severely disabled and living in nursing homes. Obviously, to implement this model, the person would have to employ some concept of continuity in the selection of activities to optimize.

Conclusion

Continuity theory's two dimensions—internal and external continuity—offer a parsimonious set of ideas about how we might expect activities to evolve in the latter part of life. Internal continuity is the development and persistence over time of mental constructs about who we are, what we are capable of, and what is satisfying to us. This evolving body of self-information is used to invest selectively in an array of activities that we expect to serve as part of our future self. In most but not all cases, continuity of ideas and orientations leads to effective adaptation. Accordingly, continuity theory is about development and adaptation, but not necessarily about successful aging.

Inner continuity and continuity of activities reinforce one another. Inner continuity leads to decisions that favor activity continuity and activity continuity produces inner experiences that reinforce inner continuity, especially continuity of identity and self-esteem. Internal continuity meets important individual needs such as security, a sense of direction, and self-esteem. It is not surprising that people value and seek internal continuity. This internal continuity predisposes people toward continuity of activities.

Activity patterns develop out of the individual's attempts to define competencies and preferences. Once developed, these patterns are generally maintained and developed even further. Continuity of activity patterns is a desirable end in itself because external continuity is an important way to minimize the negative effects of physical and mental aging, to facilitate decision making about activities, and to meet the expectations others have of us.

Aging often motivates people to restrict their activities. In doing so, they use selection processes that have served them over their entire adulthood as they experimented, developed, and refined their activities.

Thus even the process of adapting activities to meet the challenges of aging often rests on continuity of adaptation patterns from the past.

References

Atchley, R. C. (1989). A continuity theory of normal aging. *The Gerontologist, 29,* 183-190.

Atchley, R. C. (1991). The influence of aging and frailty on perceptions and expressions of the self. In J. E. Birren, J. E. Lubben, J. C. Rowe, & D. E. Deutchman (Eds.), *The concept and measurement of quality of life in the frail elderly.* New York: Academic Press.

Baltes, P. B., & Baltes, M. M. (1990). Selective optimization with compensation. In P. B. Baltes & M. M. Baltes (Eds.), *Successful aging: Perspectives from the behavioral sciences.* New York: Cambridge University Press.

Baltes, M. M., Wahl, H., & Reichert, M. (1991). Successful aging in long-term care institutions. In K. W. Schaie (Ed.), *Annual review of gerontology and geriatrics* (Vol. 11). New York: Springer.

Bengtson, V. L., Reedy, M. N., & Gordon, C. (1985). Aging and self perceptions: Personality processes and social contexts. In J. E. Birren & K. W. Schaie (Eds.), *Handbook of the psychology of aging* (2nd ed.). New York: Van Nostrand Reinhold.

Carstensen, L. L. (1991). Selectivity theory: Social activity in a life-span context. In K. W. Schaie (Ed.), *Annual review of gerontology and geriatrics* (Vol. 11). New York: Springer.

Fiske, M., & Chiriboga, D. A. (1990). *Change and continuity in adult life.* San Francisco: Jossey-Bass.

Havighurst, R. J. (1963). Successful aging. In R. H. Williams, C. Tibbitts, & W. Donohue (Eds.), *Processes of aging* (Vol. 1). New York: Atherton.

Kaufman, S. R. (1987). *The ageless self: Sources of meaning in late life.* Madison: University of Wisconsin Press.

Kelly, G. A. (1955). *The psychology of personal constructs.* New York: Norton.

Markus, H. R., & Herzog, A. R. (1991). The role of the self-concept in aging. In K. W. Schaie (Ed.), *Annual review of gerontology and geriatrics* (Vol. 11). New York: Springer.

Markus, H., & Nurius, P. (1986). Possible selves. *The American Psychologist, 41,* 954-969.

Whitbourne, S. K. (1986). *The me I know: A study of adult identity.* New York: Springer-Verlag.

2

Values as Sources of the Ageless Self

SHARON R. KAUFMAN

The voices of individual old people can tell us much about the experience of being old. In the process of conducting anthropological fieldwork with the elderly, I have heard many old people talk about themselves, their pasts, and their concerns for the future. I have observed that, when they talk about who they are and how their lives have been, they do not speak of being old as meaningful in itself; that is, they do not perceive aging or chronological age as a category of experience or meaning. To the contrary, when old people talk about themselves, they express a sense of self that is ageless—an identity that maintains continuity despite the physical and social changes that come with old age. Old people know who they are and what matters to them now. As they talk about these subjects, they may, in passing, describe themselves as "feeling old" in one context and "feeling young" or "not old" in another. This is always variable, and in my experience, it is never emphasized. Being old per se is not a central feature of the self, nor is it a source of meaning.

In my research on identity in late life, I interviewed 60 urban, white, middle-class Californians over the age of 70. Although some were not

AUTHOR'S NOTE: This chapter is adapted from Sharon Kaufman, *The Ageless Self: Sources of Meaning in Late Life* (Madison: University of Wisconsin Press, 1986).

in good physical health, they all were mentally alert and articulate. I selected individuals whom I had met over a 2-year period during visits to nursing homes, retirement residences, senior centers, and retiree support groups as well as through personal and professional referrals.

This study group represents a variety of economic, occupational, and educational backgrounds. Some individuals had impoverished childhoods while others were comfortably middle class during their youths. For some, education terminated with the high school diploma; others attained graduate professional degrees. Regardless of differences among them, study participants share some cultural characteristics that provide a context for identity development: They have all been exposed to the same major social trends and national historical events in the United States over a period of approximately 50 years, and they share certain dominant American goals, values, and expectations.

In intensive, systematic interviews over a period of 8 or 9 months with a subsample of 15 people, I found that the ageless self maintains continuity through a symbolic, creative process. The self draws meaning from the past, interpreting and re-creating it as a resource for being in the present. I came to view the self as the interpreter of experience: From this perspective, individual identity is revealed by the patterns of symbolic meaning that characterize the individual's unique interpretation of experience.

Identity is not frozen in a static moment of the past. Old people formulate and reformulate personal and cultural symbols of their past to create a meaningful, coherent sense of self, and, in the process, they create a viable present. In this way, the ageless self emerges: Its definition is ongoing, continuous, and creative.

One important source of identity and meaning in late life is values, which identify shared standards and ideals in a community or society. They are highly abstract constructs drawn from the experiences of living in a particular society during a certain historical period. Values emerge from, and in turn are shaped by, the interactions among individuals and institutions in a social system. Classic studies of values in the social sciences (C. Kluckhohn, 1951; F. Kluckhohn, 1953; Williams, 1970) describe them as guidelines for behavior and standards by which goals are chosen and decisions are made. Values provide a means of weighing and choosing solutions to everyday problems posed by living in a society and confronting adaptive dilemmas that occur over the life span. They also help give direction to behavior in situations of conflict and choice and lend justification to already performed action.

A strong activity orientation underlies the values that are shared, though to different degrees, by all members of the study group. Specific values that emerged most strongly in the intensive interviews are achievement, success, productivity, work, progress, social usefulness, independence, self-reliance, and individual initiative. As we will see in the two case studies that follow, activity-oriented values have had the greatest influence on the formation of my informants' identities in late life. While the values listed above are not necessarily "general" or "modal" American values, numerous observers of American culture have described them as characteristic of American society during the years in which my informants grew up, matured, and aged (Arensberg & Niehoff, 1975; Clark & Anderson, 1967; Epstein, 1980; Lasch, 1979; Mead, 1943).

Achievement—the attainment of a goal that brings satisfaction and heightens self-esteem—is probably a universal objective. For my informants, achievement is marked by singular, personal success in some concrete endeavor, whether the creation of a visible object, the ability to perform a task adequately, or the acknowledgment of one's expertise by others. An achievement is the result of some tangible behavior, purposefully enacted.

Achievement and success are to be reached through productive activity, especially work. It is not enough for these study participants to "keep busy"; their behavior must be oriented toward some pragmatic end to have meaning. Moreover, self-esteem is intimately related to activity and productivity. In general, my informants state that their morale is highest when they feel they are working diligently and being as productive as possible.

Characterizing himself at different life stages, Matthew, age 83, expresses his sense of self:

> As a child, I was a dreamer; as a youth, a seeker, then I was ambitious—a doer. I don't care what, but a doer. I'm still a doer. I've never gotten out of wanting to be doing work all the time. I believe that it's your God-given duty to do something, to accomplish something. No matter what. That's it.

Matthew's earliest memory is of the poverty his family experienced. He grew up on a farm in central California, the youngest of three children, the only son. Born in 1895, he recalls the drought years at the turn of the century: "It was very bad times for everyone in the farming business. Misery, poverty were not looked down upon because everyone was poor. I had a feeling of sadness about it." In 1902 Matthew's father bought his own land, and the family's economic condition began to improve. Matthew worked hard on the farm from the time he was 7. He had chores to do before and after school, and in the summertime he worked all day.

When Matthew was 15, his father died of pneumonia. The death was a terrible ordeal for the close-knit family, and Matthew missed his father a great deal in the next few years. By this time, his sisters were grown and gone from home; Matthew was left as the main support of his mother. He talks about the years following his father's death in terms of his responsibilities on the farm.

> We had about 350 acres that we farmed in barley and hay. When my father died, in the winter time, I would have to get up and harness the horses, feed them, at four in the morning. Then I'd come in and have breakfast. Then I'd have to milk the cows and do the ploughing. Then go to school. In the summertime, I'd mow the barley and hay with a mowing machine and rake it. I worked very hard.

At the insistence of his mother and with the financial aid of one of his sisters, who was a nurse, Matthew entered the university at 18. He studied philosophy and made ends meet by washing dishes and waiting on tables. He says he always had an inferiority complex regarding his intellectual capabilities. Though he was a good student, he stressed to me that he was "never a star" and was not the studious reader he might have been. World War I began during his third year, and it became the most pressing concern in his life during his last 2 years at the university. A month before graduation, he joined the American Field Ambulance Service—the United States had not yet declared war—and went off to Europe with a group of other young men to aid the British. To this day, Matthew feels guilty that he was handed his diploma without having to take his final examinations.

Matthew spent the war years in Europe, first as an ambulance driver, then in the army. When the war ended, he married an English woman and became a travel agent, organizing tours for Americans and traveling all over Europe. He enjoyed those years tremendously. When he was not touring, he lived with his wife and three children in England. When the depression struck, his business declined drastically. Finally, in 1935, with the rise of Hitler and the urging of his in-laws, he returned to the United States with his wife and children.

Matthew arrived in New York with his family, $28, and no prospect of a job. He was 40 years old. He says of that time:

> That was the lowest ebb of my life. I thought I was going to have a nervous breakdown. I would wake up in the middle of the night, crying. I had too much pride, but I had to ask my mother, who was alive then, for a hundred dollars to rent a couple of rooms and get started looking for a job.

After several miserable months, he got his break. Americans were starting to travel once more to Europe, and Matthew met a travel agent who wanted him to open an office on the West Coast. He moved his family back to California, set up an office, and was immediately successful. He told me, "I did so well in the first 4 or 5 months, they couldn't believe it in the New York office." Through his foresight and hard work, the business expanded and diversified. Matthew became a vice president and stayed with the company until he retired at age 65.

Now 83, Matthew looks 10 or 15 years younger and is extremely agile for his age. Since his retirement, he and his wife have traveled extensively in the United States and around the world. When at home, he enjoys gardening and playing energetically with his small grandchildren. He also attends to many household chores himself. During the period of our interviews, he was replacing all the rotten window frames in his home with new ones. His characterization of his entire life remains important in his old age: He says his greatest wish at present is to do more work than he has time to do.

Activity directed toward the attainment of specific goals and personal accomplishments underscores commitment to the concept of progress. My informants tend to see progress as follows: They strive for occupational success and perfection in the tasks they undertake, and they work on character development, for example, "overcoming my shyness," "getting out and being with people more often," "seeing something worthwhile in everyone," and "trying to be more patient with others." All study group members believe that, with personal effort, their temperaments can be improved, their material lives enriched, and their work made more gratifying.

In a society where progress is assumed to be possible and activity is directed toward solving human problems, humanitarian behavior, too, is evaluated in the context of performance and achievement. For example, service to community organizations, philanthropy through formal institutions, and personal acts of generosity are all pragmatic expressions of concern for others that can be measured and judged. For this study group, such behavior is defined as socially useful. That is, giving time or money to others is viewed in terms of both the results it will bring to the larger community and the contribution being made by the individual.

Bess, at 82, puts her philosophy in a nutshell: "Do the best you can. Give a little, take a little." She structures the story of her life around the philanthropic committees on which she has served over the years, her abilities as an organizer and civic leader, and her effectiveness in providing services and raising money.

Bess immigrated to the United States with her well-to-do family from Czechoslovakia in 1908. She was 12 at the time. The oldest of three children and the only girl, she says she was used to getting what she wanted and has always been stubborn, headstrong, and rebellious. Bess told me that, when her family arrived in New York, her mother wanted her to retain her upper-class European life-style and arranged for Bess to be tutored privately at home. But Bess insisted on learning English as quickly as possible and entering the public schools. Later, her mother wanted her to become a lawyer; Bess rejected that idea and took accounting, typing, sewing, and cooking classes in school.

The family moved from New York to the West Coast in 1911 when Bess's father, an inventor, decided to go into business with an uncle. When Bess finished high school, she went to work as an accountant for a manufacturing company, much to her mother's dismay, as she did not need to work. A few years later, when World War I began and the company for which Bess worked turned exclusively to war production, Bess changed jobs, noting that, at 18, with her skills and the war on, she was in great demand and could have whatever job she chose.

Bess met her future husband during the war years; when the war ended, her husband-to-be was just starting an electronics company. Bess quit her job the week before the wedding and went to work as the accountant for her husband's company. Reflecting on her past, Bess says her husband was the most influential person in her life and the only person she ever wanted to please. "He toned me down. I always did what he wanted me to do." He would never let her work for a salary, even during the early years of their marriage when they could have used the money. But, as his business became more successful and they became quite affluent, he encouraged her to do philanthropic work.

Much of Bess's account is devoted to describing her work with the Red Cross and army during World War II. Though she worked long hours, she relished the work she did in those years and apparently placed herself in charge of whatever project she was engaged in at the time. On different occasions, she organized housing, food distribution, and entertainment for the hundreds of soldiers who were stationed in her city on their way to or from the South Pacific. Bess talks about her "war work" in terms of her effectiveness in getting things done her way and her ability to organize other people to accomplish some task. "Every week I would get together with the special service officers of the army and navy to provide entertainment, and I had to allocate the talent to be fair to each place. Then I had to organize units to send out the entertainers." Beginning with her service during the war years, Bess portrays herself as influential and powerful in the community and is quite proud of those characteristics.

When the war was over, Bess became actively involved in civic and church groups. She devoted the next 40 years to fund-raising for numerous local, national, and international organizations, serving on many boards and committees, and acting as the "hostess with the mostest" by offering her large and beautiful home for fund-raising events, meetings, and gatherings of all kinds.

Now, Bess describes herself as a semi-invalid. When I asked her to describe the hardest thing about growing old, she replied:

> I just wish I could get the hell out and do more things. I still belong to 27 organizations. But I just send them checks now. I'm not very active anymore. . . . I wish I could be like my friend F.B. You should see her—90 years old, but she's always running around, never misses a meeting.

Bess's self-image and sense of worth in the world derive from her lifelong community affiliations and sense of serving others. Now, with various medical problems, she can no longer be involved in her community as she would like—by being a leader and giving her time and energy to others. Moreover, she can no longer maintain the active social life that has always accompanied her philanthropic endeavors. This is a great frustration to her.

Bess's sense of self and the structure of her life course are interpreted in a framework of social usefulness. Most informants were socialized by their mothers—regardless of religion or class—to regard humanitarian behavior as the most valued activity. By setting an example, mostly through church and community work, the mothers taught these people to give of themselves to others—and to do so with sincerity and integrity—as they went through life. Now, at the end of their lives, informants continue to place high value on social usefulness and to judge their lives in terms of it.

In American society generally, the values of achievement, productivity, work, progress, and social usefulness derive from the shared cultural background and historical period in which my informants have lived. Taken together, these values continue to provide meaning as a source of self-expression into advanced age.

These brief case studies show how values that have been held for a lifetime are accommodated amid changes that accompany aging. In late life, people have the ability to reformulate lifelong values so that they (a) take on new meaning in old age, (b) promote a sense of continuity of self, and (c) contribute to an integrated and salient account of the life course. These case studies also illustrate how a strong activity orientation underlies characteristic American values. Embedded in values, the relevance of activity extends across the life span, reaffirmed as people have the opportunity to talk about their lives and what is meaningful to them.

References

Arensberg, C. M., & Niehoff, A. N. (1975). American cultural values. In J. Spradley & M. A. Rynkiewich (Eds.), *The Nacirema* (pp. 363-378). Boston: Little, Brown.

Clark, M., & Anderson, B. (1967). *Culture and aging.* Springfield, IL: Charles C Thomas.

Epstein, J. (1980). *Ambition.* New York: Dutton.

Kluckhohn, C. (1951). Values and value-orientations in the theory of action. In T. Parsons & E. A. Shils (Eds.), *Toward a general theory of action* (pp. 388-433). Cambridge, MA: Harvard University Press.

Kluckhohn, F. (1953). Dominant and variant value orientations. In C. Kluckhohn & H. A. Murray (Eds.), *Personality in nature, society, and culture* (2nd ed., rev., enlarged; pp. 342-357). New York: Knopf.

Lasch, C. (1979). *The culture of narcissism.* New York: Warner.

Mead, M. (1943). *And keep your powder dry: An anthropologist looks at America.* New York: Morrow.

Williams, R. M., Jr. (1970). *American society: A sociological interpretation* (3rd ed., rev.). New York: Knopf.

3

Meanings of Activity

M. POWELL LAWTON

Writing about the meaning of leisure for older persons in 1992 inevitably raises the question of what advances in knowledge have occurred in the 30 years since Havighurst (1961) wrote so eloquently on this topic. Although there has been much research on leisure and aging during this period, there has been relatively little new research directed explicitly at meaning.

This chapter will therefore begin by considering "the meaning of meaning" (Osgood, Suci, & Tannenbaum, 1957) as a focus for understanding leisure behavior and will locate this construct among a variety of other facets of leisure that have been topics of empirical research. A closer link of such constructs to those used in general psychology will be sought. Finally, the bulk of the chapter will review some research that helps explicate how older people comprehend and use leisure in the service of their needs, in good and in poor health.

The Meaning of Meaning

Osgood's classic research on meaning distinguished denotative meaning from connotative meaning. Denotative meaning is derived from the observable properties of an object, that is, physical characteristics, uses, history, and so on. Connotative meaning refers to the more abstract, affective, and linguistic characteristics of the objects, dimensions by which objects of widely differing denotative characteristics may be comprehended. Osgood's research indicated that most objects were judged in terms of three major connotative dimensions: evaluation, potency, and activity. Other dimensions may be required to characterize the more subtle connotative structure of specific domains. For example, semantic differential research on environments has indicated that additional dimensions, such as physical scale or natural versus man-made, may be necessary to reflect environmental meaning fully (Ward & Russell, 1981). Little research on connotative meaning has been performed in the area of leisure, but a great variety of denotative meanings of leisure have been suggested.

Denotative Meanings of Leisure

Many classifications of leisure activity have been offered. This is understandable, considering the need for grouping the thousands of leisure activities into larger categories in such a way as to allow statistical analysis. Some have worked only with a list of ungrouped, discrete activities (Beck & Page, 1988). A more common approach has been to use very gross categories, for example, informal social activity, formal-organizational activity, and solitary activity (Lemon, Bengtson, & Peterson, 1972). Overs, Taylor, Cassell, and Chernov (1977) made an a priori classification of specific leisure behaviors into nine categories: games, education-entertainment-cultural, sports, nature, collecting, art-music, crafts, volunteering, and organizations. A group of 34 activities from the Overs et al. (1977) list were cluster-analyzed by Tinsley and Johnson (1984). Rather than empirically clustering into the denotative categories with which Overs began, Tinsley and Johnson found groupings that suggested more abstract categories: intellectual stimulation, catharsis, expressive compensation, hedonistic companionship, supportive companionship, secure solitude, routine, temporary indulgence, moderate security, and expressive aestheticism.

A number of empirical approaches to grouping activities have been taken. McKechnie (1974) began with specific leisure pursuits. Frequencies of participation were factored, resulting in factors named mechanics (male), crafts (female), intellectual, slow living, neighborhood sports, and glamour sports. Using a number of the same activities, Lounsberry and Hoopes (1988) obtained a partial replication in factors of sports/recreation, domestic activities, intellectual, easy leisure, and organizational activities. Richie (1975) selected 12 activities (the basis for their selection was not reported), which raters judged only in terms of their similarity. The ratings were subjected to multidimensional scaling, resulting in four dimensions named active/passive, individual/group, simple/difficult, and involving/time-filling. Witt (1971) factored participation frequency and identified dimensions of sports, nature, social, and aesthetic. Bishop (1970) chose to interpret only three factors from participation frequency or ratings on 26 and 32 activities. The factors' assigned names, corresponding to Osgood's activity, potency, and evaluation dimensions, seem somewhat distant from the item content.

A study dealing with elders began with a list consisting not only of leisure behaviors but also instrumental and work-related activities (Stones & Kozma, 1986). Factor analysis of frequency of participation data resulted in one instrumental factor (household independence) and four leisure-behavior factors (family involvement, solitary activity, community involvement, household activity). The Overs et al. (1977) activity list was used again with a large sample of older subjects to form cluster-analytic categories (Tinsley, Teaff, Colbs, & Kaufman, 1985). This time, clusters labeled companionship, compensation, temporary disengagement, comfortable solitude, expressive solitude, and expressive service were found. These clusters showed little congruence with those derived on the younger adult sample of Tinsley and Johnson (1984). Finally, Kelly (1987), in a telephone survey of community-resident older adults, factored frequency ratings of 28 specific activities. He extracted eight factors named cultural, travel, home-based, sport/exercise, family, outdoor, community-organizational, and social activities.

Looking at research that has dealt with denotative dimensions of leisure, there is little convergence on the identification of higher order dimensions that could be construed as basic connotative dimensions. It seems very likely that the diversity of people's preference cuts across types of activities in a way that diffuses the emergence of clear factors. It is also possible that there are too many possibilities of specific activities to allow adequate sampling of the universe of activities. In any case, the search for conceptual categories of the meaning of activities does not seem to have been advanced by factoring activity pursuits.

Connotative Dimensions of Leisure

An immense literature has been devoted to probing the dimensions of the meaning of leisure. To some extent, measures of leisure attitudes (Crandall & Slivken, 1980; Neulinger & Breit, 1969) and leisure satisfaction (Beard & Ragheb, 1980) attempt to define dimensions that give more abstract meaning to people's activities. If we really wish to focus on meaning, however, it would seem that meaning as an answer to the question, "What does the activity do for me?" is closest to the connotative meaning of leisure. From this perspective, leisure motivation, leisure need, leisure preference, leisure benefits, and leisure functions all fit the criterion of describing what the person sees an activity doing for him or her. The higher order dimensions of such functions may be abstracted on theoretical grounds or empirically by factor-analytic and related techniques.

A review of such attempts to dimensionalize meaning in this sense must be cursory to allow a focus on meaning as it applies to elders. A homemade categorization of such deductive and inductive attempts to improve order in this area follows, with appropriate references shown in Table 3.1. The names I gave to each dimension were based primarily on the modal name that appeared in the literature reviewed. Where it seemed necessary, the original authors' names for the dimensions are included to demonstrate the range of variation of a particular meaning.

It should be acknowledged that making lists characterizes the relatively early stage of development of any field. In the paradigm of science, description is the first stage. When description merges into explanation, an advance in knowledge is clearly indicated. Researchers such as Gordon, Gaitz, and Scott (1976) and Iso-Ahola (1990) argue that we can already justify a hierarchical model. Iso-Ahola (1990), for example, suggests that two dimensions can account for all leisure motivations; specific activities differ primarily in their mix of the extent to which they afford approach versus avoidance of personal versus interpersonal rewards. In the absence of sufficient empirical research, however, this scheme seems to level or obscure some dimensions whose unique characteristics should be preserved. Therefore Table 3.1 preserves a number of fairly specific categories of leisure meanings and groups then into larger categories named experiential, social, and developmental.

Experiential Leisure

Despite the usual insistence of leisure researchers that performing an activity for its own sake rather than for its consequences is a necessary defining condition of leisure, the experiential category would seem to be the only one that totally fulfills this criterion. *Intrinsic satisfaction*

Table 3.1 Experiential, Developmental, and Social Meanings of Leisure

Experiential Leisure:

Intrinsic satisfaction	Flow, Csikszentmihalyi (1975)
Solitude	Tinsley (1984); Iso-Ahola (1990); Havighurst (1961)
Diversion	Gordon et al. (1976); compensation, Ellis & Witt (1984); Tinsley & Kass (1980)
Relaxation	Gordon et al. (1976); Havighurst (1961); Ellis & Witt (1984); Pierce (1980); Witt & Bishop (1970); catharsis, Ellis & Witt (1984); passing time, Tinsley & Tinsley (1986); escape, Kelly (1983); time filling, Pierce (1980); routine temporary indulgence, Tinsley (1984).

Developmental Leisure:

Intellectual challenge	Overs et al. (1977); Tinsley (1984); learning, Gordon et al. (1976); mental activity, Lounsberry & Hoopes (1988); intellection, Pierce (1980); intellectual stimulation, Tinsley & Johnson (1984)
Personal competence	Kelly (1983); mastery, Unger & Kernan (1983); achievement, Lounsberry & Hoopes (1988) and Pierce (1980); perceived leisure competence (Ellis & Witt, 1984); skill development, Ellis & Witt (1984); self-image, Ellis & Witt (1984)
Health	Kelly, Steinkamp, & Kelly (1986); Lounsberry & Hoopes (1988); surplus energy, Ellis & Witt (1984)
Expression and personal development	Kelly (1983); Tinsley et al. (1985); Havighurst (1961); self-actualization, Tinsley & Kass (1980)
Creativity	Gordon et al. (1976); Havighurst (1961); Lounsberry & Hoopes (1988); Ellis & Witt (1984); expressive aestheticism, Tinsley & Johnson (1984)

Social Leisure:

Social interaction	Gordon et al. (1976); Kelly et al. (1986); Lounsberry & Hoopes (1988); Ellis & Witt (1984); companionship, Overs et al. (1977) and Tinsley & Johnson (1984); Havighurst (1961); intimacy, Pierce (1980)
Social status	Ellis & Witt (1984); power, Pierce (1980); Tinsley & Kass (1980); supervise others, Havighurst (1961); competition, Csikszentmihalyi (1975)
Service	Havighurst (1961); Tinsley & Kass (1980); Tinsley et al. (1985)

is exemplified by Csikszentmihalyi's (1975) concept of flow. The emotions and sensations of the activity itself are the sole source of enjoyment; the characteristics of flow—lack of awareness of time and self, focused attention, total control—characterize such experience for its own sake. Other less intense experiential aspects are related to factors of *solitude*, *diversion*, and *relaxation*. Solitude includes activities whose prime focus is either to relieve one from social contexts (see Iso-Ahola, 1990) or to affirm one's own autonomy. Relaxation may be very similar to diversion but is a special condition of diversion away from tension. Diversion is intrinsically experiential because it is the change from the usual more than the activity content that is responsible for its appeal.

Social Leisure

Virtually every system for classifying meanings of leisure has included a social category. The first of three categories is *social interaction*, where positive social contact appears to be the common thread. The second subvariety is *social status*, where the goals of the activity are competitive, the attainment of ascendancy over others. Finally, *service* (such as volunteering) is an important social category but it emerges infrequently as a statistical construct probably because of its low frequency of occurrence.

Developmental Leisure

The several categories of developmental leisure share the characteristic that the activity not only is usually enjoyed but clearly is viewed as doing something to help the person become something or change in some way. Such leisure thus possesses an instrumental component, rather than being purely intrinsic as has been often claimed. *Intellectual* pursuits are of this type. They do often involve a strong experiential feature as well, but participants seem to construe these activities as also being "good" for them. *Creativity* is also placed in this category, although one could make an equally good case for much creative activity being solely of the experiential type.

The foregoing review of meaning in leisure has dealt relatively little with aging or human development, first because it is necessary to discuss meaning in terms of its continuities (and sometimes discontinuities) across the life span. A second reason is that relatively little of the research reviewed has been performed on older people. The next section will attempt to anchor these meanings within a general view of personality and then turn to aging and meaning.

Psychological Processes and Leisure Choices

Let us begin with some processes from the field of general psychology that might lead to a better understanding of subjective meaning. Crucial to such a conception are temperament, environment, social learning, personality, and preferences.

Temperament

People appear to differ in basic biogenetic ways in the extent to which they are oriented to stimulation. Geen (1984) suggests that, although a single optimal level of stimulation characterizes all individuals, people vary widely in their baseline levels of nervous system activation, such that some people chronically require additional stimulation to reach the optimal level (extraverts) while others require reductions in stimulation for the optimal level to be achieved (introverts). To characterize this difference in terms of the familiar extraversion-introversion duality (Eysenck, 1970) goes too far. These two underaroused and overaroused states represent biological substrate that are very capable of being modified by the person's interactions with the environment.

Environment

Environment in objective terms consists of a complex of opportunities and barriers from which the person seeks optimal stimulation. The whole of all that could be called objective environment is rarely relevant to the individual. The vagaries of happenstance and the rewards and punishments provided in particular environments constitute the relevant aspects of environment for the person. A major aspect of environment is composed of the other people in physically or functionally close interaction with the person, the social norms of the environment, and the cultural values inherent in that environment.

Social Learning

The transactions between personal temperament and the environment constitute the socialization process whereby personality develops.

Personality

Personality is perhaps the most general descriptor of the behaving person. It should be clear that these processes are dynamic and therefore that personality, rather than being a fixed entity, is an ongoing process embodying both stability and change. One perspective demonstrates conclusively the continuity of personality. Costa et al. (1986) have shown that extraversion and neuroticism are highly stable over a period of decades. Yet people are also reactive to life events such as widow-hood (Thompson, Gallagher-Thompson, Futterman, Gilewski, & Peterson, 1991), relocation (Lieberman & Tobin, 1983), and natural disasters (Murrell & Norris, 1984). One can see the persistence of temperament in Costa and McCrae's research but major variations in the construct and the mood of everyday life have been shown to be the result of both major events and small events (DeLongis, Coyne, Dakof, Folkman, & Lazarus, 1982; Reich & Zautra, 1983).

Preference

Preference is a highly derived psychological process that begins in temperament, a presumed selective process whereby the person is differentially sensitive to external input and active in choosing an external environment consistent with the direction of optimal stimulation (Ellis, 1973; Furnham, 1981; Iso-Ahola, 1980). Activities and the resources necessary for their occurrence are differentially accessible in differing social environments and are differentially reinforced in different families, social strata, and cultures. In attempting to explain leisure preferences, then, one ought to be able to find components of temperament, social environment, and resource environment. That is, one learns to like activities that are consistent with both one's biological and one's socially constructed selves. Such learned preferences are relatively long lasting (leisure needs) but become activated in a contemporary setting as motivations to behave in a particular way (leisure motivation). Learned preferences thus become an inseparable aspect of personality, the consistent way in which the person deals with the world.

The temporal course of leisure preferences is thus from relatively narrowly defined gross activity preferences stemming from temperament in earliest life to a long period of fanning out of the channels that represent specific preferences. That is, early biological propensities are subjected to the joint influences of environmental and social learning. Although a basic limit on the amount of fanning remains from temperamental influences, the number of possibilities for leisure pursuits to be matched to individual needs mushrooms.

This exemplifies the multiplexity of leisure meanings. A single activity, in denotative terms, may take on a great variety of connotative meanings. Tinsley and Johnson (1984) showed that there was significant congruence between participation in factor-determined activity groups and particular activity meanings derived from the Paragraph About Leisure Questionnaire (Tinsley & Kass, 1980). On the other hand, this generalization represented only a central tendency, with every activity cluster showing a distribution of perceived meanings across most of the meaning dimensions. Thus one person's meaning of craft activities might be the opportunity for solitude, while for others it might be self-expression or security. Such multiplexity underlines why it may be difficult to obtain denotative activity clusters replicated across different research studies and methods—very different needs of different people may be served by identical participation patterns.

Another property of the multiplexity of activity meaning is that meanings may vary within the same person across different contexts or across time periods. This property serves an important adaptive function in that activity preferences, familiarity, and skills established in one period of the life span may continue as the needs served and the meaning of the activity change.

Continuity, Adaptation, and Later Life
Change in Leisure Meaning

Longitudinal Studies

Does the meaning of leisure change with age? We have few studies on which to base any conclusion. Even simple longitudinal studies are rare. Lounsberry and Hoopes (1988) performed a 5-year follow-up study of 139 adults. Although there were many changes in frequency of participation, a clear core of continuity remained. The Leisure Motivation Inventory (Tinsley, Barrett, & Kass, 1977) showed notably less stability, a finding consistent with the idea that participation and meaning may vary partially independently. This study did not, of course, deal with the later life span at all. Longitudinal studies within this age range are even fewer. The Duke Longitudinal Studies (Palmore, 1981) showed a decline in social activities over 6 years among about half of the second Duke study subjects, an increase in 17%, and no change in 32%. Some types of activity, such as organizational or religious activities, changed hardly at all. Somewhat more detailed information emerged from the Bonn Longitudinal Study (Schmitz-Scherzer, 1976), indicating a surprising degree of continuity. Only a slight decline in two social activities was noted, while eight did not change; both gardening and two passive activities, newspaper reading and television, increased after 6 years.

Cross-Sectional Studies

These bits of support for continuity stand in sharp contrast with cross-sectional data for different age groups studied at about the same calendar time. One of the most cited studies is that of Gordon et al. (1976). When analyzed by age decades, lesser participation was noted among older groups in "dancing and drinking," outdoor activities, hunting, sports, movies, traveling, and reading. No age differences were found in interaction with friends, television, and cultural activities. Elders reported a higher frequency of solitary thinking.

In the domain of leisure meaning, we have very few empirical age comparisons, the major example being separate cluster-analytic studies of participation patterns of 1,375 adults and 1,649 people 55 and over (Tinsley & Johnson, 1984; Tinsley et al., 1985). The methods differed slightly and the comparison between the two studies' results is one made by the current author, not the original researchers. Nonetheless, the factors defining activities in denotative terms appear to be roughly similar between the two age groups, and the congruence patterns between denotative (participation factors) and connotative meaning (expressed in the psychological benefits measured by the Paragraphs About Leisure Questionnaire; Tinsley & Kass, 1980) appear similar.

The denotative activity participation clusters of the younger sample were identified as intellectual stimulation, catharsis, expressive compensation, hedonistic companionship, supportive companionship, secure solitude, routine temporary indulgence, moderate security, and expressive aestheticism. These showed little correspondence with the a priori groups hypothesized by Overs et al. (1977). Clusters of elders' activities were named companionship, compensation, temporary disengagement, comfortable solitude, expressive solitude, and expressive service (Tinsley et al., 1985). Although their assigned names sometimes resembled those of the younger sample, the clusters were composed of rather different activities in the two age groups. Thus it is difficult to judge how well the age groups compared in degree of congruence between activity clusters and connotative meaning. Within the elder group, however, there were a number of pairings that indicated concordance between denotative and connotative factors: Activities classed as expressive solitude were linked in meaning to the psychological benefit dimension of self-expression; companionship to the same-named benefit dimension; compensation activities to compensation benefits; expressive service to service; and expressive solitude to solitude. As mentioned earlier, however, there were a number of instances where a single activity cluster provided multiple psychological benefits.

It is easy to conclude that information regarding continuity versus change is very ambiguous and that further study is of major importance. There is a special need to study meaning change with age in parallel with participation rate change.

Sources of Change Over Time

As new research is performed, however, it is imperative to recognize a generic obstacle to definitive information. As is well known, differences among individuals have embedded within them three components: chronological aging, cohort membership, and period of history. Cross-sectional age comparisons cannot separate the effects due to chronological age from those due to age cohort membership. Longitudinal study of the same individual over time cannot separate age changes from period changes. Awareness of this source of error has at least alerted us to the need to acknowledge and to probe the effects of each of these separate influences on the form of old age. Leisure meaning is one such form that allows analysis on theoretical, if not yet empirical, grounds.

Connotative meaning is highly subject to change in calendar time. Fad, fashion, social norms, and conceivably cultural values evolve over the life span of the individual. In general, people born during the same period of history carry with them many preferences and skills that were socially important during their period of early socialization. Such cohort-related preferences are the major source of a wish for continuity. What one learned early in life is likely to have been practiced and therefore performed with competence. Early leisure choices were unquestionably made on the basis of temperament, which gives them a strength of motivation likely to persist over time. Familiarity with particular activities provides its own motivating force in the security that comes from knowing an activity well. Early socialization experiences with activities characteristic of that period in history include preferences based on a conviction about what is morally right. One's self-concept may well hinge partly on the degree to which one spends time in leisure behaviors that affirm one's own ethics and the ethos of the society one belonged to in preadult years. In sum, one would expect a tendency, other factors being equal, for the meanings and participation patterns of leisure activities to remain relatively constant. At the very least, the Palmore (1981) and the Schmitz-Scherzer (1976) longitudinal studies affirm that the combination of chronological aging and passage of years did not disturb the continuity of some activities. Did they maintain the same meaning for these subjects over time? New research is needed to answer that question.

The opposite effect tends to be fostered by the passage of calendar time. The same changing fads, fashions, and redefined values constitute potential environmental demands on people to adopt new interests, preferences, and leisure behaviors. At the very least, such changes provide opportunities for new leisure choices not available in earlier calendar times or, conversely, the disappearance of some opportunities that were formerly available. The meaning of one's response to such external change may vary from that of preserving one's status quo to that of being an innovator or at least one who keeps up with the times.

Change within the person changes leisure opportunities only in the sense that internal factors may change the person's receptivity to, or active search for, different leisure pursuits. Intrapersonal change is an extremely important source of variance in leisure preference, however, because this source includes chronological aging and other correlated phenomena such as health changes as major determinants of perceived meaning and actual leisure behavior. One can easily think of the many intrapersonal changes that have been ascribed to chronological aging and how they may be related to leisure: physical vigor, speed of information processing, sensory and motor skill, habituation, practice, personal goals, and so on. It is less clear how the person deals subjectively with these changes. This is the major focus of this chapter, to suggest ways by which people handle psychologically continuities and discontinuities ascribed to cohort, history, and personal aging.

This process can never be understood by paying attention only to the separate influences of cohort, history, and aging on leisure behavior. Rather, we must conceive of parallel, but successively staged, marches of each cohort through historical time, with individual aging patterns constituting a distribution of differences perpendicular to the norm for a cohort at a given point in time.

Applying this concept more concretely, we must conceptualize the individual's leisure preferences and personal constructions of leisure being composed of cohort norms and shared experiences, contemporary social norms, and personal continuities and discontinuities.

Change in Leisure Behavior and Leisure Meaning

The need for security may well be expressed in maintaining the meanings of leisure in as unchanged a way as possible. Such continuity does not necessarily have to be behavioral. In fact, the adjustive capacity of people in the later stages of life may be expressed exactly in finding ways to moderate behavioral leisure while maintaining meaning. For example, the most active leisure behaviors, such as contact sports or hunting, may evolve into successively less physically demanding pursuits such as golf, fishing, spectator sport, reading about sport, television sports, conversation, and finally reminiscence. Far from representing a decline, such adaptation to biological aging may represent a psychological triumph.

Baltes (1991) and his associates have treated this process in more general terms under the label "selective optimization with compensation." The selection aspect involves self-directed decisions regarding which skills are most important to preserve. The leisure meanings summarized in Table 3.1 are selectively valued by different individuals. The multiplexity of the person's adaptational capacity is expressed in maintaining some leisure behaviors and relinquishing others. Such selective deployment of the remaining energy then can help optimize either the behavioral skill or the psychological rewards consequent to the specialization. The meanings of the relinquished activities are presumably lower in the hierarchy of importance than are the maintained activities. Finally, the compensatory aspect of the process may well be achieved in the reinterpretation of the meanings of both the optimized ("these are the activities that really count for me") and the relinquished ("these activities were not really important for me").

Thus it is often a somewhat ageistic value judgment to view the developmental change from vigorous to sedentary, from active to passive, leisure behaviors as simply a loss. In extreme cases of physical decline, for example, among chronically ill people who are housebound or institutionalized, leisure meaning may remain relatively constant in the face of gross reduction in the energy and scale of the activity. Selective optimization may occur through "miniaturization" of one's sociospatial world (Rubinstein, Kilbride, & Nagy, 1992). For such people, behavioral space is greatly restricted, but continuity may be maintained through such means as looking at photographs or iconic representations of past behavior, watching the activity of others, or recounting one's past achievements. At its best, such optimization may occur with a minimum of active regret for what has been given up.

As grouped in Table 3.1, the types of leisure meaning would seem differentially responsive to biological aging, but not necessarily to chronological aging. Experiential leisure, being primarily subjective, would seem to have the capacity to persist in the face of growing frailty. Whether preferred activities are familiar or novel, the meaning and presumed satisfaction are based on internalized criteria.

Although many of the meanings classified as developmental connote some internal or social-comparative standard, most of these meanings are easily transformed in terms of anchoring points appropriate to the person's current state. For example, to compare one's golf game with that of a peer rather than that of a young expert shows continuity of meaning together with healthy adaptation to a more appropriate standard. Physical frailty and cognitive decline are occasions for major adaptation but potentially little meaning change.

Social meaning may be most sensitive to biological aging, on the theory that proactive social behavior is demanding and likely to be moderated as frailty grows. Once more, however, continuity of meaning may be maintained in the face of behavioral decline. Such mechanisms as fantasy, reminiscence, onlooker behavior, and passive social behavior may supplant the more active forms. As John Kelly (personal communication, June 1992) has noted, no matter how passive such adaptations or compensations may appear to the outsider, the older person continues at some level in an active process of restructuring meaning to cushion the effect of major changes in form.

In conclusion, by their ability to use social meaning and personal meaning to actively direct choices of leisure behavior and interpret the experiences of leisure, people maintain a sense of continuity of the self that transcends changes in participation patterns. Although new leisure learning, leisure experience as an immediate affective experience, and enjoyment of novelty are well within the capability of most older people, there is, in fact, a dialectic between familiarity and novelty. Both biological aging and social and technological change may change the balance point increasingly toward the familiarity side. In leisure, as in other phases of everyday life, the process of selective optimization with compensation is an intrapsychic, self-regulating process of adaptation to realistic change with minimal psychological damage.

References

Baltes, P. B. (1991). The many faces of human aging: Toward a psychological culture of old age. *Psychological Medicine, 21*, 837-854.

Beard, J. G., & Ragheb, M. B. (1980). Measuring leisure satisfaction. *Journal of Leisure Research, 12*, 20-33.

Beck, S. H., & Page, J. W. (1988). Involvement in activities and the psychological well-being of retired men. *Activities, Adaptation, and Aging, 11*, 31-47.

Bishop, D. (1970). The stability of the factor structure of leisure behavior analyses of four communities. *Journal of Leisure Research, 2*, 160-170.

Costa, P. T., McCrae, R. R., Zonderman, A. B., Barbano, H. E., Lebowitz, B., & Larson, D. M. (1986). Cross-sectional studies of personality in a national sample: 2. Stability in neuroticism, extraversion, and openness. *Psychology and Aging, 1*, 144-149.

Crandall, R., & Slivken, K. (1980). Leisure attitudes and their measurement. In A. E. Iso-Ahola (Ed.), *Social psychological perspectives on leisure and recreation* (pp. 261-264). Springfield, IL: Charles C Thomas.

Csikszentmihalyi, M. (1975). *Beyond boredom and anxiety.* San Francisco: Jossey-Bass.

DeLongis, A., Coyne, J. C., Dakof, G., Folkman, S., & Lazarus, R. S. (1982). Relationship of daily hassles, uplifts, and major life events to health status. *Health Psychology, 1*, 119-136.

Ellis, G., & Witt, A. (1984). The measurement of perceived freedom in leisure. *Journal of Leisure Research, 16*, 110-123.

Ellis, M. J. (1973). *Why people play.* Englewood Cliffs, NJ: Prentice-Hall.

Eysenck, H. J. (1970). *The structure of human personality* (3rd ed.). London: Methuen.

Furnham, A. (1981). Personality and activity preference. *British Journal of Social Psychology, 20*, 57-68.

Geen, R. G. (1984). Preferred stimulation levels in introverts and extraverts. *Journal of Personality and Social Psychology, 46*, 1303-1312.

Gordon, C., Gaitz, C. M., & Scott, J. B. (1976). Leisure and lives: Personal expressivity across the life span. In R. H. Binstock & E. Shanas (Eds.), *Handbook of aging and the social sciences* (pp. 310-341). New York: Van Nostrand Reinhold.

Havighurst, R. J. (1961). The nature and values of meaningful free-time activity. In R. W. Kleemeier (Ed.), *Aging and leisure* (pp. 309-344). New York: Oxford University Press.

Iso-Ahola, S. E. (1980). *The social psychology of leisure and recreation*. Dubuque, IA: William C Brown.

Iso-Ahola, S. E. (1990). Motivation for leisure. In E. L. Jackson & T. L. Burton (Eds.), *Understanding leisure and recreation* (pp. 247-279). State College, PA: Venture.

Kelly, J. R. (1983). *Leisure identities and interactions*. London: Allen & Unwin.

Kelly, J. R. (1987). *Peoria winter: Styles and resources in later life*. Lexington, MA: Lexington.

Kelly, J. R., Steinkamp, M., & Kelly, J. R. (1986). Later life leisure: How they play in Peoria. *The Gerontologist, 26*, 531-537.

Lemon, B. W., Bengtson, V. L., & Peterson, J. A. (1972). An exploration of the "activity theory" of aging. *Journal of Gerontology, 27*, 511-523.

Lieberman, M. A., & Tobin, S. S. (1983). *The experience of old age*. New York: Basic Books.

Lounsberry, J. W., & Hoopes, L. L. (1988). Five-year stability of leisure activity and motivation factors. *Journal of Leisure Research, 20*, 118-134.

McKechnie, G. E. (1974). The psychological structure of leisure: Past behavior. *Journal of Leisure Research, 6*, 27-45.

Murrell, S. A., & Norris, F. H. (1984). Resources, life events, and changes in positive affect and depression in older adults. *American Journal of Community Psychology, 12*, 445-464.

Neulinger, J. A., & Breit, H. C. (1969). Attitude dimensions of leisure. *Journal of Leisure Research, 1*, 255-261.

Osgood, C. E., Suci, G. J., & Tannenbaum, G. J. (1957). *The measurement of meaning*. Urbana: University of Illinois Press.

Overs, R. P., Taylor, S., Cassell, E., & Chernov, M. (1977). *Avocational counseling for the elderly*. Sussex, WI: Avocational Counseling Research.

Palmore, E. (1981). *Social patterns in normal aging: Findings from the Duke Longitudinal Study*. Durham, NC: Duke University Press.

Pierce, R. C. (1980). Dimensions of leisure. I: Satisfactions. *Journal of Leisure Research, 12*, 5-19.

Reich, J., & Zautra, A. (1983). Demands and desires in daily life: Some influences on well-being. *American Journal of Community Psychology, 11*, 41-58.

Richie, J. R. (1975). On the derivation of leisure activity types: A perceptual mapping approach. *Journal of Leisure Research, 7*, 128-140.

Rubinstein, R., Kilbride, J., & Nagy, S. (1992). *Elders living alone: Frailty and the perception of choice*. Hawthorne, NY: Aldine.

Schmitz-Scherzer, R. (1976). Longitudinal change in leisure behavior of the elderly. *Contributions to Human Development, 3*, 127-136.

Stones, M. J., & Kozma, A. (1986). Happiness and activities as propensities. *Journal of Gerontology, 41*, 85-90.

Thompson, L. W., Gallagher-Thompson, D., Futterman, A., Gilewski, M. J., & Peterson, J. (1991). The effects of late-life spousal bereavement over a 30-month interval. *Psychology and Aging, 6*, 434-441.

Tinsley, H. E. A. (1984). The psychological benefits of leisure participation. *Society and Leisure, 7*, 125-140.

Tinsley, H., Barrett, T. C., & Kass, R. A. (1977). Leisure activities and need satisfaction. *Journal of Leisure Research, 5*, 67-73.

Tinsley, H. E., & Johnson, T. L. (1984). A preliminary taxonomy of leisure activities. *Journal of Leisure Research, 16*, 234-244.

Tinsley, H. E., & Kass, R. A. (1980). The construct validity of the Leisure Activities Questionnaire and the Paragraphs About Leisure. *Educational and Psychological Measurement, 40*, 219-226.

Tinsley, H. E. A., Teaff, J. D., Colbs, S. L., & Kaufman, N. (1985). A system of clarifying leisure activities in terms of the psychological benefits of participation reported by older persons. *Journal of Gerontology, 40*, 172-178.

Tinsley, H. E. A., & Tinsley, D. J. (1986). A theory of the attributes, benefits, and causes of leisure experience. *Leisure Sciences, 8*, 1-45.

Unger, L. S., & Kernan, J. B. (1983). On the meaning of leisure. *Journal of Consumer Research, 9*, 381-392.

Ward, L. M., & Russell, J. A. (1981). The psychological representation of molar physical environments. *Journal of Experimental Psychology: General, 110*, 121-152.

Witt, P. A. (1971). Factor structure of leisure behavior for high school age youth in three communities. *Journal of Leisure Research, 3*, 213-220.

Witt, P. A., & Bishop, D. W. (1970). Situational antecedents to leisure behavior. *Journal of Leisure Research, 2*, 64-77.

4

Changing Contexts of Activity

DAVID A. CHIRIBOGA
ROBERT C. PIERCE

Drawing upon data from a longitudinal study of normative transitions that spanned 12 years, the focus of this chapter is on what happens to patterns of leisure activity when the contexts of people's lives change. For example, what happens to leisure activities when people experience a psychosocial transition or when so-called life events pile up. Along the way we will also consider whether people share common profiles of activities and examine other social and personal characteristics associated with the particular profiles. Before launching into the results of data analyses, however, we will begin the chapter with a brief review of pertinent literature.

Activity, Leisure, and Change During Later Adulthood

Social activity, especially leisure activity, was a focal point in many of the early studies of middle-aged and elderly persons. The work of such pioneers as Havighurst (1957), and later Cumming and Henry (1961) and Williams (1963), demonstrated that what older people do with their leisure time has enormous implications for their well-being. Indeed, the theory of disengagement as well as Havighurst's so-called implicit theory of aging both underscore the significance of leisure activities for adjustment in later life.

Despite this early promise, gerontological research on leisure activities has not kept pace with advances in areas such as cognitive psychology, health policy, stress, and caregiving. One reason may be a lack of appreciation for the potential contribution of leisure research: Studying how often people take vacations or attend sports events may seem relatively trivial when compared with studies of health risk behaviors or the physiological substrates of exercise. On the other hand, there is growing evidence that the manner in which individuals spend their free or voluntary time is strongly associated with their physical and mental well-being (e.g., Baltes, Wahl, & Schmid-Furstoss, 1990; Holahan, 1988).

As developmental scientists consider the role of leisure among the aged of today, and tomorrow, it becomes clear that leisure activities have increased importance for those in the second half of life. What Kaplan (1979, p. 25) called the "rise of the new leisure role" parallels the development of retirement into a distinct and lengthy component of the life course resulting from increased life expectancy, a decline in numbers of the self-employed, and improved health.

Transitions as Agents of Change

The concept of transitions generally refers to periods of major change in a person's life during which his or her entire worldview is challenged and the situational context calls for a readjustment in most social roles and activities (Chiriboga et al., 1991; Schlossberg, 1984). The investigation upon which this chapter is based provided a rare chance to explore the impact of transitions upon leisure activities. Each subject was facing role changes dramatic enough to be called a transition such as departure from the family home, parenthood, or retirement.

Many studies of transitions in middle and later life have focused primarily on the potential for devastating loss. Early clinical research on the empty nest and menopause, for example, suggested that each was causally associated with a higher than expected incidence of depression and other manifestations of psychological dysfunction. Later work, drawing on community populations, largely dispelled the myth of a universal crisis but also emphasized that small but significant portions of the population did experience problems (e.g., Lowenthal & Chiriboga, 1972). One longitudinal study of the divorce process found that, in their activities as well as their mental health, middle-aged subjects were initially more disrupted than younger subjects by marital separation but generally fared better than younger subjects some 3 to 4 years later (Chiriboga et al., 1991).

Much as the myth of the "empty nest" transition being universally fraught with crisis and mental illness has been discredited, recent work suggests that retirement, considered apart from factors such as physical illness and economic crisis, is not inherently disruptive to most people. One possibility, raised by Atchley (1987), is that after retirement leisure activities may replace the work role as a source of identity. This would suggest that leisure activities become more strongly associated with at least some indices of self-concept. Further, Atchley postulates that continuity in leisure activities may offset the discontinuities experienced in the work role pre- and postretirement.

It is also possible that transitions such as retirement or the empty nest may create unique challenges and opportunities to recast leisure activities into patterns more suitable for an individual's current stage in life. Few studies, however, have actually followed people through transitions. Much of our current thinking derives from cross-sectional and panel studies.

Stress as a Model of Change in Leisure Activity

Stress conditions represent another factor that may affect leisure activities in later life and indeed in earlier adulthood as well. Theorists and researchers have often viewed stress in terms of its relevance for short-term changes in physical and social function. In study after study of bereavement, amputation, relocation, divorce, and other social traumas, the typical investigation evaluates respondents, at the most, from 1 to 2 years after the stress event. More recently, students of adult development and aging are beginning to recognize the long-term impact of stress. It has been found, for example, that the social activities, relationships, and mental health of many adults are still strongly influenced by marital dissolution 4 to 10 years after the divorce (e.g., Chiriboga et al., 1991; Wallerstein & Blakeslee, 1989). The relevance of stress to leisure activities is less defined.

When reviewing patterns of continuity and discontinuity in leisure styles over the adult life course, Kelly, Steinkamp, and Kelly (1986) identify three types of people: those whose trajectories show a certain normative evolution over time, those whose trajectories seem to have been markedly altered by one specific life event, and those whose lives followed a "zigzag" trajectory resulting from the impact of multiple life events. Such stress exposure has been found to reduce the stability or continuity over time of personal attributes such as self-concept and morale (e.g., Fiske & Chiriboga, 1990).

A Longitudinal Study of Transitions and Stress

Late in 1968 a group of social and behavioral scientists began a life span study of what happens to average, community-dwelling people over time. One rather unique feature of the study was that we sampled according to where people stood in relation to one of four normative and therefore predictable life transitions instead of selecting subjects according to age. Two of the respondent groups were in the early stages of adulthood: (a) 52 high school seniors who were facing graduation and entry into adult status and (b) 50 men and women whose first marriage was less than 1 year old and who would presumably be dealing with issues of parenting within the next few years. We also included persons at earlier and later stages of middle age: (c) 54 men and women whose youngest child was a high school senior and who therefore were likely to face the proverbial "empty nest" and (d) 60 men and women who either were expecting to retire within 5 years or who had a spouse about to retire.

A Study of Ordinary People

One desire of the research team was to study ordinary people, because many longitudinal studies have been based on relatively elite sample populations. To simplify the sampling design, we began by selecting the most homogeneous district of one West Coast city: San Francisco. The district we selected was composed, with a few exceptions, of lower-middle-class and blue-collar workers of Caucasian descent.

The five contacts. The first interviews began in 1968 and usually required a total of from 6 to 8 hours to complete. Each of the four remaining interviews was designed to fit within a single 3-hour session. The second interview was conducted in 1970-1971. The third interview was conducted in 1974, while the fourth was in 1977. The fifth and final set of interviews was completed in 1980. During these multiple contacts, we lost some respondents. By the time of the last contact, our sample was reduced to 168 persons—78% of the original sample. Not unexpectedly, 18 respondents had died, mostly older ones.

We ended up with a sample generally representative of traditional blue-collar workers. Being for the most part upwardly mobile, their ways of living resembled those of the middle and lower-middle classes. They lived in their own small homes in a neighborhood distinguished by the homogeneity of its architecture. The primary concern for most lay with the family, both nuclear and extended. Aside from those who were high school seniors at the first interview, a majority had some technical or general education beyond high school, but few had completed college. Not surprising, the newlyweds were better educated than the middle aged, who in turn had more schooling than the preretirees. Also reflecting national trends, the older respondents were more likely to have many siblings but only two to three children. Most acknowledged some religious affiliation, with more women than men attending services; many parents who did not participate themselves sent their children to Sunday school or synagogue. More than three fourths of the women had jobs, frequently part time.

The Activities Checklist

The focus of this chapter will be a measure that deals with leisure activities: the 33-item Activities Checklist. An initial factor analysis (Lowenthal, Thurnher, & Chiriboga, 1975) produced five scales:

1. Housework: This scale included three items—shopping, cooking, chores (alpha = .56).
2. Solitary Activities: This scale included five items—crafts, solitary activities, playing a musical instrument, helping others, and self-improvement activities (alpha = .48).
3. Sports: This scale included six items—participant sports, exercise, spectator sports, playing cards, dancing, and lower levels of reading (alpha = .56).
4. Social Activities: This scale included nine items—cultural activities, travel, picnics, visiting, being visited, parties, eating out, talking, and going to the movies (alpha = 70).
5. Contemplative Activities: This scale included five items—walking, praying, daydreaming, reminiscing, and writing (alpha = .58).

A factor analysis also suggested two additional scales with low internal reliabilities that were retained for exploratory purposes:

6. Outdoor Activities: This scale included scores for three items—interaction with pets, general outdoor activities, and listening to the radio (alpha = .33).

7. Passive Activities: This scale included only two items—resting and watching TV (alpha = 28).

Together these seven scales bear a strong resemblance to those arbitrarily defined by Kaplan (1970) as well as leisure scales developed by Kelly and his colleagues (e.g., Kelly et al., 1986).

Measures of Stress Exposure

Two measures of life events formed the basis of our assessment of stress exposure.

Life events coding. The first was a 168-item Life Events Inventory, developed for our baseline interviews as a result of content analysis of randomly selected cases (Lowenthal et al., 1975). Coding was for experiences that created conditions of change in the past 4 years. For this chapter, two measures derived from this coding effort were included: total negative life events and total positive events.

Life events inventory. The second was a 139-item Life Events Questionnaire, which respondents completed at the third, fourth, and fifth contacts (Fiske & Chiriboga, 1990). In addition to checking off each event that occurred over the past year, respondents also noted whether it was a positive or negative experience.

Assessment of Transitions

At the third contact, approximately 5 years into the study, ratings were made concerning whether subjects had undergone the transition for which they had originally been selected: leaving the family home, parenthood, departure of the youngest child from the family home, and retirement (Fiske & Chiriboga, 1990).

Personal and Health Characteristics

Measures from four instruments explored a variety of personal characteristics:

(1) Psychological symptoms. A 42-item checklist of symptoms had been developed for the study by three geriatric psychiatrists (see

Lowenthal et al., 1975). Drawing heavily on the Cornell Medical Index, this checklist generated several indices, including the total or summary score used in this chapter.

(2) Bradburn scales. Included here are the Bradburn (1969) Affect Balance Scale and a general question ("In general, how happy are you these days? Very happy, somewhat happy, or not too happy").

(3) Self-reported health. Two questions with structured responses asked (a) how often the subjects had visited the doctor during the past 12 months and (b) how healthy they thought they were compared with others their age.

(4) Adjective Rating List. A 70-item instrument was derived from the Block (1961) Q-Sort method but changed to a 3-point rating system. Factor analysis yielded seven scales: socially polished, amiability, hostility, assertiveness, control, dysphoria, and insecurity (Lowenthal et al., 1975). In addition, four global scores were created. These included two scales assessing positive and negative self-concept (generated by the initial principal components analysis) and masculine and feminine identity scales (generated by including items that significantly differentiated men from women).

Activity and the Life Course

The Pretransitional Period

At the first interview, well before they embarked on the normative transition of interest to the investigators, significant life course differences were evident on all but one variable: outdoor activity. For outdoor activity, the only difference found was that men were far and away more likely to be involved than were women.

Of the six scales demonstrating life stage differences, there were four in which one or both of the two younger groups were more active in the specific leisure area than were the two older groups. Specifically, the younger subjects were more involved in social activities (newlyweds more than anyone else), contemplative activities (high school seniors were highest; preretirees were lowest), solitary activities (the two younger groups were higher than the two middle-aged groups), and sports (high school seniors scored highest; preretirees, lowest).

Newlyweds reported the greatest involvement in maintenance activities and the high school seniors the least. And, as might be expected, women were more likely than men to be involved in such activities. More important, however, an interaction of life stage and gender was found (p < .01); multiple range tests indicated that the differences between men and women were more pronounced among the two middle-aged groups.

The last scale to be considered summated the two most passive forms of activity on our checklist: resting and watching television. Results indicated that the two older groups were significantly more involved in these than were the newlyweds, while the high school seniors fell into the middle.

Stability and Stress

To begin considering the influence of stress exposure on changes in social activities, a series of correlations were computed between activity scale scores for the initial and 5-year interview contacts. Correlations were computed separately for three subgroups: (a) 28% who reported low levels of negative life events at either the initial or the 5-year contact; (b) 45% who reported high levels of negative events at only one of the contacts; (c) 27% who reported high levels of negative life events at both the first and the 5-year contact. These analyses drew upon both younger and older subjects.

As shown in Table 4.1, among those who reported low levels of negative stress exposure, there is one very clear finding: The correlation between baseline and 5-year scores for the same scales is consistently in the moderately high range and is consistently significant. In addition, being higher in contemplative activities at baseline was not only a strong predictor of subsequent contemplative activities but predicted lower levels of the more passive activities (resting and watching TV).

As also shown in Table 4.1, among those who were categorized as being intermediate in stress exposure, the pattern of autocorrelations over time began to break down. Significant correlations between time 1 and the 5-year follow-up scores were found only for five scales; the two that were lowest in internal reliability, outdoor and passive activities, now do not correlate significantly over time. In addition, people who scored higher on passive activities at baseline were more likely at the follow-up to score higher in social activities.

When considering subjects reporting exposure to high levels of stress at both contacts, the correlations once again were not significant for the scales assessing outdoor and inactive activities. Social activities were

Table 4.1 Correlations Between Baseline and Five-Year Scores

	Low-Stress Context	Intermediate-Stress Context	High-Stress Context
Household	.51**	.54**	.55**
Sports	.64**	.51**	.51**
Social	.60**	.40**	.12
Contemplative	.56**	.53**	.51**
Solitary	.64**	.52**	.48**
Outdoor	.42*	.16	.32
Inactive	.42*	.24	.26
(Group N)	(47)	(79)	(48)

NOTE: Correlations are between the same measures, as assessed at baseline and 5-year follow-up, for persons who reported the lowest levels of negative life events at both T1 and T3, intermediate levels, and high levels. One-tailed significance: * = .01; ** = .001.

also uncorrelated over time. Another finding of interest, not shown in Table 4.1, is that two cross-scale correlations were now significant. Those higher in contemplative activities at baseline were not only more contemplative at the 5-year contact but also more likely to participate in solitary activities. Further, those who were more inclined toward inactive pursuits at baseline were more likely to be lower in sports activities at the follow-up.

Overall, these results suggest that stress exposure does have some impact on activities, especially outdoor activities, in the more passive activities such as resting and watching TV, and in social activities. Knowledge of the participation in these three areas of activity at one point may not provide much information concerning their subsequent status in the same area if they are in a high-stress context.

Predictors of Change in Leisure Activities

We used hierarchical regression analyses as another means of considering the degree of change in activity levels over the first 5 years of the study, here using data drawn only from the two oldest groups of subjects. The analytic model used to identify and order sets in the hierarchical analysis was a simple one: The first set consisted of initial status on the same activity scale.

After partialing out the component of 5-year status that could be attributed to initial status, the next step was to enter three variables reflecting demographic characteristics: stage (i.e., empty nest versus retirement), gender, and educational level. Third, the seven factor-derived self-concept scales were added. Fourth, baseline levels on psychological symptoms, happiness, and affect balance were entered. Fifth, measures were included that assessed potential change agents: levels of positive and negative events reported for the year preceding the 5-year interview and a measure indicating when (and if) the normative transition under study had been undergone.

Results will be presented here only for the two older samples. Further, to save space and provide the most parsimonious view of the data, results were rerun for each type of activity with the reanalyses including only the significant predictors of 5-year status.

Social activities. Approximately 50% of the variance in social activities at the time of the 5-year follow-up was accounted for by initial status in social activities (entry beta = .58, p = .00) at baseline contact. Life stage (entry beta = −.16, p = .07) and transitional status (entry beta = .20, p = .05) at the fifth year also contributed. Total variance accounted for was 63%. In less technical terms, higher levels of social activities at the 5-year follow-up were predicted by higher levels of social activities at baseline, being in the younger of the two middle-aged groups, and having gone through the transition earlier than others.

Sports activities. For sports, the only significant predictor was status at the baseline contact. Initial levels of sports activity accounted for 43% of the variance in the same scale some 5 years later (beta = .65, p = .000). The lack of association with any other variable, including education and gender, suggests that an interest in sports has its own inner drive.

Maintenance activities. Maintenance activities at the 5-year follow-up were predicted by initial level of maintenance activities (beta = .60, p = .00), which explained 36% of the variance in maintenance activities at the third contact. In addition, stage (beta = .26, p = .00) and gender (beta = .30, p = .00) contributed to the prediction of subsequent levels of maintenance activities together accounting for an additional 13% of the variance. Finally, when time 3 negative events for the last year (beta = −.17, p = .04) and transitional status at T3 (beta = −.16, p = .06) were added, the two together added a final 4% to the variance. Overall, the regression equation predicted 53% of the variance.

With over half the variance in the 5-year levels of maintenance activity accounted for, the prediction model seems to have been appropriate. Being higher in maintenance activities was associated with higher levels of participation at baseline, being a woman and in the older of the two middle-aged groups, lower levels of stress exposure, and having experienced the anticipated transition relatively recently.

Contemplative activities. Initial levels of contemplative activities (beta = .70, p = .00) accounted for 49% of the variance in contemplative activities at the third contact. Perception of oneself as socially polished added 4% to the variance (beta = −.19, p = .01). Finally, addition of the psychological symptoms variable added 2% of explained variance (beta = −.15, p = .05). The overall explained variance for contemplative activities was 53%.

Solitary activities. When attention turned to prediction of more solitary activities, again the best predictor was initial level of solitary activities (beta = .49, p = .00), which accounted for approximately 24% of the variance. Nothing else was associated with the level of solitary activities after 5 years.

Outdoor activities. Level of involvement in outdoor activities was predicted by initial involvement (beta = .40, p = .00), although only about 16% of the variance was accounted for. Two self-concept attributes—feelings of hostility (beta = −.32, p = .00) and amiability (beta = −.28, p = .01)—together accounted for 11% of the variance (p = .00). The Bradburn (1969) happiness score added 3% to the variance (beta = −.19, p = .05). With less than a third of the variance accounted for, the predictive model was less adequate in predicting outdoor activities than it was for other variables. Results did suggest, however, that older individuals who are initially higher in outdoor activities, who feel themselves to be simultaneously low in hostility and in amiability, and who generally feel happier are more likely to end up being involved in outdoor activities at a future date.

Passive activities. Although the prediction was not very strong, initial levels of passive activities predicted approximately 6% of the variance (beta = .24, p = .05) in such activities 5 years later. Perceiving oneself to be more hostile (beta = .20, p = .05) was also linked with higher levels of passive activities accounting for an additional 4%. Total variance accounted for in the predictive analysis, however, was only 10%.

Leisure as a Predictor of Self-Concept

In the introductory section, we mentioned Atchley's (1987) hypothesis that in retirement leisure activities may play a more important role in shaping the self-concept of men and women. When a major source of self-esteem and identity is taken away, activities of a more discretionary nature may (a) simply become more influential in the absence of work-related activities and/or (b) provide a more accurate reflection of self-related interests because the retired person theoretically has more choice about what activities to pursue.

To begin exploring this hypothesis, we selected a subgroup of the oldest cohort who had actually retired by the 5-year follow-up—44 of the 50. For these people, we used a hierarchical regression procedure to predict, for baseline and for the 5-year follow-up data, overall positive self-image, overall negative self-image, masculine self-image, and feminine self-image. In the regression, we first entered gender and educational level and then entered the seven activity scales as a set. For prediction of self-concept indices at the first, or baseline, interview, we included baseline indicators of activity; in the prediction of self-concept at the 5-year follow-up, we used the follow-up activity scales.

In the case of positive self-image, the results provided some confirmation of Atchley's theory. In the prediction of initial levels of positive self-image, the activities set did not contribute (R-square change = .21, p = .13) but the demographic set played a significant role: The more educated subjects were less positive about themselves (beta = −.45, p = .01). By the 5-year follow-up, however, the situation had changed: Demographic variables did not contribute significantly but activities did (R-square change = .28, p = .05). Specifically, those who were more positive about themselves were more likely to be engaged in outdoor (beta = .35, p = .05) and social activities (beta = .48, p = .01) and tended to be lower in the more contemplative activities (beta = −.29, p = .10).

Toward a Typology of Activity

In addition to life course studies of individual activity scales, some studies have focused on more comprehensive life-style issues. Life-style research typically tries to pull back a step from the level of individual scale measurement and to evaluate the significance of various activity patterns for the individual. Reichard, Livson, and Petersen

(1962, p. 170), for example, classified retired men into categories such as the "rocking chair" aged and the "armored."

A Leisure Typology: Initial Findings

While classification of individuals into groups can be based on qualitative approaches such as content analysis, cluster analysis is a more empirically based approach. Cluster-analytic strategies evaluate the overall similarity across individuals of scores on multiple measures (Chiriboga & Krystal, 1985; Tryon & Bailey, 1970). The seven leisure scales were subjected to a cluster analysis (SPSS/PC Version 4.0) in an effort to determine whether groups could be empirically obtained that shared similar profiles of scores. A five-cluster solution was judged to provide the optimum differentiation.

Cluster 1 (N = 24) was the highest in maintenance activities (chores, cooking, shopping) but also scored relatively high on the sports/playing and social scales. They were the lowest on contemplative, solitary, and outdoor activities. A surprise, they averaged the highest score on the "passive" activity scale that included resting and watching TV. From a leisure point of view, they seem to adhere to a relatively active but uncomplicated pattern of leisure activities. We called them the "simple pleasures" group.

The simple pleasures group had the highest proportion of women (62%) and was most likely to have a spouse (79%), most educated, next to lowest on self-perception as being a hostile person, highest in their perceived health, second lowest in reports of psychological symptoms, and second highest in reports of positive life experiences over the past 4 years.

Cluster 2 (N = 42) stands out as being lowest in social activities and also were low in contemplative and maintenance activities. They were roughly average in all other activities. We called them the "socially restricted" or "minimalists."

The socially restricted group was the second most likely to have men as members (79%), least likely to see themselves as insecure, on the low end on self-perceived hostility, second to the bottom on perceived health, and below average in the number of reported psychological symptoms but tied for lowest in reports of positive life events. Overall, these were relatively self-confident people, mostly men, who were not very healthy and whose lives did not seem to be providing much positive stimulation. The majority, 69%, were from the two middle-aged groups.

Cluster 3 (N = 95), the largest group, were highest of all groups in solitary activities and among the highest in maintenance, contemplative, and outdoor activities. They were the group least likely to participate in passive activities. We called them the "creatively engaged" because their activity pattern seemed to focus on doing things that were of special interest to them and involved some creativity.

The creatively engaged group had the highest proportion of women (72%), was second highest in educational attainment, most likely to feel insecure, second highest in self-perceptions of hostility, most likely to report psychological symptoms, and relatively high on positive experiences over the past 4 years.

Cluster 4 (N = 6), the smallest group, stood out as being least likely to be involved in maintenance and sports activities while also being low in contemplative, solitary, and outdoor activities. In contrast, they were second highest in social and passive activities. In some ways, they were mildly withdrawn from anything that seems physically or intellectually challenging. We called them the "socially focused," although physical disengagement also characterized this group.

The socially focused group contained the highest proportion of older subjects, all were either in the empty nest or retirement stage, and all were married men. They had the lowest level of educational attainment, were second lowest in insecurity, and the lowest in self-perceived hostility. They reported having the lowest overall health compared with others their age but also were lowest in psychological symptoms. Finally, they scored lowest in reports of positive life experiences. Overall, this was a group of relatively uneducated older men who seemed to manifest the possible later life "mellowing out" but who were not obtaining many pleasurable experiences—possibly because of physical restrictions.

Cluster 5 (N = 42) members stand out as being highest on activities related to sports and games, social activities, contemplative activities, and outdoor activities, and next to highest in solitary activities. The only area in which they scored substantially below the other groups was on passive activities. We called them the "vigorously engaged."

The vigorously engaged were the youngest group (52% were in the high school group), were more likely to consist of men, least likely to be married, second lowest in educational attainment, highest in self-perceived hostility, highest in self-reported health, among the highest in psychological symptoms, and had the highest reports of positive life experiences over the past 4 years.

A Look at Long-Term Outcomes

In addition to considering the characteristics that defined the five groups at the first interview contact, we were also interested in whether group membership helped us to understand people's circumstances some time later. At the end of 12 years, these five groups differed in several ways. For example, the "socially focused" group of older men reported the fewest positive life experiences and projected (probably with some realism) the fewest years into the future. Despite these apparent liabilities, however, they were happiest in terms of satisfaction with current activities and with goal attainments. It was the younger "vigorously engaged" group that was least satisfied with current activities and goal attainment. Although scoring highest in positive life experiences, it is noteworthy that the vigorously engaged also were scoring with the most negative stressors as well. Perhaps their lives were most stressed and complex as well as most active.

The two groups with the fewest negative stressors reported at follow-up were the "socially restricted" and the "socially focused." It is important to point out, however, that, while the socially focused were also lowest on positive life experiences, the socially restricted were second highest. In balance, the latter group seems to have fared better.

Summary and Implications

In this chapter we have explored several characteristics of leisure activities, both from an adult life span perspective and also from the perspective of later life. When first interviewed, the younger subjects were more active in four of the seven areas of leisure developed for this chapter: social, contemplative, solitary, and sports activities.

To put these cross-sectional results in perspective, we then considered whether stress exposure produced a destabilizing force on leisure activities. Over a period of 5 years, the leisure activities of subjects who had been exposed to relatively few stressors generally seemed to be more stable than the activities of subjects exposed to intermediate or relatively high stress conditions. Subsequent analyses focused on the two older groups. It was found that, apart from the two scales with very low internal reliability—outdoor activities and passive activities—the best predictor of activity over a 5-year period was initial status on the same activity. In two cases—sports and solitary activities—initial level was the only significant predictor. Men and women who experienced the departures of their children or who retired earlier than others were more likely to be high in social activities at the 5-year contact. In contrast, and perhaps because they still had not adjusted to their new circumstances, maintenance activities were highest in those who had made the transition relatively recently.

The next step, one that raises some intriguing glimpses into the complex transactions that help shape our lives, was to consider the specific case of retirement. Drawing on continuity theory, the hypothesis was examined that retirement might heighten the influence of leisure activities upon self-concepts. Only four indices of self-concept were considered, but findings provided some evidence that leisure activities are indeed more strongly associated with positive self-concept in the years following retirement.

Finally, attention turned to the possibility that individuals might share common profiles of scores across our measures of leisure. Our own findings reinforce the utility of cluster analysis, and we found several groups relevant to middle age and aging.

The socially restricted group, consisting largely of middle-aged men, was of particular interest. When first evaluated, this group seemed to have more than their share of health problems and generally were not encountering many positive situations in their lives. Some 12 years later, however, they were doing quite well; in fact, they had the enviable position of experiencing few negative stressors and very high levels of positive experiences.

In contrast, consider the vigorously engaged group. At first contact, they not only were actively involved in many spheres of leisure activities but were experiencing many benefits from this involvement. Some 12 years later, these men and women, nearly half of whom were now about 30, were encountering more than their share of problems. One conclusion suggested by these findings is that the same "style" of leisure activities may shift in outcomes as people move across the life course.

Of particular interest in these life-style-oriented analyses was that the pattern of leisure activities seemed to play a role in determining the degree to which subjects later were exposed to life stressors, both positive and negative. This relationship was not unexpected, because other analyses from the same study had found life-style characteristics were linked to current stress exposure (e.g., Lowenthal et al., 1975). The reason for the relationship of life-style to stress is not explained by the data. One possibility is that persons who are subject to consistently high or low levels of stress may simply adapt to circumstances. Persons laboring under sustained and severe stress, for example, may find themselves voluntarily or involuntarily restricting their lives so they have more time to deal with their problems. The proverbial 36-hour day of caregivers of demented patients is an example.

Another possibility is that patterns of leisure activities may predispose individuals to differing stress experiences. The pattern of activities, in turn, may be shaped by such personality characteristics as the self-concept. Some support for this notion comes from investigations conducted a number of years ago. Beiser (1971) described a category of people whose lives were dedicated to preservation of the status quo. They sought stability by restricting their lives and input from external sources. When change was forced upon them, their first consistent response was to reestablish a new life as close as possible to the old. In this research, our socially restricted group bears some resemblance to those people described by Beiser; results suggest that social restriction is not necessarily a bad thing.

In concluding this chapter, one last point deserves emphasis. The results strongly reinforce the idea that longitudinal designs can add important dimensions to the study of leisure. Research on leisure activities generally either has relied on cross-sectional designs or has followed subjects for relatively brief periods. As can be seen from the current investigation, availability of data from extended periods of time can help us to conceptualize leisure as an evolving process. The varying significance of activities and patterns of activities, at different points in time, only becomes accessible to study when longitudinal data are available.

References

Atchley, R. C. (1987). *Aging: Continuity & change* (2nd ed.). Belmont, CA: Wadsworth.

Baltes, M. M., Wahl, H., & Schmid-Furstoss, U. (1990). The daily life of elderly Germans: Activity patterns, personal control and functional health. *Journal of Gerontology, 45*(4), 173-179.

Beiser, M. (1971). A study of personality assets in a rural community. *Archives of General Psychiatry, 24,* 244-254.

Block, J. (1961). *The Q-Sort method in personality assessment and psychiatric research.* Springfield, IL: Charles C Thomas.

Bradburn, N. M. (1969). *The structure of psychological well-being.* Chicago: Aldine.

Chiriboga, D. A., Catron, L. S., and Associates. (1991). *Divorce: Crisis, challenge or relief?* New York: New York University Press.

Chiriboga, D., & Krystal, S. (1985). An empirical taxonomy of symptom types among divorcing persons. *Journal of Clinical Psychology, 41*(5), 601-613.

Cumming, E., & Henry, W. (1961). *Growing old: The process of disengagement.* New York: Basic Books.

Fiske, M., & Chiriboga, D. A. (1990). *Change and continuity in adult life.* San Francisco: Jossey-Bass.

Havighurst, R. J. (1957). The social competence of middle-aged people. *Genetic Psychology Monographs, 56,* 297-375.

Holahan, C. E. (1988). Relation of life goals at age 70 to activity participation and health and psychological well-being among Terman's gifted men and women. *Psychology and Aging, 3*(3), 286-291.

Kaplan, M. (1979). *Leisure: Lifestyles and lifespan.* Philadelphia: Saunders.

Kelly, J. R., Steinkamp, W., & Kelly, J. R. (1986). Later life leisure: How they play in Peoria. *The Gerontologist, 26*(5), 531-537.

Lowenthal, M. F., & Chiriboga, D. A. (1972). Transition to the empty nest: Crisis, challenge or relief? *Archives of General Psychiatry, 26,* 8-14.

Lowenthal, M. F., Thurnher, M., & Chiriboga, D. A. (1975). *Four stages of life.* San Francisco: Jossey-Bass.

Reichard, S., Livson, F., & Petersen, P. G. (1962). *Aging and personality.* New York: John Wiley.

Schlossberg, N. K. (1984). *Counseling adults in transition: Linking practice with theory.* New York: Springer.

Tryon, R. C., & Bailey, D. E. (1970). *Cluster analysis.* New York: McGraw-Hill.

Wallerstein, J., & Blakeslee, S. (1989). *Second chances: Men, women and children a decade after divorce.* New York: Ticknor and Fields.

Williams, R. H. (1963). Styles of life and successful aging. In R. H. Williams, C. Tibbitts, & W. Donahue (Eds.), *Processes of aging: Social and psychological perspectives* (Vol. 1, pp. 335-371). New York: Atherton.

5

Later Life Activity From European Perspectives

WALTER TOKARSKI

In the decades to come, there will be fewer children and greatly increased numbers of elderly. Every aspect of American life will be affected, including: the family, women, intergenerational relationships, health care and ethical choices, minorities and the economy. Will we have a better society or a worse one? It depends on us. (Pifer & Bronte, 1986, front cover)

This short text summarizes well the current situation not only in America but in the whole so-called Western industrialized world. Moderate future perspectives on one hand and very explosive predictions on the other hand stand in opposition to each other. The most pessimistic expectations of the future are expressed by young people who do not accept the individual and social changes in older peoples' lives that have occurred in Europe in the past 15 to 20 years.

This chapter is based on European discussions in the field of later life activity. It outlines and summarizes research results as well as conceptual and social-political approaches. Because of limited space and the fact that this chapter has only one author, it cannot be a "classical research report" with detailed information about the state of the art in the different European countries.

The "Activating People" Perspective in Europe

Analyzing changes and working on possibilities of coping with these changes have always been the main topics of social gerontology concerning the individual and social processes of aging (Tokarski, 1991). Today there is worldwide agreement that being active is the main characteristic of the "new" old in changing societies. It is also agreed that being active or becoming active again is the best way to reach a high quality of later life. In nearly all European countries, activating older people is the leading concept in social policy and in health care. Often there is a big difference between demand and reality, but what is important is that at least the concept is generally accepted. Some years ago this was not the case.

The idea of activating older people and helping them to stay active leads to the question: Activating them for what? It can be said without any contradiction that this will become one of the great questions in gerontology. Looking for adequate roles for people in later life will be at the center of gerontological discussions. Until now gerontological efforts had not succeeded in working out adequate roles for the elderly. In the meantime, more older individuals have taken the initiative and created such roles themselves by initiating social groups, private activities, self-help groups, and social movements. Many of these groups do not seek any support from the public sector. The fact that many of the "new" old are finding adequate roles for themselves is more or less the "mystery" of the new ways of living and organizing life in old age: Most younger people cannot imagine that the elderly are able to do this. European pension systems and social policy for the elderly have been improved during the last decades. Older people live in better conditions than in the past. But we have not succeeded in developing qualitatively new approaches that give orientation to older people for later life activities. Official policy for the elderly has defined aging as a social status of being dependent, segregated, and in need of state aid. That is why policy for the elderly has enlarged the depth of the split between young and old and between employed and retired people (Guillemard, 1992).

Conceptual Perspectives

There are traditional ways of viewing aging and life in old age in many European countries. But in most countries attention has increased since the end of the 1970s. The actual state of information about the aging process differs from country to country. In all European countries gerontology exists in theoretical and practical forms (Amann, 1984; Tokarski, 1989b). Especially in the leisure field, however, information is as underdeveloped as in many of the other fields that are relevant for everyday life and activity.

Most of the differences in regard to the process of aging result from different views of the elderly: Older people are not seen as a so-called problem group in all European countries as they are in Germany. It is not clear whether the elderly have problems because they are old or the young have problems because they cannot understand aging. In many countries aging is seen as the most natural thing in the world and problems are identified only with special groups of the elderly: the disabled, the poor, the frail, and those in institutional care.

Structural Changes

Structural changes are responsible for the fact that in most countries aging has become a political and scientific topic. The number of those over 65 years old in the European Community will increase from 13.7% in 1982 to 19% in the year 2020 (Guillemard, 1992). In some European countries the numbers today are nearly as high as those previously predicted for 2020 or will be as high as those predicted earlier than 2020, especially if the numbers of those currently over 60 years old are taken into consideration (Tokarski, 1989a).

It is also important to examine the development of younger generations to see the whole extent of the phenomenon. A comparison of United Nations surveys from 1950 to 1980 shows that the population structure in the European Community has changed dramatically: The number of children under 15 dropped 3.6% while the number of those over 60 increased 3.5%. The total European Community population increased 40% during this time period, but the number of those over 60 increased 80%. The number of those over 60 in Western Europe is projected to increase from 35 million in 1950 to 79 million in 2025 (130%), in Eastern Europe from 26 million to 82 million (225%), and in Southern Europe from 7.5 million to 35 million (365%; De Quijano-Caballero, 1986). These demographic changes are accompanied by changes in life-styles and life circumstances. For the West European countries, seven aspects of structural changes can be identified (Tokarski, 1991), as follows.

1. *Early retirement* has characterized the working situation in many European countries for 10 to 15 years. The reduction of working life and the prolonging of later life have changed expectations and demands of retired people, especially toward leisure and activity. Increased variety in leisure facilities combined with the social-political concept of activating people has led to increasing participation in activities that were reserved for young people in the past: overseas traveling, learning, entertainment, play, fitness, and sport activities.

2. The process of *"singularization"* is a common phenomenon in nearly all European countries. There are few extended families in the West European countries, and even in Southern and Eastern Europe the number of extended families is declining. The generations tend to live their own lives; the members of each generation seek to be independent from the others. Family life takes place over distances; only 20% of the elderly in Germany live with younger relatives. On the other hand, being with people and having social contacts are two of the most common aims of the elderly when they look for activity.

3. In most of the Western European countries, the *pension systems* are rather good and the amount of money that is available for retired people is normally much higher than is needed to survive. Nevertheless, a large number of people in Europe are poor. Either they live in the Eastern European countries with economies not yet recovered from structural problems or they exist on welfare in wealthier countries. For most of the elderly, however, life has improved since World War II. There are better chances for consumption, leisure activities, and education, more mobility, and a better self-image. Many of the new leisure facilities use these characteristics for animation: Even sport for the elderly no longer consists of only gymnastics, walking, and swimming as in former times. More and more there is golf, cross-country skiing, tennis, badminton, and leisure activities that require financial investment.

4. *Life expectancy* is still increasing in Europe but differs among countries (Tews, 1990). This change is accompanied by better health conditions and delaying of frailty. Ten years ago gerontologists assumed that older people started to become ill and multimorbid by the age of 75. Studies today show that this process more often starts after people are 80 and older. Even the majority of people older than 85 in

Germany are not ill, handicapped, or disabled. One development in Europe is that more and more older people—especially women—live to be 85, 90, and older. The number of people who are advanced in years is growing rapidly. There are not enough facilities for these aged people to be active because the facilities are developed for the young old but not for the old old.

5. *The higher level of education* among older people has led to higher levels of demand and expectation that have become relevant in the educational field. Not only do traditional institutions like open universities and universities of the "third age" gain from this but also commercial institutions, self-initiated groups, and even regular universities and colleges. In 1988 nearly 95% of the 53 West German universities offered special educational programs for the elderly (Tokarski, 1989a). In other Western European countries, similar numbers can be found.

6. *Life-style diversification* among the elderly makes it impossible to view them as a homogeneous group. Life-style diversification leads in developed countries to the situation in which some people over 65 have more similarities with younger generations than with their own generation. Cohorts no longer seem to be the best category for analyzing aging processes in Western industrialized countries: Life-style management and experiences during the last 40 years have become too diverse. Social and technological developments are too rapid and too contradictory to produce identical life-styles within any one cohort. Society today is not built by horizontal but by vertical dimensions. International gerontological research has found that age is not a variable that discriminates life or leisure styles. Such research has demonstrated that attitudes and the meaning of leisure activities are much more relevant for life-style than sociodemographic factors or the activities themselves. Links in the field of leisure and sport occur more often among life-styles and common interests than age. This is why in some leisure situations older persons have more problems with other old people than with younger people.

7. The results of psychological research in the field of aging show that the new old are *more flexible and have more intellectual possibilities* at their disposal than former generations. The mental abilities of the new old are higher and decrease later than was the case decades ago. Many studies show that the flexibility of behavior and attitudes and the fluidity of associations are significantly greater than in former generations. Two possible consequences are that

Table 5.1 Free Time in OECD Countries per Working Day (in hours, 1981)

Country	Retired People		Over 65 Years
	Men	*Women*	
Austria	7.7	6.2	6.7
Finland	8.8	7.4	—
France	6.7	5.2	5.7
The Netherlands	9.8	8.8	—
Norway	7.0	5.7	5.8
Switzerland	8.7	6.9	7.4
United States	7.3	7.1	6.7

(a) more can be expected of older people, and

(b) leisure and sport facilities should be organized more like those for younger participants.

Time Perspectives

In 1986 retired people in West Germany said that they had 9.7 hours per day of free time (after subtracting time for sleeping, eating, cleaning, housework, and work). This is the highest amount of free time hours in Europe (Tokarski, 1989b).

Looking for social contacts and being with others are the main motivations of the elderly for leisure activities. Time for social contacts varies internationally. Social contacts cover between 10% and 80% of the total free time of the elderly (Tokarski, 1989b).

Activity Perspectives

Culture, media, sport, and tourism are the main types of leisure activities in general. Participation by older persons, however, varies among the forms of activity.

Table 5.2 Time for Social Contacts in OECD Countries per Week (in hours, 1980)

Country	45-54 Years	55-64 Years	Over 65 Years
France	7.6	8.3	8.3
Switzerland	6.9	6.6	7.0
United States	5.3	6.6	6.8
Finland	7.0	8.0	—
Austria	7.3	8.3	8.6
The Netherlands	9.7	11.9	14.6
Norway	11.5	11.7	12.2

Cultural activities are primarily characterized by learning and other educational elements. Most of the Western European countries have thoroughly planned education systems that comprise "preparation for life in old age" for the young old, special educational programs and preparation for volunteering, as well as classical learning (languages, arts, writing, discussion groups, reading, and so on). The main conceptual approach is of lifelong learning as an instrument to enhance independence in later life by increasing competence in certain fields among the elderly.

Media play an important role in old age. In all industrialized countries, watching TV, listening to the radio, and reading newspapers and journals are common activities for more than 90% of adults. Only a few countries, such as Sweden and the United Kingdom, have special newspapers, journals, and TV programs for older citizens.

Most of the older people know about the importance of *sport and fitness* for the quality of later life. Germany has a participation rate of approximately 10% in physical activity. Other countries have half of this participation rate or less. It is obviously very difficult to motivate older people to engage in sport. Most of the clubs, organizations, and institutions are not ready to offer adequate sport and fitness facilities to the elderly (Tokarski, 1991).

Tourism is a developing area for senior leisure. In the Western European countries, about 55% of people over 60 travel more than one week per year, and the number of older people going overseas is increasing. Most of the travel agencies have special travel programs for the elderly. For short holidays, many communities have their own programs. A special aspect of travel is the migration of older people to the South: in the United Kingdom, to Kent and Sussex; in France, to the Riviera; in Germany, to the Bodensee and to Spain. The coming integrated Europe will increase this trend.

The role of *volunteers* in the European countries is different. While the United Kingdom, the Netherlands, and Scandinavia have a higher number of elderly volunteers, in Germany this number is lower. Considerable research shows that volunteering keeps people mobile, flexible, and competent and leads to a higher degree of quality in later life. It is difficult, however, to motivate older people to work as volunteers.

In general, in Europe there is increased attention being paid to the significance of activity for the quality of later life. Both conditions and later life-styles are changing. The emerging cohorts of older persons may well be both more active and more varied in their engagement patterns.

References

Amann, A. (Ed.). (1984). *Social-gerontological research in European countries: History and current trends.* Berlin: Deutsches Zentrum fuer Altersfragen.

De Quijano-Caballero, C. (1986). News from the United Nations. *ELRA News, 14*(1), 20-21.

Guillemard, A. (1992). Europaeische Perspektiven der Alterspolitik. In P. B. Baltes & J. Mittelstrasse (Eds.), *Zukunft des Alterns und gesellschaftliche Entwicklung* (pp. 614-639). Berlin: De Gruyter.

Pifer, A., & Bronte, L. (Eds.). (1986). *Our aging society.* New York: Norton.

Tews, H. P. (1990). Neue und alte Aspekte des Strukturwandels des Alters. *WSI-Mitteilungen, 8,* 478-491.

Tokarski, W. (1989a). *Zur gerontologischen Ausbildung and Hochschulen der Bundesrepublik* (Kasseler Gerontologische Schriften 7). Kassel: Gesamthochschulbibliothek.

Tokarski, W. (1989b). *Freizeit und Lebensstile aelterer Menschen* (Kasseler Gerontologische Schriften 10). Kassel: Gesamthochschulbibliothek.

Tokarski, W. (1991). Neue Alte, alte Alte: Alter oder neuer Sport? Seniorensport im Zeichen des Umbruchs. In W. Tokarski & H. Allmer (Eds.), *Sport und Altern* (pp. 5-21). Sankt Augustin: Academia Verlag.

PART II

Social Contexts of Activity

Activity is more than individuals doing something that produces a personal meaning or outcome. Considerable activity, usually called "leisure," is focused on the experience itself, on "intrinsic" meaning. Other activity is more "developmental," with meanings of longer-term outcomes, of "becoming." And considerable activity is social, in which the meaning is inextricably tied to sharing, companionship, communication, and interaction with other persons. Many kinds of activity are, more than anything else, a context for expressing, building, and enjoying social relationships. The most important factor in enjoying an event is often who else is present and the quality of the interaction rather than the activity itself.

This approach to activity as the context for social interaction is given several different slants in this part. What is significant for understanding aging is the connection. What makes for really satisfying later life? Some research suggests that, beyond income and health, what is most important is being active. Other research points to "meaningful integration" with other persons, relationships of trust and sharing. It seems likely that the two elements cannot be separated. We are usually involved in a variety of activity with those who are closest to us. Caregivers, support networks, and confidants are most often those with whom we do other things. Those mutual activities may be familial, informal, and unstructured. Or they may be quite directed and specific.

Social activity is more than filling time. It is a context of social bonding. It is sharing and feeling deeply related to others. It is mentoring and feeling of value. It is having a community of reliable others with whom to share the discontinuities of the later life course. Again, the issue is one of meaning more than amounts of time.

Rebecca Adams, in Chapter 6, has found that older women's friendships commonly have an activity base. Histories of common activity have continuity. There is considerable variety in what older women do together, but informal interaction is most common. Both friendship and activity patterns are processes with trajectories that are altered through the later life course. In that process, activity, contexts, and the relationships themselves have a career with intersecting elements. Research, however, has not focused on the ways in which the meanings of the activity and relationships are related. What really happens in the process? Aging is, after all, freedom from some responsibilities as well as limitation. Some activities would seem to be environments for meeting new friends, while others are social spaces for developing continuing friendships. As older women find their former friendship networks diminished through the years, activities become part of the reconstituting process of social bonding and expression. Later life friendship is a process that includes cognitive and social role elements as well as affect and emotion.

In Chapter 7 Carol Cutler Riddick uses her own and other research to deal with the particular circumstances of aging women. It seems clear that activity engagement does contribute to quality of life and to mental health. Again, social activity seems most salient, a fact that is underlined by the likelihood that women will outlive their male partners. Further, women are most likely to have their activity patterns limited throughout the life course by caregiving, first for children and later for older adults. As a consequence, women often express the need for "time for me." This suggests that in general they have been less able than men to determine their schedules and segregate time for their own chosen activities. What are the differences in the life course of women that bring them to later life activity with values, orientations, and histories different from men's? Are women less likely to feel "entitled" to activity that is really their own and for their own sake? Is the activity of older women more likely to be home based and home related? Research on the leisure of adult women suggests that there are common constraints related to women's roles that have limited their opportunities to learn and find satisfaction in some kinds of activity. Further, their gender-role socialization may have oriented them to different meanings in leisure activity, more directed toward relationships, sharing, communication, and even nurturing rather than to competition and achievement. Leisure is less separated from the common round of life and more often meshed with roles and relationships. Women and men enter later life with different histories, in activity as well as in work and family. New attention to women and listening to the voices of women in research will likely produce new sets of issues. For example, what are the relationships of male-defined acceptable body images of women and definitions of physical competence to the willingness to risk later life physical activity?

Most women become widows. Helena Znaniecka Lopata draws on her long experience of research on widows in Chapter 8. Widows' activities are different than those of married women in significant ways. The social definition of not being "a couple" changes everything, not just immediate companionship but also the social contexts of access and invitation. This is especially true for those whose social niche has been primarily as a spouse. No longer being married may alter social status as well as financial and social resources. On the other hand, some new freedom is possible as the central spousal role is ended. Being a wife provides resources and also limiting norms. Perhaps there is a dialectic between the themes of community and of independence that are drawn with particular poignancy for many widows. Again, being a widow is more than loneliness. Activities are one element in the process of "recomposing a life."

Generations are linked in many ways. In Chapter 9 Douglas Kleiber and Robert Ray address the issue of generativity. At the heart of the subject is the continued desire of many older persons for a life that has value, a life of meaning and accomplishment. Some of that meaning may be found in contributing to the lives of others, especially those of succeeding generations. The orientation of generativity is contrasted with escapism and stagnation. Can older persons go on growing? One way is through generativity, through "mentoring" broadly conceived. It may be that there is a gender factor here too. Men may approach mentoring with more of a sense of separation from a defined "other" than do women with more of a sense of relatedness. Generative activity may be contrasted with kinds of leisure that are more disengaged and intrinsic. It is more relational in the sense of finding its meaning in the relationship. For many, it may be based on family or work roles. As such, it suggests that such relationships are positive, not "constraints" to leisure activity. The extent to which older persons hope to "leave a mark" on life that will last beyond their own deaths probably varies. What would seem to be common is that nonwork activity provides one context for generativity. The mark on the lives of others may be in the arts, sport, natural environment immersion, or some other interest or skill as well as in the work and family domains.

In a study of the retirement lives of a small sample of men and women workers in the Midwest (Kelly & Westcott, 1989), informal interaction with family and friends was at the center of the meaning of activity as well as of time allocation. The relatively high levels of satisfaction were not based on extraordinary investments in exotic activity or on radical reorientations of life in retirement. Rather, "ordinary retirement" tended to be quite social. Continuity was found both in relationships and in activity. The ordinary ties of common life together were the fabric on which individual patterns of life were imprinted. In this part of the book, primary attention has been given to women. There is some evidence, however, that friendships become increasingly important to men in later life and that such friendships are frequently activity based. In any case, it is evident that the social dimension of later life activity is central.

Reference

Kelly, J., & Westcott, G. (1989). Ordinary retirement: Commonalities and continuity. *International Journal of Aging and Human Development, 32*(2), 81-89.

6

Activity as Structure and Process

Friendships of Older Adults

REBECCA G. ADAMS

Older people meet friends while participating in leisure activities. Some of their friendships are activity based—they would not exist or continue if the older adults were to cease spending time in the relevant settings or to stop pursuing certain interests. These commonsense observations are not based on reported research findings. Although gerontologists have had a long-standing interest in the leisure activities of older adults (Kelly, 1987) and, more recently, an interest in their friendship patterns (Adams, 1989; Blieszner & Adams, 1992), they have not systematically examined what older people do with their friends.

Ethnographers have observed groups of older people participating in activities together (e.g., Hochschild, 1973). Researchers have not, however, systematically synthesized the findings of ethnographers or used their observations to generate or test hypotheses about friendship activities. Furthermore, ethnographers generally have not described the people they have observed as "friends." They may or may not have considered themselves as such. People have different conceptions of what friendship is (Adams, 1989), and the defining criteria are often intimate processes that occur only when the friends are alone (Adams, 1983). It is thus difficult to study what friends do together using only observational methods.

Survey researchers interested in explaining why some older people are better adjusted or have higher morale than others have used participation in leisure activities and in friendship each as predictors. Even the researchers who have reported on both types of activity have measured them separately. For example, in the classic Kansas City Study of Adult Life, Havighurst and Albrecht (1953) asked questions about various leisure activities centered in clubs, church, and the community and, separately, about time spent with friends. Methodologically, this classic approach is problematic because the two types of measures are not independent—people spend time with friends while pursuing leisure activities. Nonetheless, successive generations of gerontological researchers have used this approach.

A few survey researchers specifically interested in friendship have included questions in their research instruments about what older people do with their friends. These friendship researchers, however, either have failed to report these findings in subsequent reports on their data or have grouped activities in ways that obscure details.

So, the question becomes: Why has no one reported systematic and detailed data on what older people do with their friends? Researchers probably would have examined this topic if they had had a compelling theoretical reason for doing so. Even the few friendship researchers who have asked questions about what older people do with their friends have done so without theoretical motivation and thus have phrased questions in ways that have produced uninteresting data. (I include myself in this category and will use some of my data below to illustrate the limitations of atheoretical approaches.)

Building on recent friendship literature, it is now possible to construct a theoretical purpose for studying what older people do with their friends. The argument is two-staged. First, it is important to understand older adult friendship patterns, because researchers have demonstrated that they affect social support and psychological well-being (see Crohan & Antonucci, 1989; Larson, 1978), which are just two of myriad possible outcomes. Second, knowing what older people do with their friends will help us understand why they have the friendship patterns that they do. In this chapter, I argue that activities both provide the context for meeting and making friends and are processes shared by friends. Understanding what types of activity contexts and what types of shared activities contribute to the development and maintenance of friendships thus becomes the theoretical rationale for studying what older people do with friends. So, the main purpose of this chapter is to outline a theoretical framework for examining how participation in different leisure activity contexts affects friendship patterns and for determining which shared activities enhance friendship development and maintenance.

Gender, class, race, and a variety of other factors also affect leisure participation and thus the trajectory of individual friendships and friendship network patterns. In this chapter I outline the importance of one such characteristic—age. Furthermore, I discuss the potential effects on friendship activity of structural and cultural context (period) and of the way in which people are socialized (cohort).

Illustrative Data

Data suitable for illustrating the approach developed in this chapter are not available. The data from my 1981 Study of Nonmarried Older Women's Friendships illustrate the limitations of typical approaches to the study of activities shared by friends and provoke thoughts about future research directions.

The respondents were 70 white, nonmarried, female older adults who lived in Oak Park, Illinois, a middle-class suburb of Chicago. None of the women was employed at the time of the study. About two thirds of the women were widows, a fifth had never been married, and the rest were divorced or separated. Half of the women lived in age-segregated housing, and the rest lived elsewhere in the community.

Using their own definitions of friendship, the respondents listed a total of 678 friends. The 67 women who named at least one friend named an average of 10.1 friends. After they had listed their friends, they indicated whether the members of each pair knew and were friends with one another. By quickly sketching sociometric diagrams, it was possible to identify friendship groups within each respondent's larger network. Each respondent was asked to choose one friend from each cluster of friends (or friendship group). The respondents then answered detailed questions about each of their group representative friendships. They reported a total of 304, 228 of whom they had seen within the year. The data reported in this chapter concern these 228 active group representative friends. The respondents answered an open-ended question about what they did with each of them.

Treating these friendships as representative of groups assumes that the activities in which the women participated with these friends are the

Table 6.1 Activities in Which Older Women Participated With Friends
(N = 67)

Type of Activity	Percentage Who Did Activity With at Least One Friend	Average Percentage of All Friends With Whom They Did Activity
Talking	83.6	51.4
Eating meals	68.7	43.4
Recreational activities	50.7	26.7
Clubs	49.3	23.0
Outings	43.7	18.7
Cultural events	37.3	15.4
Instrumental support	16.4	6.0
Social gatherings	11.9	4.6
Exercise and sport	7.5	2.4

same as those in which they participated with other members of the group. Even for descriptive purposes, it would have been better to have obtained activity data for each of the 678 friendships or to have asked questions about friendship group activities rather than about activities with individual friends.

Table 6.1 lists the types of activities in which the women reported participating with friends, the percentage who shared each type of activity with at least one friend, and the average percentage of all of their friends with whom they shared each type of activity. The activities are arranged in order of decreasing occurrence.

With the exception of the category of talking, explanations of the specific activities are warranted. Eating meals includes those at the respondents' or friends' homes, in restaurants, at the Nutrition Center, in the cafeteria of age-segregated buildings, and during picnics. Recreational activities include watching television, singing, playing bingo, playing instruments, playing cards, playing games, and making crafts. Clubs include volunteer and political organizations, church activities, hobby groups, and classes. Outings include walking, riding in automobiles, shopping, riding on buses, and going to parks. Cultural events include travel, sight-seeing, movies, theater, sports events, musical performances, and races. Instrumental support is help given to the friend by the respondent or to the respondent by the friend. Social gatherings include parties, weddings, and funerals. Exercise and sports include swimming, bowling, tennis, and workouts.

Leisure Activities as Structure

Not all friendships are based on participation in leisure activities, so a limited amount of the variation in friendship patterns can be explained by the approach outlined in this chapter. One step in explaining the variation in friendship patterns, however, is to discover why some people have activity-based friendships and others do not. To do this, one must first determine why people do or do not participate in leisure activities and then ascertain why people are able to make and maintain friendships in some of the leisure contexts in which they participate and not in others of them. Goodale and Witt (1989) argued that the characteristics of specific leisure contexts can encourage or discourage participation in activities. In this section I argue further that participation in some leisure activities provides more opportunities for meeting and maintaining friendships than participation in others. Specifically, I propose that the social structural characteristics of the group involved in a given activity affects the opportunities for friendship. This argument is the social parallel to Cheek and Burch's (1976) observations about the effect of physical setting on social interaction in various leisure locales. In addition to building on the argument made by Goodale and Witt, this proposal elaborates on recent findings by friendship scholars.

In the friendship literature, researchers repeatedly report that friendship networks tend to be homogeneous. In other words, people tend to have networks composed of friends who are sociologically similar to themselves and to one another (e.g., Usui, 1984). Most of the literature on homogeneity assumes that people voluntarily select status-similars as friends. Researchers have recently challenged this assumption and have concluded that, though choice definitely contributes to homogeneity (McPherson & Smith-Lovin, 1987), the context in which friendships are formed affects network homogeneity as well (Feld, 1982; Fischer, 1982). Of particular interest here is Feld's (1982) finding that most relationships originate in activities that bring together homogeneous groups of people. The more homogeneous these sets of people are, the more homogeneous are the resulting friendship networks.

The discussion about the effect of the characteristics of the context on friendship formation has been focused exclusively on the homogeneity of the participants. Other social structural characteristics of the context might affect friendship formation and maintenance as well. For example, the higher the proportion of people in a context who know one another (density), the closer they feel to one another (solidarity), the more equally they regard and treat one another (equality), and the more similar their attitudes, values, and beliefs (similarity), the greater the opportunities for friendship in the context might be (see Blieszner & Adams, 1992, for a more detailed discussion of these concepts). The size of the context might also affect friendship opportunities, but it is not clear how. The literature on community size, for example, suggests two opposing hypotheses. On one hand, a smaller context might be more conducive to the formation of friendship ties, because people are more likely to participate in them actively (Lang, 1987; Wicker, 1979). On the other hand, a large context increases the number of people from whom to choose and might therefore improve friendship opportunities (Fischer, 1982). To test these hypotheses, in addition to information on their friendships, the researcher would have to ask respondents for a list of all of their leisure activities (regardless of whether any of their friends are involved), about the social structural characteristics of each leisure context, and for a list of the friends who participate in each of them.

Unfortunately such data do not currently exist. Note the inadequacy of the two previously used approaches for studying the effects of the characteristics of leisure contexts on friendship. The classic approach (e.g., Havighurst & Albrecht, 1953) involves asking respondents for a list of their leisure activities, but not about which ones involve interaction with friends, let alone about the characteristics of the contexts in which these activities take place. On the other hand, the respondents who participated in my Study of Nonmarried Older Women's Friendships listed activities that involved interaction with friends, not other activities, and they did not describe the contexts in which the activities took place. For example, it is not possible to determine whether the women were least likely to name exercise and sport as a context for friendship (see Table 6.1) because they were least likely to participate in that type of activity or because the characteristics of the context in which this type of activity took place were not conducive to friendship.

An additional problem with both of these approaches is that they do not involve distinguishing among the several contexts in which a given activity might take place. For example, in my study some of the women were involved in several different clubs, the structural characteristics of which probably varied. Because I separated the responses by type of activity alone rather than also separating them by setting, it would not have been possible to collect data on the characteristics of the contexts.

Leisure Activities as Processes

Leisure activities provide a structural context for friendship, but participation in them is also a component of friendship interaction itself. Leisure activity thus both provides structure for friendship and is friendship process. Processes are overt behavioral events and covert cognitive and affective responses that occur when people interact (Kelley et al., 1983).

Participation in leisure activities is thus a behavioral process. Behavioral processes are the action components of friendship (Blieszner & Adams, 1992). They are the deeds people do with, for, and to their friends. In addition to shared activities, they include such behaviors as self-disclosure, resource exchange, and displays of affection, but also concealment, competition, and conflict. Participation in a given activity might include one or more of these behaviors or others.

Viewing leisure activities only as behavioral processes is overly simplistic. Leisure activities might foster cognitive and affective processes as well. Cognitive processes reflect the internal thoughts that each partner has about self, the friend, and the friendship. These thoughts might include the evaluations and judgments that one person makes of another's attractiveness, character, similarity to the self, and other important attributes. Affective processes encompass emotional reactions to friends and friendships. Empathy, indifference, joy, anger, loyalty, and jealousy are all examples of affective processes (Blieszner & Adams, 1992).

Leisure activities vary in the processes and combinations of processes they foster. For example, some sports and games might foster competition and others might foster cooperation. Helping one another might contribute to affective processes such as empathy, joy, or even irritation or anger. The type of activity does not entirely determine the processes involved (individual circumstances certainly intervene), but the type of interaction involved in participation in specific leisure contexts leads to the more frequent occurrence of certain types of processes than of others. To my knowledge, researchers have not studied this variation in the relationship processes fostered by different types of activities.

Instead, survey researchers have typically used proxy measures of friendship process rather than direct measures of the behavioral, cognitive, and affective components of interaction. Proxy measures are measures of how often and how long processes occur (the length of acquaintance, the frequency of contact, the recency of contact, and the average length of each contact) and of the variety of activities in which friends participate (multiplexity). In other words, researchers have been concerned with whether interaction has taken place, but not with the nature of the processes involved (Blieszner & Adams, 1992). The underlying assumption seems to be that a larger quantity and variety of processes is better than a smaller one.

Both groups of gerontologists who have done research relevant to this topic, those using the classic approach and those interested primarily in friendship, have used proxy measures. They have not studied which behavioral, cognitive, and affective processes are involved in various types of activities shared with friends. Those using the classic approach have used proxy measures of the processes involved in various leisure activities, one of which is friendship. Those primarily interested in friendship have used proxy measures of overall friendship process and measures of process in relationships with specific friends. So, the classic researchers have ended up with data on how much time people spend doing different types of activities and on the variety of activities in which people engage. They often scaled these measures of participation in various activities together as measures of engagement or leisure involvement. In contrast, those primarily interested in friendship have ended up with data on the quantity of interaction and variety of activities shared with all friends or with specific friends. So, for example, my Study of Nonmarried Older Women's Friendships included questions about how much time they spent with each friend and what they did with each friend, but not questions about how much time they spent participating in each activity with friends. Neither the classic nor the friendship researcher approach has yielded data on the quantity of interaction with friends while sharing specific activities.

Although using proxy measures of processes to the exclusion of measures of the behavioral, affective, and cognitive components of interaction is not adequate, this does not mean that researchers should omit proxy measures of process from their instruments. Knowing that people routinely see friends by virtue of regular participation in activities illustrates the intersection of structure and process. On one hand, routine participation in an activity becomes a structural factor. It facilitates interaction with others without requiring forethought and planning on the part of the friends or potential friends. On the other hand, routine interaction allows for behavioral, cognitive, and affective processes to occur.

So, the researcher interested in studying the processes involved in activities shared by friends should include measures of quantity of time spent in each activity context and a list of friends who participate in each of them. In addition, he or she should include measures of the behavioral, cognitive, and affective processes fostered by each activity. With these data, it would then be possible to map the effect of the processes involved in leisure activities with friends on the trajectory of individual friend relationships and on friendship network patterns.

Aging, Period, Cohort, and Activities with Friends

Up to this part of the discussion, the framework has applied to people of all ages. We know, however, that for both developmental and sociological reasons, older people may behave differently than people in earlier stages of life. In this section I briefly explore how aging, period of history, and cohort membership might affect findings about activity with friends. To examine these propositions, researchers would need to conduct longitudinal studies of multiple age groups over a substantial length of time.

Aging affects us psychologically, physically, and socially. These changes, in turn, probably affect our predispositions, capabilities, and opportunities to participate in various types of activities with friends. Certain friendship activities may seem more or less interesting, sensible, and possible at different ages.

Allan and I (Allan & Addams, 1989) outlined the effects on friendship patterns of the sociological changes associated with entering old age. Our basic argument was that sociological aging can lead to new constraints on friendship but can also result in new opportunities. For example, retirement limits income and eliminates that one sphere of interaction with friends and potential friends. Relocation to a warmer environment or to be near family members might disrupt old friendship ties and create a need to generate new ones. Widowhood means no longer interacting with friends as part of a couple. On the other hand, my Study of Nonmarried Older Women's Friendships showed that entering old age also freed the women from the demands and normative constraints of work, family, and community and thus provided them with opportunities to pursue friendships in new ways (Adams, 1987).

Neither one of these discussions examined the ways that sociological aging might affect opportunities for participation in specific activities with friends, but one can imagine ways in which it might. For example, living on a limited income, no longer being part of a couple, or being geographically separated from one's closest friends might make it less likely that one could participate in certain activities with friends. On the other hand, having more time for leisure, being free to pursue activities unencumbered by a spouse, and entering into new relationships with people lacking preconceptions about one's interests might afford opportunities to pursue new activities with friends. The list of activities in Table 6.1 would have been substantially different if the women had not all been retired or widowed and if half of them had not relocated to age-segregated housing. Research is needed on how various aspects of aging affect participation in leisure activities and thus friendship.

The period of history can also affect activities shared with friends. For example, in recent times recreation centers and nutrition centers for senior citizens have provided contexts for leisure activities. Many of the older women I interviewed reported spending time at these centers solely to avoid isolation. They would not have played bridge, made crafts, played musical instruments, and so forth if the centers had not scheduled such activities. The figures reported in Table 6.1 thus reflect such opportunities. The availability of contexts for leisure activities in a given structural and cultural context thus needs to be examined.

Cohort membership might also affect participation in certain types of friendship activities. For example, the women in my study reported a relatively low rate of exercise and participation in sports with friends. This could be, as previously mentioned, because the contexts in which these activities take place are not conducive to friendship or because declining health prevented the women from vigorous activity. On the other hand, this low rate might reflect the way in which the women were socialized in their youths—young women did not exert themselves then as they do now. Another example of a cohort effect on friendship activity from my study concerns the women's tendency to report very few friendships with men (Adams, 1985), largely because they were socialized to view cross-sex relationships as romantic. As a result, most of their activities tended to be sex segregated. Perhaps in future generations older men and women will be friends and thus participate in a wider range of activities.

Conclusions

In this chapter I have outlined a theoretical approach to the study of activities with friends. Leisure activities both provide social structural contexts for friendship and are processes shared by friends. Some contexts are more conducive to friendship or to certain types of friendship patterns than are others. Activities vary in the behavioral, cognitive, and affective processes involved. Certain types and combinations of friendship processes lead to different individual friendship trajectories and to different friendship network patterns. Routine participation in a leisure context facilitates unplanned interactions with friends and potential friends and allows for behavioral, cognitive, and affective processes to occur. Thus one step in understanding variation in friendship patterns is to examine variation in the types of activities in which people participate with friends and in the extent of their participation in them. Understanding this variation is important because friendship patterns predict well-being and possibly other outcomes.

Previous studies of friendship activity have been without theoretical purpose. Asking how much time is spent with friends and separately asking how much time is spent pursuing various leisure activities or asking what activities are shared with friends is not adequate. Lists of friendship activities such as the one in Table 6.1 are superficial, because they do not help us understand why people participate in specific activities with friends and not in others or how participation in them affects friendship trajectories and patterns.

Instruments designed for studies of activities with friends using the theoretical approach outlined in this chapter would need to include measures of friendship network patterns and information on the dyads that compose them (see Blieszner & Adams, 1992), structural descriptions of each of the leisure contexts in which respondents participate (regardless of whether they have friends in the context), a list of the friends who participate in each of the leisure contexts, measures of the quantity of interaction with each friend in each leisure context, and measures of the behavioral, cognitive, and affective processes fostered by each type of activity. This would make it possible to use the characteristics of activity contexts and the processes fostered by activities as predictors of which activities people share with friends, the trajectory of individual friendships, and friendship network patterns.

Understanding the effect of aging, period in history, and cohort on participation in leisure activities with friends poses a further challenge. One cannot make inferences about what older people do with their friends from lists such as the one in Table 6.1. Such lists are merely descriptions of what people of various social ages, living in a given structural and cultural context after having been raised in another such context, did with their friends. Although it is unlikely that a longitudinal study of the friendship activities of different age groups over a substantial period of time will be conducted in the near future (or perhaps ever), certain steps can be taken to gain better understanding of the effects of age, period in history, and their interaction with one another. Researchers need to examine the age-related factors constraining and facilitating participation in different types of activities with friends, the characteristics of the activity contexts available for older people in today's world, and the way in which the current and future generations of older people have been socialized to regard leisure pursuits. Together, these explorations will bring us closer to understanding why older people tend to participate in some leisure activities with friends more than in others and, ultimately, will help explain variation in the friendship patterns of older adults and in their consequences.

References

Adams, R. G. (1983). *Friendship and its role in the lives of elderly women.* Unpublished doctoral dissertation, University of Chicago.

Adams, R. G. (1985). People would talk: Normative barriers to cross-sex friendships for elderly women. *The Gerontologist, 25,* 605-611.

Adams, R. G. (1987). Patterns of network change: A longitudinal study of friendships of elderly women. *The Gerontologist, 27,* 222-227.

Adams, R. G. (1989). Conceptual and methodological issues in studying friendships of older adults. In R. G. Adams & R. Blieszner (Eds.), *Older adult friendship* (pp. 17-41). Newbury Park, CA: Sage.

Allan, G., & Adams, R. G. (1989). Aging and the structure of friendship. In R. G. Adams & R. Blieszner (Eds.), *Older adult friendship* (pp. 45-64). Newbury Park, CA: Sage.

Blieszner, R., & Adams, R. G. (1992). *Adult friendship.* Newbury Park, CA: Sage.

Cheek, N., & Burch, W. R., Jr. (1976). *The social organization of leisure in human society.* New York: Harper & Row.

Crohan, S. E., & Antonucci, T. C. (1989). Friends as a source of social support in old age. In R. G. Adams & R. Blieszner (Eds.), *Older adult friendship* (pp. 129-146). Newbury Park, CA: Sage.

Feld, S. L. (1982). Social structural determinants of similarity. *American Sociological Review, 45,* 797-801.

Fischer, C. S. (1982). *To dwell among friends.* Chicago: University of Chicago Press.

Goodale, T. L., & Witt, P. A. (1989). Recreation non-participation and barriers to leisure. In E. L. Jackson & T. L. Burton (Eds.), *Mapping the past: Charting the future* (pp. 421-449). State College, PA: Venture.

Havighurst, R. J., & Albrecht, R. (1953). *Older people.* New York: Longman, Green.

Hochschild, A. R. (1973). *The unexpected community.* Berkeley: University of California Press.

Kelley, H. H., Berscheid, E., Christensen, A., Harvey, J. H., Huston, T. L., Levinger, G., McClintock, E., Peplau, L. A., & Peterson, D. R. (1983). Analyzing close relationships. In H. H. Kelley et al., *Close relationships* (pp. 20-67). New York: Freeman.

Kelly, J. R. (1987). *Peoria winter: Styles and resources in later life.* Lexington, MA: Lexington.

Lang, J. (1987). *Creating architectural theory.* New York: Van Nostrand Reinhold.

Larson, R. (1978). Thirty years of research on the subjective well-being of older Americans. *Journal of Gerontology, 33,* 109-125.

McPherson, J. M., & Smith-Lovin, L. (1987). Homophily in voluntary organizations. *American Sociological Review, 52,* 370-379.

Usui, W. M. (1984). Homogeneity of friendship networks of elderly blacks and whites. *Journal of Gerontology, 39,* 350-356.

Wicker, A. W. (1979). *An introduction to ecological psychology.* Monterey, CA: Brooks/Cole.

7

Older Women's Leisure Activity and Quality of Life

CAROL CUTLER RIDDICK

The purpose of this chapter is twofold. First, what is known about leisure and the quality of life of older women will be reviewed. Second, ideas for future research and practice will be identified.

Background

Before examining the literature on how leisure influences older women's lives, some background information is needed. In particular, the amount of attention devoted to females in gerontological research will be addressed, followed by a section summarizing a definitional approach to the term *quality of life.*

Gerontological Female-Focused Research: A Void

When reviewing the gerontological literature prior to 1980, one discovers a lack of focus on the conditions of older women. For example, Szinovacz (1982) notes that research on retirement was largely limited to "male only" samples into the later 1970s.

The decade of the 1980s, however, could be characterized as a period in which research activity, especially related to caregiving, on older women escalated (Cutler Riddick & Keller, 1991). Nevertheless, our knowledge about how the aging process influences the lives of older females in American society is not very advanced.

The same problem exists in the study of leisure activity. Henderson (1990) reflects on this situation by noting that it has been widely assumed that the findings of leisure studies involving males would also hold true for females. There has been little attention given to the particular conditions of women's leisure over the life span. Perhaps the crux of the explanation is best summarized by Henderson (1990, p. 229), who notes that "researchers who have studied women's leisure over the past ten years have faced a double problem because frequently neither the study of women nor the study of leisure is taken seriously."

Defining Quality of Life

One recurring theme in gerontological research has been the identi- fication of factors in the "quality of life of older persons." While most of us probably have a feel for what constitutes the "good life," the reality is that there has not been universal agreement regarding what is meant by the term *quality of life* (George & Bearon, 1980). Neverthe- less, one of the more popular approaches adopted in research undertak- ings is to define quality of life from the subjective evaluations of individuals. Myriad ways have been used to measure the different dimensions of subjective evaluation including the use of such concepts as successful aging, adaptation, life satisfaction, morale, well-being, happiness, self-concept, and self-esteem.

An examination of over four decades of research on the well-being of older (albeit predominantly male) Americans reveals that a number of factors, including leisure, have an effect on subjective evaluations dealing with quality of life (Cutler Riddick, 1982, 1985a, 1985b; Cutler Riddick & Daniel, 1984; Henderson, Bialeschki, Shaw, & Freysinger, 1989; Larson, 1978). Given the influential nature of leisure on an older person's quality of life, a review of the leisure literature was conducted and is reported in three parts: time usage, effects of leisure activity on quality of life, and experiences related to leisure. The following litera- ture review was limited to studies that specifically reported including females in the sample (either entirely or partially).

Literature Review

Time Usage

Time usage studies can focus on either how much leisure is available or how much time people devote to specific leisure undertakings. Regarding the former focus, a review of the earliest time budget studies concludes no overall gender differences in the amount of adult leisure time (Shaw, 1985). In an effort to overcome some methodological weakness of these earlier works, Shaw (1985) conducted a study of middle-aged adults (X age = 40) and reported that (a) males have significantly more leisure time than females on weekends and (b) there is little difference between homemakers and employed women in the amount of leisure time experienced.

Kelly, Steinkamp, and Kelly (1986) examined participation patterns by querying 400 adults age 40 and above. Among other things, it was reported that for the older compared with the younger women involved in the study: (a) Constriction or disengagement characterized certain activities, especially sport and exercise as well as outdoor recreation, and to a lesser degree cultural activity and travel; (b) there was continuity (with one exception) in a core of social, home-based, and family activities. It is important to note, however, that about 60% of the oldest old (or 75+ age group) females versus 85% of the younger age female groups reported participation in family activities; and (c) rates of participation in community organizations expanded or increased.

Effects of Leisure Activity in General as Well as Specifically on Quality of Life

It has been observed that leisure activity is a significant element in the lives of older adults (Neugarten et al., 1964; Tinsley, Colbs, Teaff, & Kaufman, 1987). A number of studies have concluded that there indeed is a direct positive relationship between participation in leisure activities (as measured in global or a cumulative fashion) and older men's and women's quality of life (Cutler Riddick, 1985a; Kelly et al., 1986; Ragheb & Griffith, 1990).

At least three studies have been conducted to assess the relative contribution of leisure activities to the quality of life of older women. Examinations of nationally representative samples of older women of varied employment backgrounds revealed that leisure activity emerged as an important predictor of life satisfaction for older homemakers and female retirees (Cutler Riddick, 1982, 1985b; Cutler Riddick & Daniel, 1984). In particular, for older female homemakers and retirees (but not older female workers), leisure roles emerged as the most important explanatory variable of life satisfaction. These results suggest that different life satisfaction mechanisms are operating for older female homemakers and retirees than for older women in the paid labor force.

Additionally, efforts have been directed at determining how specific leisure activities affect an older person's life. In particular, older women's well-being has been positively associated with three types of activities: informal activity/friendship interactions (Elwell & Maltbie-Crannell, 1981; Kelly, Steinkamp, & Kelly, 1987; Longino & Kart, 1982), formal activity in community and volunteer organizations (Hoyt, Kaiser, Peters, & Babchuk, 1980), and solitary activity (Sauer, 1977). Participation in specific types of leisure activity has not, however, consistently emerged as improving an older person's quality of life (Okun, Stock, Haring, & Witter, 1984).

Experiences Related to Leisure

The experiences older women have in leisure activity can include a number of dimensions. For this review the literature will be presented on leisure entitlement, meanings/motivations/needs/reasons given for participating, and constraints associated with leisure.

Turning to how women value leisure, Henderson (1991, p. 370) cites several studies that conclude women feel they are not "entitled" to leisure. That is, either women feel they have no right to leisure or they report feeling guilty about putting their own leisure preferences ahead of demands made on them by significant others.

Chambers's (1986) study of female British textile workers found that, although the surveyed women desired to be more active in leisure activities, they believed they were not entitled to it because family responsibilities resulted in a "lack of time." This lack of time was traced to having domestic obligations and secondarily to out-of-home employment demands. The little time found for leisure was channeled into pursuits that reinforced domestic responsibilities. That is, working women reported taking up family-centered activities (rather than socializing with friends) and home-based hobbies that could be characterized as "constructive" (e.g., sewing, knitting, gardening) rather than those focused on personal pleasure.

Focusing on the experiential aspects of leisure, Allison and Duncan (1987) compared the leisure experience of professional and blue-collar women. For both groups of women: (a) Intense involvement or "flow" most frequently occurred in nonwork activities, especially in the inter-personal family domain and particularly with children; (b) the second type of activity where the greatest flow was experienced was in sport and other creative endeavors; and (c) important factors associated with "flow" were sense of control and autonomy and freedom in tasks and activities selected.

Allen and Chin-Sang (1990) also completed a study on the meanings of leisure for women. In qualitative interviews with 30 older (X age = 75) African American women, the sampled individuals characterized leisure as freedom from constraint of needing to work to survive (or "free time") and also as "time for me" or using leisure as an outlet for self-expression.

Kelly et al. (1986) also conducted an investigation on motivations underlying leisure pursuits. Based on a study of adult men and women (age 40 and over), it was reported that, regardless of gender and age, adults valued leisure activities that involved interaction with significant others as well as those activities that enabled them to display previously gained competencies. It was also noted that adult females were less likely than males to rank health/exercise and skill development as reasons for engaging in leisure.

In an effort to examine the psychological benefits derived by older adults from participation in 18 commonly chosen activities, Tinsley et al. (1987), using nonprobability sampling, queried 771 females and 878 males ranging in age from 55 to 75. Three benefits associated with activity were companionship and social interaction, recognition and opportunity for self-expression, and advancement and power. Further, women over age 65 reported companionship to be the principal benefit they received from leisure. Women in the 55-65 age range were more likely than men to report recognition to be the principal psychological benefit received from their leisure activities. And men and women over 65 years of age, from higher socioeconomic backgrounds, were more likely than those from lower socioeconomic backgrounds to report satisfaction of their need for power through their leisure experiences.

In their unique study, Allen and Chin-Sang (1990) examined the needs met through leisure of African American women. The needs and activities that fulfilled the expressed needs of this group were affiliative activity pursued in community institutional settings (in particular, involvement in church and attending senior centers), passive solitary activity (primarily watching television), and active solitary activity (doing crafts).

It has been observed that experiencing leisure constraints—anything that inhibits people's ability to participate in leisure activities—affects quality of life (Peppers, 1976). At least seven studies have been conducted that have examined leisure constraints experienced by females.

In an effort to investigate the reasons older persons did not participate in leisure activity, McGuire (1984) completed a study using a systematic random sample of older individuals (X age = 64) listed in a midwestern telephone directory. The constraints to leisure involvement noted by both females and males were time, external resources (lack of equipment, facilities, information), approval from family and friends, limited abilities, and not having someone to accompany them to the activity.

Focusing on barriers encountered to recreation participation, Searle and Jackson (1985) used a sample randomly drawn from Canadians listed in a telephone book. Women, when compared with men, evaluated the following barriers as more significant obstacles to recreation participation: lack of partners, family commitments, lack of information, shyness, physical abilities, and lack of transportation.

Though gender differences were not reported, Mannell and Zuzanek (1991) collected data on the constraints experienced by 92 physically active older (X age = 69) men and women living in Canada. They found: (a) The most frequently reported constraint for not exercising was time or being "too busy;" (b) constraints that were reported were more likely to reflect intervening constraints (e.g., lack of time, too busy) rather than antecedent constraints such as personality, mental states, and prior socialization; and (c) factors perceived to inhibit participation were variable and temporary in their influence over the course of a day.

Two studies were located that focused on barriers to recreation participation in later life cycle stages. Buchanan and Allen (1985) used a stratified sample of four communities in Chicago to survey older men and women. They reported that the most significant reasons cited by female and male "retirees" (age 60-69) and "postretirees" (age 70+) for nonparticipation in leisure activities were fear of crime, not "having enough time," and health-related problems.

McGuire, Dottavio, and O'Leary (1986) in a secondary analysis of national survey data found that respondents aged 61-75 were limited in their outdoor recreation participation by lack of time and health. Respondents over the age of 75 were primarily limited from leisure involvement by health.

Only two research projects could be located that focused on leisure barriers experienced exclusively by females. Deem (1982) initiated an investigation of constraints to leisure by interviewing 195 women living in a new community in Great Britain. The most frequently cited constraints to recreational participation were partner's attitude toward women going out alone or with friends (especially evening activities that involved mixed gender groups such as going to a bar, social club, or dance), absence of private transportation, and absence of a friend or relative to accompany them.

Henderson, Stalnaker, and Taylor (1988) conducted a study that involved 500 randomly selected female university students, faculty, and staff ranging in age from 18 to 66. What emerged in the findings was that time was reported as the largest barrier to recreation for women, followed by money, facilities (not convenient or available), family concerns (including family obligations, expectations), awareness (for example, knowledge of resources and opportunities), interest (including social uneasiness in recreation, previous "poor" experiences, reluctance to get involved, and feelings of boredom), decision making (including items related to having no direction concerning leisure interests, inability to plan recreation, not knowing how to use time), and body image (not having the physical skills needed, lack of self-confidence, and not being fit enough).

Recommendations

Given the preceding review, one may wonder how we can increase our understanding of how leisure affects older women's quality of life as well as increase responsiveness in providing leisure services that foster well-being. One way to frame responses to these two questions is to divide them between two categories or recommendations for future research and recommendations for practice.

Future Research

An array of possible topics for further research exist. Among the possible strategies are the following.

1. Compare the leisure activities, social settings, and physical locations of men and women across the life span and examine why differences exist including gender and age stereotyping about "appropriate" leisure activities, feelings about entitlement to leisure, conflict between family/domestic demands versus employment outside the home, and other possible inequalities (Henderson, 1990; Kane, 1990; Kelly et al., 1986; Samdahl, 1988; Shaw, 1985).

There are at least two approaches for examining how gender-based leisure repertoires develop over the life span. A simple resource approach views the leisure repertoire developing as a response to available resources, both personal and community.

A second approach is to view the leisure of older women as reflecting a sequential, age-related developmental process (Kelly et al., 1986). In other words, does leisure activity assist women with managing or coping with life change? One of the transitions, for instance, confronting most older women is the death of a spouse (see Chapter 8). Patterson and Carpenter (1991) recently found that, in the two years following the death of a spouse, widows and widowers alike report lower frequency of participation in leisure activities. These same individuals reported that when they again resumed leisure activity it was to keep busy and involved, avoid the loneliness of an empty house, help others in need through voluntary work, and meet friends and acquaintances through social activities.

2. Determine the effects of leisure activity in general and specific leisure activities in particular on the quality of life over the life span while taking into account the heterogeneity of older women's backgrounds (e.g., ethnicity, health status, sexual orientation and marital status, employment background, socioeconomic status, caregiving responsibilities, quantity and quality of family interaction, social support for leisure involvement, knowledge of leisure resources, and acquisition of leisure skills) (see Cutler Riddick, 1982, 1985a, 1985b; Cutler Riddick, Cohen Mansfield, Fleshner, & Kraft, in press; Henderson, 1990, 1991; Lee & Markides, 1990; Okun et al., 1984).

3. Ascertain the "leisure needs" of women as they age. Two frameworks for undertaking this line of research are the updated model of older adult development published by Erikson, Erikson, and Kivnick (1986) and the androgyny model outlined by Neugarten et al. (1964). The former model proposes that the primary needs of older women are integrity, generativity, intimacy, identity, industry, initiative, autonomy, and trust. The androgyny model, on the other hand, posits that at

the later stages of life women become more like men and men become more like women (e.g., women become more aggressive and men experience nurturing needs). The fundamental questions deserving additional study are identifying the social psychological needs of aging women and determining how these needs can and are met through leisure.

4. Document constraints that operate or influence the activity patterns of aging women. Little is currently known either about women's leisure nonparticipation or why older women cease participation in leisure (Henderson, 1991). For example, even though many older women assume or are assigned formally caregiving responsibilities, little is known about how caregiving roles affect the individual's leisure life (Cutler Riddick et al., in press). Execution of family responsibilities, especially when coupled with employment outside the home, can and does have spillover affects into leisure.

One framework (Henderson, 1991; Henderson et al., 1988) that can be used for conceptualizing and measuring the cumulative effects of social, psychological, and cultural constraints is to view constraints in terms of antecedent constraints (e.g., gender-role socialization, personality, body image, and lack of interest) and intervening constraints (such as time, money, lack of interest).

An alternative model for explaining and understanding constraints is proposed by Szinovacz (1992). In this paradigm, gender differences in leisure constraints are tied to the societal domain, the familial domain, and personality. Gender differences in leisure opportunities and constraints, at the societal level, are tied to gender stratification in the occupational sphere. Such stratification results in economic disadvantages that constrict leisure, work style that may remain dominant in retirement leisure (e.g., women employed in the service sector may pursue people-oriented leisure whereas males who are engaged in manual labor take up activities that involve manipulation of things or symbols), and discontinuous work histories that delay achievement of occupational goals resulting in older women seeking out retirement activities such as volunteering that can provide a sense of achievement and accomplishment. Additionally, using this paradigm at the familial level, leisure is deemed affected by a household division of labor. That is, the model incorporates the fact that most women are typically most involved in household and caregiving tasks, which limit the amount of leisure time available and direct possible leisure time toward family responsibilities. Finally, the model, at the personality level, proposes that men and women are influenced by gender-role socialization into gender-differentiated activities.

Future Practices

The practices of those providing leisure programs and services for older women can directly and indirectly affect the psychological well-being of female clientele. Among suggested practices are the following:

1. Service agencies should strive in their program offerings as well as in social environments to fulfill the social psychological needs of older women. While the research literature is not definitive on this topic, some consistent themes appear to have emerged including fulfillment of social, self-expression, and power needs (see Allen & Chin-Sang, 1990; Allison & Duncan, 1987; Kelly et al., 1986; Tinsley et al., 1987).

2. Leisure education and counseling programs should be designed for older women that take into account their unique history and preferences. Older women may have moved through life involved with family and/or employment roles, with little or no time left for leisure pursuits, especially those with an individual focus. Deem (1982) has observed that many married women have put aside their own leisure to make their male partner's or children's leisure possible. A female entering later life stages can thus be constrained by any number of factors including values, stereotypes about "appropriate" activities for older women, perceived abilities, time management skills, awareness of leisure opportunities in the community, and a support system that does not promote optimal involvement in activity. Drawing on the work of Henderson (1990, 1991), it would seem advisable that these leisure education and counseling programs should address entitlement (feeling that one deserves or has a right to pursue leisure), equality (freedom from role constraints or obligations), and empowerment (providing knowledge, skills, and self-confidence to carry out preferred leisure activities).

3. Research should evaluate the impacts of recreational programs on the health of elderly women. Moreover, the methodological shortcomings of earlier studies (see Cutler Riddick & Keller, 1991) should be avoided. In addition, replication studies using larger samples need to be conducted to establish the external validity of earlier studies that have reported "efficacious" recreational activities, programs, or treatments.

Conclusion

To maintain equilibrium, societies pressure people to act out expected stereotypical behaviors. Through history women and men have been socialized in terms of appropriate and expected behaviors through the life cycle, including what is prescribed for being "female" and as "age appropriate." With the mid-1960s publication of Friedan's (1963) *The Feminine Mystique,* coupled with the emergence of "gray power," the world began to consider achievable roles for women (Rubin Wainrib, 1992) as well as reexamine roles ascribed to age. Rubin Wainrib (1992, p. xix) has captured the essence of the issue by noting that we are experiencing an "impact of the interaction between life-cycle development, social change, and gender role." Because of changing attitudes of and about women, coupled with the diverse backgrounds and personal histories of each cohort, several themes for further study emerge: (a) What are the evolving changes in the leisure time, activity, and experiences of women as they age? (b) How does leisure activity throughout the life course influence quality of life, including mental, social, and physical health? (c) How can the provision of services and public policy become more responsive to enhancing the recreational activities of females of all ages?

References

Allen, K., & Chin-Sang, V. (1990). A lifetime of work: The context and meanings of leisure for aging black women. *The Gerontologist, 30,* 734-740.

Allison, M., & Duncan, M. (1987). Women, work, and leisure: The days of our lives. *Leisure Studies, 9,* 143-161.

Buchanan, T., & Allen, L. (1985). Barriers to recreation participation in later life cycle stages. *Therapeutic Recreation Journal, 19,* 39-50.

Chambers, D. (1986). The constraints of work and domestic schedules on women's leisure. *Leisure Sciences, 5,* 309-325.

Cutler Riddick, C. (1982). Life satisfaction among aging women: A causal model. In M. Szinovacz (Ed.), *Women's retirement: Policy implications of recent research* (pp. 45-59). Beverly Hills, CA: Sage.

Cutler Riddick, C. (1985a). Life satisfaction determinants of older males and females. *Leisure Sciences, 7,* 47-63.

Cutler Riddick, C. (1985b). Life satisfaction for older female homemakers, retirees, and workers. *Research on Aging, 7,* 383-393.

Cutler Riddick, C., Cohen Mansfield, Y., Fleshner, C., & Kraft, G. (in press). Caregiver adaptations to having a relative with dementia admitted to a nursing home. *Journal of Gerontological Social Work.*

Cutler Riddick, C., & Daniel, S. (1984). The relative contribution of leisure activities and other factors to the mental health of older women. *Journal of Leisure Research, 16,* 136-148.

Cutler Riddick, C., & Keller, J. (1991). The benefits of therapeutic recreation in gerontology. In K. Coyle, W. Kinney, B. Riley, & J. Shank (Eds.), *Benefits of therapeutic recreation: A consensus view* (pp. 151-204). Philadelphia: Temple University Press.

Deem, R. (1982). Women, leisure and inequality. *Leisure Studies, 1,* 29-46.

Elwell, F., & Maltbie-Crannell, A. (1981). The impact of role loss upon coping resources and life satisfaction of the elderly. *Journal of Gerontology, 36,* 223-232.

Erikson, E., Erikson, J., & Kivnick, H. (1986). *Vital development in old age.* New York: Norton.

Friedan, B. (1963). *The feminine mystique.* New York: Norton.

George, L., & Bearon, L. (1980). *Quality of life in older persons: Meaning and measurement.* New York: Human Sciences.

Henderson, K. (1990). The meaning of leisure for women: An integrative review of literature. *Journal of Leisure Research, 22,* 228-243.

Henderson, K. (1991). The contribution of feminism to an understanding of leisure constraints. *Journal of Leisure Research, 23,* 363-372.

Henderson, K., Bialeschki, M., Shaw, S., & Freysinger, V. (1989). *A leisure of one's own: A feminist perspective on women's issues.* State College, PA: Venture.

Henderson, K., Stalnaker, D., & Taylor, G. (1988). The relationship between barriers to recreation and gender role personality traits for women. *Journal of Leisure Research, 20,* 69-80.

Hoyt, D., Kaiser, M., Peters, G., & Babchuk, N. (1980). Life satisfaction and activity theory: A multidimensional approach. *Journal of Gerontology, 35,* 935-941.

Kane, M. (1990). Female involvement in physical recreation-gender role as a constraint. *Journal of Physical Education, Recreation, and Dance, 61,* 52-56.

Kelly, J., Steinkamp, M., & Kelly, J. (1986). Later life leisure: How they play in Peoria. *The Gerontologist, 26,* 531-537.

Kelly, J., Steinkamp, M., & Kelly, J. (1987). Later life satisfaction: Does leisure contribute? *Leisure Sciences, 9,* 189-200.

Larson, R. (1978). Thirty years of research on the subjective well-being of older Americans. *Journal of Gerontology, 33,* 109-135.

Lee, P., & Markides, K. (1990). Activity and mortality among aged persons over an eight-year period. *Journal of Gerontology, 45,* 539-542.

Longino, C., & Kart, C. (1982). Explicating activity theory: A formal replication. *Journal of Gerontology, 37,* 713-722.

Mannell, R., & Zuzanek, J. (1991). The nature and variability of leisure constraints in daily life: The case of the physically active leisure of older adults. *Leisure Sciences, 13,* 337-351.

McGuire, F. (1984). A factor analytic study of leisure constraints in advanced adulthood. *Leisure Sciences, 6,* 313-326.

McGuire, F., Dottavio, D., & O'Leary, J. (1986). Constraints to participation in outdoor recreation across the life span: A nationwide study of limiters and prohibitors. *The Gerontologist, 26,* 538-544.

Neugarten, B., & Associates. (1964). *Personality in middle and later life.* New York: Atherton.

Okun, M., Stock, W., Haring, M., & Witter, R. (1984). The social activity/well-being relation. *Research on Aging, 6,* 45-65.

Patterson, I., & Carpenter, G. (1991, July). *Participation in leisure activities by older adults after the death of a spouse.* Paper presented at the First International Leisure and Mental Health Conference, Salt Lake City, UT.

Peppers, L. (1976). Patterns of leisure and adjustment to retirement. *The Gerontologist, 16,* 441-446.

Ragheb, M., & Griffith, C. (1990, October). *The contribution of leisure participation and leisure satisfaction of older persons.* Paper presented at the Leisure Research Symposium, Phoenix, AZ.

Rubin Wainrib, B. (1992). Introduction. In B. Rubin Wainrib (Ed.), *Gender issues across the life cycle* (pp. xvii-xxii). New York: Springer.

Samdahl, D. (1988). Interactionist model of leisure: Theory and empirical support. *Leisure Sciences, 10,* 27-39.

Sauer, W. (1977). Morale of the urban aged: A regression analysis by race. *Journal of Gerontology, 32,* 600-608.

Searle, M., & Jackson, E. (1985). Socioeconomic variation in perceived barriers to recreation participation among would-be participants. *Leisure Sciences, 7,* 227-249.

Shaw, S. (1985). Gender and leisure: Inequality in the distribution of leisure time. *Journal of Leisure Research, 17,* 266-282.

Szinovacz, M. (1982). Introduction: Research on women's retirement. In M. Szinovacz (Ed.), *Women's retirement: Policy implications of recent research* (pp. 13-21). Beverly Hills, CA: Sage.

Szinovacz, M. (1992). Leisure in retirement: Gender differences in limitations and opportunities. *World Leisure Recreation Association Journal, 12,* 14-17.

Tinsley, H., Colbs, S., Teaff, J., & Kaufman, A. (1987). The relationship of age, gender, health, and economic status to the psychological benefits older persons report from participation in leisure activities. *Leisure Sciences, 9,* 53-65.

8

Widows

Social Integration and Activity

HELENA ZNANIECKA LOPATA

This chapter addresses the basic question of how the social integration
and activity of widows differ from those of other members of society.
Most of the answers come from studies of widows in American society
with some reference to situations elsewhere in the world.

A widow is a woman who has been married, whose husband has died,
and who has not remarried. This definition highlights four basic characteristics: gender, age, former marriage, and current status as a widow.
In all societies many, if not most, activities of women differ from those
of men due to historically developed divisions of labor and often
divisions of the symbolically constructed world into private and public
domains. Even leisure activity, which often bridges the two spheres,
may contain gender-specific limitations. A typical example is the activity area of games: Although many games are played by both genders
together, a game such as poker is often identified as the province of
men, while mah-jongg is more often seen as feminine. A woman,
widowed or not, would not be welcome at an all-male poker table any
more than a man would typically try to enter a mah-jongg game played
by women.

Although this separation is allegedly in the process of slow and often
painful change, household-maintaining activity is also gender specific,
as is involvement in many occupations and community work.

Age obviously influences activity, as this volume documents in many places. Widows must have reached a certain minimal age because societal norms, even laws, prevent marriage at what is considered an inappropriate age. Married women enter activities, both as work and as leisure, in many ways different than those of unmarried women. In modern American urban circles, a considerable amount of the activity is tied to being a married woman and being married to a particular man. Sociologists have extensively studied the impingement of a man's occupation on the economic situation, space, time, work, and friendships of his wife in the top social classes (Finch, 1983; Lopata, 1991, in press). Couple companionate socializing is also typical of traditional women who are often dependent upon the husband's needs for most of their leisure activity. Although there is an increasing tendency on the part of "modern" married women to spend a great deal of time independently of the husband, role conflict is still assumed to be resolved in favor of motherhood and wifehood.

Widowhood and Activity

It is in widowhood that a woman's activities can become quite divergent from those of other members of society. The divergence varies considerably by the age and stage of life of the woman and of her children (if any), the degree of her prior dependence upon the husband and the role of wife, social class, race, ethnicity, and religion, and many other factors. To organize these variations among older widows, we must first look at the society and community within which they are located, then focus on their personal resources.

To accentuate the uniqueness of widowhood in urban America, we can briefly examine other situations. Many societies force upon a widow a strong loss of status and limitations of activity. Continuity of social involvement is simply not possible in many areas of life. For example, the child widow in upper-caste traditional India who had not borne any sons and did not commit suttee, simply became an ill-treated servant in the home of her parents-in-law and was forbidden to remarry (Guyral, 1987; Lopata, 1987a). Even now, according to Patil's (1990) *Hindu Widows: A Study of Deprivation*, the life of a widow is totally dependent upon the in-laws, who are not likely to treat her with respect or to allow any but subservient activity. A similar fate for widows is reported in many developing societies, especially those dominated by fundamentalist religions. Widows are often dependent upon an adult son. Those women lacking sons may continue being workhorses in family households, even in old age. As Cowgill and Holmes (1972), Simmons (1945), Fry (1981), and other anthropologists have long ago concluded, the status of the elderly, which usually means elderly widows, depends to a great extent on the evaluation of their contributions to family, community, and society.

The Activity of Widows in America

The social integration and activity of widows in American society are very different than those of still developing or modernizing societies. In many urban communities, the loss of status and consequent stigma surrounding widowhood have diminished considerably. In fact, there are no distinguishing symbols of widowhood, such as wardrobe, which make possible public control of their behavior. The attempts to separate the private sphere of life from the bureaucratized, rationalized domain means that many people with whom a woman interacts—on the job, as a consumer, as a member of a voluntary association, or in politics—may not even know that she is a widow. Such identification, however, may affect her private interaction, as in the case of leisure activity. An older worker may find that her married coworkers do not want interaction after job-related hours when husbands are involved. In fact, widows studied in many locations in America report strain in, and even cessation of, activity with married friends, even those who were not brought into prior companionate relations by the late husband (Lopata, 1973a, 1979; see also Lopata, 1987b).

Even when not forced by the community or personal associates to change her activity because of widowhood, a woman may find herself lacking the resources to continue doing what she had been doing in the past. Financial constraints may accompany the loss of the husband's earnings or other income. Such a drop in income can result in residential changes, cutting off interaction with former neighbors and making difficult continued affiliation with religious or other groups. A widow of a man who had been a high executive in a major corporation reported to me that about the only thing she can now do with former associates is play bridge (Lopata, 1975). She can no longer afford the clubs to which she belonged when he was alive. In addition, she is no longer invited to many social events because past invitations were dependent upon his presence. Other widows also complain bitterly that their prior contributions to the organization were discounted and their personal attributes redefined as unimportant (Lopata, 1979). Widows can also face restrictions on life because of other dependencies; some older ones never learned to drive or were too uncomfortable to venture out into public leisure-time places without a male escort. As one said, "It takes two to Tango." Unpaid male escorts are hard to find, especially by older widows, due to the shorter life span of men and the likelihood that they are still married. Several widows in the Chicago area studies explained that they did not want "what is left over," comparing available men unfavorably with the often idealized image of the late husband (Lopata, 1980). The combination of grief and restrictions on activity can produce deep feelings of loneliness not only for the late husband but also for the whole former life-style (Lopata, 1969, 1980; Lopata, Heinemann, & Baum, 1982).

At the same time, women can continue many activities into widowhood, as Atchley (see Chapter 1) points out. Church affiliation can be quite meaningful, especially in the African American community (Lopata, 1973b). Ethnic subcommunities may contain many relationships and activities that maintain social integration even, or especially, among elderly widows (Lopata, 1977). Of course, there is a problem in American cities in that younger generations of ethnic groups move out to be succeeded by people of very different backgrounds. Older widows accustomed to limiting their activity to friends made in youth or to the family can continue doing so only as long as such relations remain easily available.

Voluntary Changes and Expanded Life Spaces

Widows can, on the other hand, experience freedom and expansion of the whole life space within which their roles and activities take place (Lopata, 1979, in press). Many wives are highly restricted in marriage, by the husband, by the duties of the role of wife, and by limitations imposed by the community in its many representations. Even when the duties of household maintenance and socializing are decreased by the husband's retirement, the very presence of a husband is restrictive

(Szinovacz, 1989). He may place personal limitations through his own tastes and problems. His long illness can confine the wife to the home for years. These restrictions are lifted by his death. Several widows also reported that this event resulted in more discretionary income, derived from social security or other sources now under their own control.

One of the dramatic characteristics of widowhood in America is the ability of the woman to live alone. We cannot be sure, of course, to what extent her wish to do so is influenced by the declared or assumed unwillingness of family members to move in with her or to have her move in with them. In any case, a high majority of older widows live alone and declare that they do so by their own choice (Chevon & Korson, 1972; Lopata, 1971). One basic reason is that children now move out of the "ancestral home" to set up their own households (although there is some reversal in recent years as housing costs make it impossible for adult children to find comparable space). In fact, the parents are likely to have moved out of a house large enough to keep children and their families of procreation. This means that the widow would have to become a peripheral member of a household managed by another woman, a daughter, or, even worse, a daughter-in-law. This would deprive her of rights concerning space, time, rituals, sleeping, and eating. Her activities would be controlled by others. In fact, many of my respondents explained that such a move would force them to return to the role of housekeeper and child rearer. They had done all that once, and now they wanted to have minimal work and maximum leisure time (Lopata, 1971, 1979). Anticipated strain and even conflict with the adult children, in-laws, and grandchildren also encouraged them to live alone. Of course, some widows could not do so, lacking the resources for independent residence. This was particularly true of women socialized into a different culture, another society, or rural areas of this one and who lack the education that provides competence in modern life.

Those women who develop multiple personal resources earlier in life can function in complex life spaces in modern society. They can "bloom" personally, paying attention to themselves, their looks, and their capacities (Lopata, 1986). They can reconstruct their self-concept, finding support from new social roles and relations, rather than being tied down to people who saw them through a past prism. They report feeling whole and venturing into new activities. They travel, join new groups, and try new ventures.

Conclusions

In all, the social integration of widows varies considerably not just by their activities as women and as wives but also by the changes they are forced into experiencing in consequence of the illness and death of the husband and related events and those they undertake on their own once the period of heavy grief is over. There are widows whose lives really do not change much, because they were not dependent upon the husband, being a wife, and the overall situation while he was around. They can be immersed in other family roles, neighboring, friendship, a career, or other forms of social engagement. Others may be devastated by the death of the husband who served as a connecting link to the rest of the world and around whom they built their whole lives. Some restrict their activities to interaction with a very limited support network, often becoming heavily dependent upon a daughter or, less often, a son. Social isolation or what Cumming and Henry (1961) defined as social disengagement is very likely for women who never had been socialized to replace members of support networks with new contributors or to initiate social engagement in later life. Loneliness for the husband and past life-styles, however, does not inevitably lead to a withering of social activity. The numbness of grief can be replaced by initiating action and lead to a "blooming" of self-concept and life-style, as past restrictions are removed and new avenues of social engagement explored.

References

Chevon, A., & Korson, H. (1972). Widows who live alone: An examination of social and demographic factors. *Social Forces, 51,* 45-53.

Cowgill, D. O., & Holmes, L. D. (Eds.). (1972). *Aging and modernization.* New York: Appleton-Century-Crofts.

Cumming, E., & Henry, W. E. (1961). *Growing old: The process of disengagement.* New York: Basic Books.

Finch, J. (1983). *Married to the job: Wives' incorporation in men's work.* Boston: George Allen & Unwin.

Fry, C. (Ed.). (1981). *Dimensions: Aging, culture and health.* Westport, CT: Bergin & Garvey.

Guyral, J. S. (1987). Widowhood in India. In H. Z. Lopata (Ed.), *Widows: The Middle East, Asia and the Pacific* (pp. 43-55). Durham, NC: Duke University Press.

Lopata, H. Z. (1969). Loneliness: Forms and components. *Social Problems, 17,* 248-262.

Lopata, H. Z. (1971). Living arrangements of urban widows and their married children. *Sociological Focus, 5,* 41-61.

Lopata, H. Z. (1973a). *Widowhood in an American city.* Cambridge, MA: Schenkman.

Lopata, H. Z. (1973b). Social relations of black and white widowed women in a northern metropolis. *American Journal of Sociology, 78,* 241-248.

Lopata, H. Z. (1975). Couple companionate relationships in marriage and widowhood. In N. Glazer-Malbin (Ed.), *Old families/new families* (pp. 119-149). New York: Van Nostrand.

Lopata, H. Z. (1977). Widowhood in Polonia. *Polish American Studies, 34,* 7-25.

Lopata, H. Z. (1979). *Women as widows: Support systems.* New York: Elsevier.

Lopata, H. Z. (1980). Loneliness in widowhood. In J. Hartog, J. R. Audy, & Y. Cohen (Eds.), *The anatomy of loneliness* (pp. 237-258). New York: International Universities Press.

Lopata, H. Z. (1986). Becoming and being a widow: Reconstruction of the self and support systems. *Geriatric Psychiatry, 16,* 203-214.

Lopata, H. Z. (1987a). *Widows: Vol. 1. The Middle East, Asia and the Pacific.* Durham, NC: Duke University Press.

Lopata, H. Z. (1987b). *Widows: Vol. 2. North America.* Durham, NC: Duke University Press.

Lopata, H. Z. (1991). Which child? The consequences of social development on the support systems of widows. In B. B. Hess & E. W. Markson (Eds.), *Growing old in America* (pp. 39-49). New Brunswick, NJ: Transaction.

Lopata, H. Z. (in press). *Circles and settings: Role changes of American women.* Albany: SUNY Press.

Lopata, H. Z., Heinemann, G. D., & Baum, J. (1982). Loneliness: Antecedents and coping strategies in the lives of widows. In L. A. Peplau & D. Perlman (Eds.), *Loneliness: A sourcebook of current theory, research and therapy* (pp. 310-326). New York: Wiley Interscience.

Patil, G. D. (1990). *Hindu widows: A study in deprivation.* Unpublished doctoral dissertation, Karnatak University, Dharwad, India.

Simmons, L. (1945). *The role of the aged in primitive society.* London: Oxford University Press.

Szinovacz, M. (1989). Retirement, couples and household work. In S. J. Bahr & E. T. Peterson (Eds.), *Aging and the family* (pp. 33-58). Lexington, MA: Lexington.

9

Leisure and Generativity

DOUGLAS A. KLEIBER
ROBERT O. RAY

When, if ever, is leisure *generative*? Or, to take Erik Erikson's meaning of that word, when, in the course of adulthood, is leisure directed toward "cultivating strength in the next generation?" (1982, p. 67). Under what circumstances does leisure support productivity, creativity, or the growth and development of others? The purpose of this chapter is to consider critically the generative potential of leisure for adults in contemporary society. In so doing, we will consider both prevailing leisure meanings and patterns of leisure activity as well as interpretations of leisure that are more or less consistent with generativity. To examine the relationship between leisure and generativity, after addressing each of those concepts separately, we will use gender differences and contemporary value shifts to shed light on optimal conditions for supporting a generative function in leisure.

Generativity

Erikson (1963) presents the issue of *generativity versus stagnation* as the seventh in an eight-stage epigenetic sequence. Erikson's working assumption is that development is a lifelong process characterized by the resolution of a series of crises that are likely to emerge at certain times in the life course. Generativity is the issue that is most likely to preoccupy people in middle adulthood. It precedes and sets up the issue of the final stage of life: ego integrity versus despair—whether one has a sense of connectedness with and acceptance of all that has come before. Generativity is set up *by* the problem of early adulthood, which is finding intimacy, where establishing a family is a common outcome. But Erikson sees generativity as more than procreation. It is, he says,

> the concern in establishing and guiding the next generation, although there are individuals who, through misfortune or because of special and genuine gifts in other directions, do not apply this drive to their own offspring. And indeed, the concept generativity is meant to include such more popular synonyms as productivity and creativity, which however, cannot replace it. (1963, p. 267)

The failure to move in this direction is reflected in *stagnation*, which is equated with self-concern, self-indulgence, and personal impoverishment and is reflected in "the lack of some faith, some 'belief in the species,' which would make a child appear to be a welcome trust of the community" (p. 267).

The suggestion that generativity can be established in activity that is not directly nurturant of others—that is, in personal productivity and creativity—is somewhat confusing and has led others (e.g., Schaie & Geiwitz, 1982) to see *generativity* as simply another word for *self-actualization*. But Erikson is quite clear that it is the virtue and ethic of *care* that is at issue here, "a widening commitment to *take care of* the persons, the products, and the ideas one has learned *to care for*" (1982, p. 67). Even when one's ideas and products do not have any immediate beneficiary, midlife maturity is reflected in a concern that one's efforts will have some impact on and value for the generations that will follow. In fact, it is the concern for impact on the world, whether in terms of the success of one's children or the endurance of one's inventions and policies, that makes generativity a very instrumental purpose, one apparently antithetical to the more expressive tendencies to be found in leisure.

Leisure as a Context for Generativity

Leisure is best reflected in a composite of perceived freedom, relaxation, and enjoyment (Shaw, 1985) with the daily experience of leisure reflecting varying degrees of those components. There are also various purposes that frequently emerge in the context of leisure that do not compromise and may even enhance the experience. These include competence, relatedness, creativity, celebration, and solitude among others (Kelly, 1987).

Such variations notwithstanding, a sense of relative freedom from obligation is traditionally regarded as the *essence* of leisure (e.g., deGrazia, 1962; Neulinger, 1981).[1] Is leisure, so considered, capable of supporting the sense of responsibility that generativity implies, or even the more general ethic of care? Adding the other commonly recognized characteristics of leisure—relaxation and enjoyment (Gordon, Gaitz, & Scott, 1976; Shaw, 1985)—would not change the issue. Hedonism has manifold social and biological justifications and escapism can be regarded as socially adaptive if its alternation with responsible behavior leads to greater effectiveness in that direction. Furthermore, self-expression is thought to be important to identity formation. But the self-indulgent character of most of leisure would in itself seem to be inconsistent with generativity. In truth, it may be more readily associated with generativity's antithesis, stagnation, as in this statement by Kivnik (1985):

> Each individual's middle adulthood is viewed, in these terms, as focusing on a struggle to balance Generative expressions (e.g., creativity, procreativity, productivity) with expressions of Stagnation (e.g., relaxing, focusing on oneself, taking time out, or, in California, laying back and mellowing out). (p. 95)

And even when leisure is portrayed in terms of its more active variants and its more social contexts, the question of privatism and flight from responsibility often comes up. In *Habits of the Heart,* Robert Bellah and his associates (Bellah, Madsen, Sullivan, Swidler, & Tipton, 1985) discuss leisure as one of the primary contexts for individualism and isolationism in contemporary American culture:

> With the weakening of the traditional forms of life that gave aesthetic and moral meaning to everyday living, Americans have been improvising alternatives more or less successfully. They engage, sometimes with intense involvement, in a wide variety of arts, sports, and nature appreciation, sometimes as spectators but often as active participants. Some of these activities involve conscious traditions and demanding practices, such as ballet. Others

such as walking in the country or jogging, may be purely improvisational, though not devoid of some structure of shared meaning. Not infrequently, moments of intense awareness, what are sometimes called "peak experiences," occur in the midst of such activities. At such moments, a profound sense of well-being eclipses the usual utilitarian preoccupations of everyday life. But the capacity of such experiences to provide more than a momentary counterweight to pressures of everyday life is minimal. Where these activities find social expression at all, it is apt to be in the form of what we have called the lifestyle enclave. The groups that form around them are too evanescent, too inherently restricted in membership, and too slight in their hold on their members' loyalty to carry much public weight. (pp. 291-292)

If there is little generativity to be found in most of what we associate with free time activity, perhaps there are *aspects* of leisure in other contexts that are more typically and clearly generative, in work, for example, or in family settings. Is generativity ever served in these contexts in ways that emphasize intrinsic enjoyment and self-expression? To begin with the context of work, the subjects of mentoring and volunteerism offer some interesting possibilities for revealing the generative *potential* of leisure.

Mentoring

Mentoring would appear to be an excellent vehicle for generativity, especially for those without children to nurture or for those whose children have grown up and left home (Barnett, 1984; Levinson, Darrow, Klein, Levinson, & McKee, 1978). The literature on mentoring (Carden, 1990; Merriam, 1983) indicates that its use in professional, corporate, and educational contexts has become institutionalized to a great extent, with formalized programs in some cases, and has been shown to contribute to knowledge enhancement, emotional stability, problem solving and decision making, corporate morale, and productivity. It is, however, at least as used in this literature, entirely task related. Nevertheless, a distinction is made (Carden, 1990) between the corporate version that is purely instrumental and career oriented and may even be organizationally prescribed and the type that has a more expressive, intrinsic, or "psychosocial" quality and builds relationships outside of and beyond that which is task oriented (see also Clawson, 1980; Kram, 1985).

Still, the focus of mentoring, for all its variations, is almost always on career success. Are there other mentorlike roles to be found in the context of leisure, where the emphasis is on enjoyment and the "mentor" may not feel particularly obligated to bring about the success of those being sponsored? We might consider coaching children in recreational soccer or voluntarily teaching a pottery class to offer such conditions. Even as learning and the development of competence are the objectives, a recognition of the intrinsic rewards of the activity for both the tutor and the tutored reflects a large degree of leisure. But then are such situations truly generative? As the investment in products and outcomes—skills acquired, victories achieved—is deemphasized, how much is really being generated?

Volunteerism

A similar question can be raised of any kind of volunteer work. Chambré (1987) makes the case that volunteering contributes to a sense of personal integrity and serves as a mechanism for passing experiences from one generation to the next. Thus it can be personally meaningful and intrinsically enjoyable; but is it then an expression of leisure? While its voluntary quality and potential for intrinsic enjoyment may be critical to underlying motivation, it is usually a sense of necessity and responsibility that draws a person to volunteer work. In fact, those who volunteer rarely regard their experience as leisure; and those who are "working" voluntarily in the context of leisure (organizing interest groups, for example) are not likely to see their activity, however effortful, as volunteering (Hoggett & Bishop, 1985; Parker, 1987). Whether motivated by pure altruism or the potential to gain marketable skills and useful references, when volunteerism is outcome oriented it tends to be distinguishable experientially from leisure.

Child Care

Perhaps the clearest place for generativity in leisure is in the nurturance of children, whether one's own or others (e.g., in scouting). The experience of shared enjoyment of activities that are challenging and intrinsically interesting may serve to shape a faith in the future. Activities such as music, photography, sports, and games have been shown to have qualities of experience, such as effort and intense concentration, that offer a prototype for optimal experience (at work and play) in the future (Csikszentmihalyi & Larson, 1984; Kleiber, Larson, & Csikszent-mihalyi, 1987; see also Mannell, Chapter 10). Important in such activities is the *sponsorship* of adults, for it is in the recognition of such activities as valuable in the eyes of adults that they become "transitional activities," linking childhood and adulthood (Csikszentmihalyi & Larson, 1984; Kleiber et al., 1987). While the emphasis of this line of research has been on children and adolescents, a recognition of these effects by the adults involved would most likely reinforce a sense of generativity while still retaining an appreciation for the activity as play and leisure. In offering a repeating cycle reconceptualization of Erikson's stage theory, Logan (1986) points to the similarly instrumental orientations of the *industry* motives of preadolescents and adults dealing with generativity as often effecting a kind of symbiotic "cog-wheeling" that makes the coaching relationship so potentially effective during these periods (p. 128). Of course, it is important to note that there are probably as many failed relationships between would-be "mentors" and the youth they would influence, especially in adolescence (Larson & Kleiber, 1992). This is especially true if the adult is exclusively outcome oriented in his or her approach.

A Question of Gender

The business of child care has traditionally involved men differently than women, of course, and the same may be said of leisure. As noted earlier, most interpretations of leisure emphasize freedom from role obligation as an essential characteristic (e.g., deGrazia, 1962; Kleiber, 1985) and many studies of leisure behavior identify escape and solitude as important leisure needs (Driver, Tinsley, & Manfredo, 1991). But this view appears to reflect a clearly "androcentric" perspective of leisure, ignoring the experience of most women (Bella, 1989). According to Bella, leisure is inherently androcentric to the extent that it emphasizes freedom from obligation and opposition to work in its definition and conceptualization, given that women working in the home and being consistently involved in matters of caregiving are most likely to enjoy life and find personal meaning in activities that are interpersonally responsive. She questions the relevance of the word *leisure* for women and prefers to recognize intrinsic enjoyment in social contexts as *relationality*.

It might be argued that generativity is itself androcentric, as has been suggested of Erikson's theory more generally (e.g., Gilligan, 1982). Men are more likely than women at midlife to feel a deficiency in their responsiveness to others, as a result of having focused on more instrumental career-oriented purposes, and to attempt to redress the situation with greater attention to others (Gutmann, 1977), thus giving a heightened profile of the caring aspects of generativity. Indeed, there is evidence that women are less conscious of generativity in the sense of nurturance at midlife than men and more oriented to other instrumental purposes (Gilligan, 1982; Gutmann, 1977).[2] This may then be reflected in an increase in "relationality" for men, even as that style of leisure may continue for women. But perhaps this is too limited an understanding of generativity, as well as leisure, for both genders.

Reconsidering Generativity

As with other stage models of adult development, the empirical evidence in support of Erikson's theoretical framework is limited (Ryff & Heincke, 1983); the strength of the model is in its heuristic value in highlighting the ascendence of certain themes as the life course progresses. It is also a misrepresentation of Erikson's epigenetic sequence to suggest that the issue of one stage is addressed exclusively during that period. In fact, Erikson and his more recent interpreters (e.g., Logan, 1986) discuss the repetition and recapitulation of themes across stages. Erikson points to identity, especially, as being reflected in different ways in each of the preceding and following periods; and Logan (1986) points to two unifying themes, instrumental and existential, that link Erikson's other stages in a repeating cycle. In Logan's view, ego integrity belongs to a wholeness/continuity theme with identity and basic trust while generativity is regarded as a "replay of initiative and industry" (p. 125), clearly instrumental orientations. The social interest of generativity in that sense is less a matter of expanding relatedness than the extension of social influence, the exercise of what Neugarten (1977) refers to as "executive powers." *Agency* is being served here to a greater extent than *communion* (Bakan, 1966).

Nevertheless, it is important to recognize the value of both aspects of generativity, even as one may receive more emphasis in a given theoretical interpretation. In fact, in an interview study of middle-aged adults, McAdams, Ruetzel, and Foley (1986) found that higher levels of generativity were associated with the *sum* of power and intimacy motives on the Thematic Apperception Test. They concluded that generativity "implies a blending of agency and communion in human experience" (p. 800). The two factors may exist in varying degrees and may emerge at different times in people, but both are reflections of generativity.

Disengagement

The issue of generativity is not completed in any real sense in middle age. It is likely to continue on into later years, but with a somewhat different character. Labouvie-Vief (1981) makes the point that, from a life span perspective, the deteriorative regression of aging is often consistent with, rather than oppositional to, growth and adaptation. Conservatism and rigidity, for example, are adaptive to the extent that external influences are disruptive to integrity. "Issues of commitment, specialization and channeling one's energies in the service of social system stability become mature concerns" in middle and later adulthood (p. 217) in contrast to what Schaie referred to as the "acquisitive flexibility" of youth (Labouvie-Vief, 1981, p. 218). Even the *relatively* later life purposes of generativity may become regarded as youthful dissipation. As Labouvie-Vief notes, these midlife "preoccupations with executive power and competence," however generative, represent that stage's own version of egocentrism and may come to be viewed by many as "chains of their past." He refers to Carl Jung in noting the realization of the middle-aged adult that "even the integration of generativity was the result of a specific social fabric with its pressures toward restraining the process of individuation" and that "later life . . . brings the most crucial turning point—a chance for freedom from, and transcendence of, those constraints" (p. 218).

Labouvie-Vief gives greater credibility to disengagement as an adaptive process in aging than do other investigators (e.g., Cath, 1975; Hochschild, 1975; Maddox, 1965). It can be argued that the earlier research that led to a rejection of Cumming and Henry's (1960) hypothesis did not adequately take the matter of choice and control into account. More research is needed to test the proposition, but continuing unwanted commitments and expanding social involvement have the potential to undermine some of the deeper meaning and value of the more intimate interactions that contribute to ego integrity. There is, in fact, considerable evidence that higher amounts of social interaction in later life are *not* associated with subjective well-being (Larson, 1978) and have even been shown to be negatively related in some cases (Longino & Kart, 1982). The *quality* of interaction and the intensity of commitment, on the other hand, *are* related (Larson, Zuzanek, & Mannell, 1985; Ray & Heppe, 1986). Nor is aloneness itself inherently problematic or necessarily indicative of social isolation. In their study of the experience of solitude and togetherness in later life, Larson et al. (1985) found that, with respect to married couples, being alone "was a positive opportunity, a chance for focused thought and absorption; it is likely that some of this focused attention on reading, reflection, hobbies or whatever may well have been directed toward other people and ultimately will contribute back to the human community" (p. 380).

Generativity and disengagement are actions that operate dialectically in response to developmental interests, but they are not entirely antithetical. In the simplest manifestation, one seeks collective involvement and influence at certain points while retracting from involvement at others. What should be recognized, however, is that continuing generativity—whether defined in terms of individual creativity, group productivity, protégé success, the sharing of meaningful traditions, or some other criterion—does not come about without some degree of *discrimination*, deciding who or what *not* to attend to. As priorities and circumstances change, some degree of disengagement is frequently necessary to facilitate engagements that are more conducive to generative purposes later in life.

Optimizing Leisure for Generativity

Considering Erikson's work in relation to the world's religions and philosophical thought, Bellah (1978) argues that generativity is associated with the active life and that integrity is associated with the contemplative (p. 63). Leisure has also been associated historically with the latter, especially in the thinking of Augustine (p. 69) as well as Plato and Aristotle (deGrazia, 1962). This is consistent with seeing leisure as a product of selective disengagement, relaxation, and private enjoyment (Kleiber, 1985). But there are important traditions for the more socially integrative and generative aspects of leisure as well. It is a misrepresentation of classic thought on leisure to emphasize only its contemplative aspects. According to Hemingway (1988), the leisure (*schole*) of

Plato and Aristotle was the context in which citizens sought to cultivate the *civility* necessary to exercise the rights of citizenship most responsibly and effectively. It was, in Hemingway's words, "a great counterexample to the isolation and fragmentation of modern society" (1988, p. 188).

Leisure has been described as "the basis of culture" where celebration and affirmation ensure its continuance (Pieper, 1952) and where the ritualization of playfulness offers new cultural forms (Huizinga, 1955). These are classical ideas of leisure, running in some contrast to contemporary manifestations. But in recognizing the importance of generativity in people's lives and the current stresses on the social fabric, the power of a context that encourages openness and responsiveness to others in ways that are mutually agreeable and supportive should not be ignored. Such experiences may serve quite instrumentally, though often unintentionally, as the bindery that allows the best products of one's generativity to endure.

Notes

1. It is important to note, however, that this view is regarded by some as exceedingly androcentric, applicable largely to male role structures in Western culture (Bella, 1989), a point to which we will return.

2. This pattern is clearly changing, however, as female career patterns have become more consistent with males'. Nevertheless, gender differences no doubt still obtain with respect to both generativity and leisure.

References

Bakan, D. (1966). *The duality of human existence*. Boston: Beacon.

Barnett, S. (1984). The mentor role: A task of generativity. *Journal of Human Behavior, 1*(2), 15-18.

Bella, L. (1989). Beyond androcentrism: Women and leisure. In E. Jackson & T. Burton (Eds.), *Understanding leisure*. State College, PA: Venture.

Bellah, R. (1978). To kill and survive or to die and become: The active life and the contemplative life as ways of being adult. In E. Erikson (Ed.), *Adulthood*. New York: Norton.

Bellah, R., Madsen, R., Sullivan, W., Swidler, A., & Tipton, S. (1985). *Habits of the heart*. New York: Harper & Row.

Carden, A. (1990). Mentoring and adult career development: The evolution of a theory. *The Counseling Psychologist, 18*(2), 275-299.

Cath, S. H. (1975). The orchestration of disengagement. *International Journal of Aging and Human Development, 6*, 199-213.

Chambré, S. (1987). *Good deeds in old age*. Lexington, MA: Lexington.

Clawson, J. (1980). Mentoring in managerial careers. In C. Derr (Ed.), *Work, family and career: New frontiers in theory and research* (pp. 144-165). New York: Praeger.

Csikszentmihalyi, M., & Larson, R. (1984). *Being adolescent*. New York: Basic Books.

Cumming, E., & Henry, W. (1960). *Growing old: The process of disengagement*. New York: Basic Books.

deGrazia, S. (1962). *Of time, work and leisure*. New York: Anchor.

Driver, B., Tinsley, H., & Manfredo, M. (1991). The Paragraphs About Leisure and Recreation Experience Scales: Results from two inventories designed to assess the breadth of perceived psychological benefits of leisure. In B. Driver, P. Brown, & G. Peterson (Eds.), *Benefits of leisure*. State College, PA: Venture.

Erikson, E. (1963). *Childhood and society*. New York: Norton.

Erikson, E. (1982). *The life cycle completed*. New York: Norton.

Gilligan, C. (1982). *In a different voice*. Cambridge, MA: Harvard University Press.

Gordon, C., Gaitz, C., & Scott, J. (1976). Leisure and lives: Personal expressivity across the lifespan. In R. Binstock & E. Shanas (Eds.), *Handbook of aging and the social sciences*. New York: Van Nostrand Reinhold.

Gutmann, D. (1977). The cross-cultural perspective: Notes toward a comparative psychology of aging. In J. Birren & K. W. Schaie (Eds.), *Handbook of the psychology of aging*. New York: Van Nostrand Reinhold.

Hemingway, J. (1988). Leisure and civility: Reflections on a Greek ideal. *Leisure Sciences, 10,* 179-191.

Hochschild, A. R. (1975). Disengagement theory: A critique and proposal. *American Sociological Review, 40*, 553-569.

Hoggett, P., & Bishop, J. (1985). Leisure beyond the individual consumer. *Leisure Studies, 4*, 27-36.

Huizinga, J. (1955). *Homo ludens*. Boston: Beacon.

Kelly, J. (1987). *Freedom to be: A new sociology of leisure*. New York: Macmillan.

Kivnik, H. (1985). Interpersonal relations: Personal meaning in the life cycle. *Contributions to Human Development, 14*, 93-109.

Kleiber, D. (1985). Motivational reorientation in adulthood and the resource of leisure. In D. Kleiber & M. Maehr (Eds.), *Motivation and adulthood*. Greenwich, CT: JAI.

Kleiber, D., Larson, R., & Csikszentmihalyi, M. (1987). The experience of leisure in adolescence. *Journal of Leisure Research, 18*, 165-176.

Kram, K. (1985). *Mentoring at work: Developmental relationships in organizational life*. Glenview, IL: Scott, Foresman.

Labouvie-Vief, G. (1981). Proactive and reactive aspects of constructivism: Growth and aging in life-span perspective. In R. Lerner & N. Busch-Rossnagel (Eds.), *Individuals as producers of their own development*. New York: Academic Press.

Larson, R. (1978). Thirty years of research on the subjective well-being of older Americans. *Journal of Gerontology, 33*, 109-125.

Larson, R., & Kleiber, D. (1992). Free time activities as factors in adolescent adjustment. In P. Tolan & B. Cohler (Eds.), *Handbook of clinical research and practice with adolescents*. New York: John Wiley.

Larson, R., Zuzanek, J., & Mannell, R. (1985). Being alone versus being with other people: Disengagement in the daily experience of older adults. *Journal of Gerontology, 40*, 375-381.

Levinson, D., Darrow, C., Klein, F., Levinson, M., & McKee, B. (1978). *The seasons of a man's life.* New York: Knopf.

Logan, R. (1986). A reconceptualization of Erikson's theory: The repetition of existential and instrumental themes. *Human Development, 29*, 125-136.

Longino, C., & Kart, C. (1982). Explicating activity theory: A formal replication. *Journal of Gerontology, 37*, 713-722.

Maddox, G. (1965). Fact and artifact: Evidence bearing on disengagement theory from the Duke Geriatrics Project. *Human Development, 8*, 117-130.

McAdams, D., Ruetzel, K., & Foley, J. (1986). Complexity and generativity at midlife: Relations among social motives, ego development, and adults' plans for the future. *Journal of Personality and Social Psychology, 50*(4), 800-807.

Merriam, S. (1983). Mentors and protégés: A critical review of the literature. *Adult Education Quarterly, 33*(3), 161-173.

Neugarten, B. (1977). Personality and aging. In J. Birren & K. W. Schaie (Eds.), *Handbook of the psychology of aging.* New York: Van Nostrand Reinhold.

Neulinger, J. (1981). *The psychology of leisure.* Springfield, IL: Charles C Thomas.

Parker, S. (1987, October). *Volunteering as serious leisure.* Paper presented at the NRPA Leisure Research Symposium, New Orleans.

Pieper, J. (1952). *Leisure: The basis of culture.* New York: Pantheon.

Ray, R., & Heppe, G. (1986). Older adult happiness: The contributions of activity breadth and intensity. *Physical and Occupational Therapy in Geriatrics, 4*(4), 31-43.

Ryff, C., & Heincke, S. (1983). Subjective organization of personality in adulthood and aging. *Journal of Personality and Social Psychology, 44*, 807-816.

Schaie, K. W., & Geiwitz, J. (1982). *Adult development and aging.* Boston: Little, Brown.

Shaw, S. (1985). The meaning of leisure in everyday life. *Leisure Sciences, 13*, 33-50.

PART III

Varieties of Activity

From the beginning, activity has been defined inclusively. Narrow limits or stereotypes do not represent the wide variety of things that older people do to maintain a sense of identity, reconstitute schedules in retirement, fill unobligated hours, present an acceptable self to others, and be a part of communities of interaction and caring. One thing that is evident is that age-designated and age-segregated activities take a relatively small place in the overall life patterns of most older adults. In the 1984 National Health Interviews, less than 10% of those age 60 and over were found to participate regularly in senior centers. When we look at the activity of older adults, it is necessary to include the entire community, all the mass media, a full range of travel destinations and styles, home electronics, churches and schools, and places where grandchildren play as well as all the informal social spaces of interaction. In short, older adults are everywhere, doing almost everything, but at rates and in styles that fit their age-related abilities, interests, and resources. So much for bingo and sing-alongs.

The context is one of continuity. In the earlier years of retirement, most men and women go on doing pretty much what they did before, but with the timetables revised to fill and take advantage of the blocks of time opened by leaving the strictures of employment (Kelly & Westcott, 1989). They interact with much the same family and friends, give priority to the same TV favorites, do more of activities that had been limited to weekends (but not as much more as they had anticipated), take a trip or two that had been postponed, and finally get to some projects around the house. Community involvement, the exercise of long-developed skills, and nurturing activity may be expanded, but usually on a previously established base. Of course, there are those who move to new environs and respond to the opportunities and norms of a recreation-based community. But most "age in place" and demonstrate more continuity than change.

Some of the basis for that pattern has already been offered. There is no age or event that causes older people to suddenly and dramatically redefine themselves. In fact, most don't want to. Why should they disrupt their life-styles and commitments to redefine themselves as "old" so they can enter age-segregated environments euphemistically labeled "golden," "senior," or in any way denigrating? They are still themselves, persons who have competently constructed their own lives, nurtured the lives of others, and done the work of the world. They recognize that age has its impacts. There may be some constriction of activity, usually limited to those with particular requirements for resources that age may reduce. But the "active old," those with adequate financial and health resources, demonstrate more continuity than change. They are, after all, still the same persons.

Of course, there are significant changes. Being widowed makes a difference in both manifest and subtle ways. Retirement incomes are usually smaller. The incidence of health problems increases and requires coping. Yet, the multiple meanings of activity (see Chapter 3) still are a significant part of life and contribute to its overall quality. And some kinds of activities are more important than others, especially those with other persons who are important to us and those that yield a sense of ability and competence. Activity is more than filling time. Even frail older persons, those with severe limitations, respond to social engagement and challenging activity. Community and communication remain important. There are many kinds of activity. One issue concerns which kinds are appropriate, possible, and most valuable?

In Chapter 10 Roger Mannell argues that some kinds of activity are better than others. What are the activity involvements that contribute to a quality of later life that is more than ordinary? The kinds of activity that seem to really make a difference are those that are characterized by involvement, commitment, and skill. Depending on the aspect to be stressed, they may be referred to as "high investment," "serious," or "flow." Whatever the label of emphasis, they involve sustained commitment, developed competence or mastery, and challenge. They provide not only an experience of meaningful engagement, but they tend to yield a self-definition of ability and worth and lead to the formation of communities of action. Commonly, those engaged in such activity find all or most of their friendship groups in its practice, support, and action. Action is the basis of interaction. Such activity, whatever its nature, can make a special contribution to life, especially for those who have left the competence, status, and reward arena of work. Such commitment and standards of performance may run counter to images of leisure that stress immediate "fun" rather than longer term satisfaction. The outcomes may, however, transform the entire idea of retirement into one of opportunity to become deeply invested in the most satisfying kind of activity rather than meeting the requirements of the product-oriented workplace. If such "serious leisure" seems to be a contradiction in terms, that does not transform it into "work." Work remains directed toward products of economic value. The primary product of serious leisure is the person.

Stephen Cutler and Nicholas Danigelis in Chapter 11 address the activity context of community organizations. They analyze several national studies to draw a number of pertinent conclusions. The most common community organization for older adults is the church, which is not age segregated. They find about 15% of older adults related to senior programs of some sort. Senior centers are different from more general programs because participation is related to age, gender, and income level and may reflect relative social marginality. Age alone does not appear to be an overriding determinant of participation in organizational activity. Rather, the type of organization makes a difference. Volunteering decreases little to age 75. Further, the image of organizations is significant. Volunteering provides a context for retaining continuity in a sense of worth and value and may be especially significant for the "young (active) old." The selection effect causes firm conclusions about the values of community organization participation based on correlations to be somewhat suspect. Nevertheless, those involved in the community and especially in churches are usually found to be healthier and happier. Further, there is no support for a policy of age segregation in such findings.

In Chapter 12 Francis McGuire and Rosangela Boyd focus on the frail, who are most likely to be institutionalized. For them, activity is a context of interaction and communication. The issue becomes one of process: What happens in the activity? They argue that humor is one dimension of communication and interaction that can make a difference even to the frail and severely limited. It becomes a perspective on communication and on life. The frail are still in their life course, coping with change. The humor of irony and incongruence may help deal with even the drastic change of institutional life. It may involve remembering as well as dealing with the day. Life has so many limitations in the nursing home, but humor offers some transcendence and even a sense of mastery. Further, it facilitates interaction and the development of relationships. One implication of this approach is to avoid placing arbitrary limits on the frail old. Another is that affect and emotion are an important part of activity at any age and in any condition.

For both community-dwelling and institutionalized older persons, a variety of creative arts offer activity contexts that provide challenge, community, a sense of ability, and even an existential sense of developmental becoming. The vast range of possibilities of creative activity is addressed by Nancy Osgood in Chapter 13. The arts in their manifold forms may offer opportunities for expression, exploration, growth, reminiscence, socializing, and outright enjoyment. The arts may be enjoyed as others produce and perform. More important from an activity perspective, they offer opportunities for effective action that is unique to the individual. They often involve the whole being—mind, body, and spirit. There is feedback that may yield a sense of efficacy. The arts are a special realm of activity in which to exercise the "Ulyssean" spirit of later life, one in which there remains the creative adventure of making and remaking some part of the world. Again, the variety seems infinite, not only in forms but also in levels and contexts of meaningful action. The arts may be "done" at all levels of skill. Chapter 10, however, reminds us that there seems to be a relationship between skill and satisfaction. It should never be assumed that age means incompetence or lowered standards. Singing may mean Bach chorales rather than sing-alongs. Older persons may seek continuity based on previous levels of skill. Groups gathered around doing some form of art not only build community but also are a context for the demonstration of personal expression and creation, growth and development, integration and competence. In the limits of a single chapter, Osgood is able to give only a small sample of the countless valuable programs in the creative arts. Again, the message is that no arbitrary limits should be based on age. One question is the extent to which opportunities for creative activity are available and accessible for older persons.

It is clear that no type of activity is as likely to be abandoned or avoided by the old as regular physical exercise. Contexts for exercise such as sports are difficult or unavailable for many. Yet, the health and psychological benefits of regular physical activity have been fully documented. In Chapter 14 Edward McAuley uses his line of research to stress that there is more to persistence in physical activity than trying harder. The values of regular physical activity are well documented. The catch is that most older persons don't do it. McAuley has found that a sense of "self-efficacy" is at the center of continued activity. Those who have found a sense of ability and positive results in activity are most likely to continue; they are those who have a "positive mastery experience," a positive self-definition of ability. Programs that provide positive feedback are most likely to retain adherents. Those who have a personal history demonstrating physical competence most often exercise in later life. (Those playing "age 55+" softball have been good players in the past.) The message is one of positive reinforcement that is both immediate and cumulative. For the 80%-90% of older adults who are not active, recruitment remains a problem. One implication of the emphasis on self-efficacy would be to identify and offer contexts of exercise that are accepting and reinforcing rather than threatening, perhaps walking more than sports. This may also be a gender issue because women currently in old age cohorts came through school in the days when females were protected against and even shut out of demanding physical activity.

One theme of these chapters is to warn against placing arbitrary age-based limits on older adults. Such limits are especially counterproductive when they close access to activities that call for high levels of skill, commitment, experience, involvement, and even exertion. The kind of activities that make the most difference in later life seem to be the most demanding and involving. They have challenge and yield a sense of worth and ability. They engage us with other persons, sometimes in organized contexts and frequently in taking on some responsibility for others. They may be creative for the mind and spirit. They may call for bodily action. They are both existential and social. They involve self-development and community.

This does not mean that the ordinary round of later life is to be packed with strenuous and demanding activity, a time of stress and strain. It does suggest that the ordinary round of activity that may fill all available time quite nicely may not be enough. For those whose later lives are more than "OK," there seems to be a dimension of involvement. Preferably challenging mind and body, social and personal skills, such activity does far more than fill time.

Reference

Kelly, J., & Westcott, G. (1989). Ordinary retirement: Commonalities and continuities. *International Journal of Aging and Human Development, 32*(2), 81-89.

10

High-Investment Activity and Life Satisfaction Among Older Adults

Committed, Serious Leisure, and Flow Activities

ROGER C. MANNELL

On the Politics and Nature of "Good" Leisure Activities

"Freedom to choose never guarantees happiness. The growth of leisure does not automatically enhance the quality of life. It merely bestows the opportunity and thereby underlines the urgency of enquiring how individuals can be assisted to derive maximum benefits from their scope for choice" (Roberts, 1981, p. 61). Underlying Roberts's statement is the assumption that some of the activities with which people choose to structure the free time in their daily lives are *better* than others. Presumably, then, there are "good" and "bad" leisure choices, activities, and life-styles. Also implied by this statement is the belief that we can both discover the nature of good choices and develop strategies to help people make them.

Social scientists have belonged to two camps concerning the appropriateness of making judgments about whether leisure and cultural activities are essentially good or bad (Kando, 1980). On the one hand, there are those who feel that the leisure and cultural behavior of individuals and groups is simply a difference in life-style reflecting social values and choices and that social scientists should remain value-free and not make judgments. These judgments can be ethnocentric, a source of conflict between individuals and groups with different leisure and cultural values, and restrictive of the individual's freedom. As Csikszentmihalyi and Kleiber (1991) have pointed out, this view is often accompanied by the belief that it is important to allow "people their freedom, even if its exercise leads to 'wasting' time or to personal harm" (p. 97). On the other hand, there are those who argue that certain forms of leisure and cultural behavior are better because they are exploratory and creative, reflect a society's important traditions, and are superior in engaging the human intellect and engendering quality of life. Acceptance of this view requires a more critical look at the choices people make and how these choices affect their lives.

These two perspectives need not be in conflict for the social scientist. If we specify the nature of the outcomes we value, some leisure activities can be "good" in the sense of fostering valued outcomes more than others. Empirical social science methods can then be used to study the nature of "good" activities and their links with valued outcomes. What are not available for empirical testing by the social scientist, but need to be debated, are the outcomes to be valued.

In this chapter I assume that the life satisfaction of older adults is a valued outcome. First, I will review recent social science theory and research that may help us understand the nature of those leisure activities that may be particularly "good" or effective in contributing to quality of life. Second, with the use of data collected as part of a larger study of the life-styles of retired older adults, I will examine the occurrence of these activities in everyday life, the conditions that foster participation in these "good" activities, and differences in the extent to which the daily lives of respondents reporting various levels of life satisfaction are colored or structured by the experience of these activities.

Candidates for "Good" Leisure Activity

When we look at the leisure and life-style choices of older retired adults, current prescriptions for high life satisfaction include staying active. Recent reviews of the activity theory of aging conclude that there is substantial support for the hypothesis that, the more active people are in their later years, the greater will be their subjective well-being (Kelly & Ross, 1989; Kelly, Steinkamp, & Kelly, 1987; Lawton, 1987). Activity theory is not very precise, however, on how "more active" should be defined and whether participation in all types of activities contributes to being more active or has equal value for well-being (Kelly et al., 1987). The process by which leisure activities contribute to life satisfaction is also unspecified (Kelly & Ross, 1989).

What are the best candidates for "good" leisure activities? Two hypotheses can be suggested that characterize the view examined in this chapter. The first hypothesis is that retired older adults who experience higher levels of subjective well-being and life satisfaction are more involved in freely chosen activities that challenge their knowledge and skills and require an investment of effort. I use the term *high-investment* activities to label these. Kelly and his associates coined the term *high-investment activities* and suggested that they are activities that have been developed over time, require a great deal of effort and resources and the acquisition of skill, and are most likely to yield outcomes of an enhanced sense of competence and worth (Kelly & Ross, 1989, p. 57; Kelly et al., 1987, p. 194). A second related hypothesis is that there are certain conditions that must be met by these activities if they are to successfully entice high investment from participants in their freely chosen pursuits. Consequently, high-investment activities are those that involve commitment, obligation, some discipline, and even occasional sacrifice.

To put it simply, we could say that, *the more you invest in the activities that you choose to participate in, the more you get out of them.* Of course, this idea is not new. It is an adage that many of us probably heard from parents, teachers, and coaches. This second hypothesis suggests that, in those moments in daily life when people are confronted with the opportunity for free choice, there is some natural resistance or "psychological inertia" to overcome in choosing to engage in activities requiring higher levels of investment of effort. Important to overcoming this inertia is having a repertoire of high-investment activities in which one has developed a sense of commitment or feels a sense of obligation. The growing belief among researchers that leisure needs to be more than simply a pleasant, diversionary, escape-oriented experience if it is to contribute substantially to the quality of life (Csikszentmihalyi & Kleiber,

1991; Haworth, 1986; Kelly et al., 1987; Mannell, Zuzanek, & Larson, 1988; Shamir, 1988; Stebbins, 1992; Tinsley & Tinsley, 1986) has led to substantial interest in the constructs of "commitment" (Becker, 1960), "serious leisure" (Stebbins, 1982), and "flow" (Csikszentmihalyi, 1975). This triad of constructs provides a theoretical basis for understanding the nature of these "good" high-investment leisure activities and the social psychological mechanisms by which they contribute to well-being.

Commitment

The construct of commitment was formally introduced into the social psychological literature by the sociologist Becker (1960). While there has been some debate over definition and terminology, commitment can be described as an attitudinal or motivational state to continue participating in an activity and to invest effort in it regardless of the short-term costs and benefits of participation. Becker (1960) suggested that commitment develops over time as a consequence of many small decisions or "side-bets." He argues that the committed person has staked something of value on being consistent in her or his behavior. The consequence of inconsistency will be more expensive than the short-term costs of choosing to participate. These short-term costs could include fatigue, possibility of physical injury and failure, forgoing other more immediately enjoyable activities, and financial expense. It has been noted that while commitment, which denotes obligation, duty, and routine, may seem to be incompatible with the commonly understood characteristics of leisure such as freedom, spontaneity, variety, and pleasure, there is still freedom as to the actual behavior that can be engaged in during participation (Shamir, 1988) as well as the freedom to chose not to participate.

Buchanan (1985) and Haworth (1984) have provided reviews and analyses of commitment and its relevance for understanding leisure activity. Buchanan demonstrated the importance of commitment for understanding and integrating theories dealing with recreation conflict, substitution, and specialization. Particularly, his discussion of the role of commitment in recreation specialization is relevant to our analysis of high-investment activity as it refers to the process by which an individual becomes willing to invest time and effort in an activity. The notion of recreation specialization was originally proposed by Bryan

(1977) and suggests that individuals undergo a "career" within a recreation activity. Commitment is thought to covary with specialization and to increase as people move along the "specialization continuum" from "occasional participants" through "generalists" and "technique specialists" to "technique and setting specialists" (Buchanan, 1985, p. 409).

Recently, a variety of terms denoting commitment to a leisure activity, program, service, or product have emerged in the leisure marketing and consumer behavior literature, for example, *loyalty* (Backman, 1991) and *involvement* (Havitz & Dimanche, 1990; McCarville, 1991). Researchers have focused on issues such as measurement, explaining continuing participation in an activity and willingness to pay to participate. No explicit theoretical link between commitment to activities and subjective well-being has been suggested or explored in this research.

Haworth (1984, 1986), rather than being concerned with the process of becoming committed to or specialized in an activity, has focused more on the role that commitment to a leisure activity plays in quality of life. He has argued that participation in these types of leisure activities can counter the "detrimental effects on psychological well-being, including increased susceptibility to mental illness and lowered self-esteem" of being unemployed, retired, or employed in an unsatisfying or alienating job (p. 281). In the studies reviewed by Haworth, committed leisure activities included home improvements, gardening, hobbies, learning new activities, active leisure, games and sports, and voluntary activities. The mechanism linking commitment and subjective well-being, according to Haworth, is the opportunity provided for status recognition and self-development. Shamir (1988) elaborates this argument and suggests that acting in accordance with one's commitments leads to satisfaction in "maintaining and presenting a valued self-image" (p. 248). Tinsley and Tinsley (1986) have also suggested that "personal commitment" to an activity "is necessary in order to achieve the intense involvement that can contribute to personal development" (p. 14).

In a recent review, Shamir (1988) concluded that little empirical evidence has been provided to support Haworth's (1984) premise that committed leisure activity can replace work as a source of well-being in the lives of people who are dissatisfied with their jobs, unemployed, or retired. He argues that, when committed leisure activities have been found to be associated with higher levels of psychological well-being, it is a rare occurrence and the experience of only a minority of individuals.

Serious Leisure

Commitment is at the core of Stebbins's (1992) theory of "serious leisure." In fact, the construct provides a clear picture of what being committed to a leisure activity entails and the characteristics of those activities most likely both to require and to foster commitment. He proposed the construct following his early studies of amateurs and during the past decade has completed a number of extensive qualitative studies of amateur and professional participants in various types of sport (baseball, football), arts (music, theater), variety arts (magic and stand-up comedy), and science (archaeology, astronomy) activities. Recently, Stebbins (1992) has provided a summary and reappraisal of the construct based on this work. He defines serious leisure "as the systematic pursuit of an amateur, hobbyist, or volunteer activity that is sufficiently substantial and interesting for the participant to find a career there in the acquisition and expression of its special skills and knowledge" (Stebbins, 1992, p. 3). Like Shamir (1988), he does not see commitment to a serious leisure pursuit as incompatible with freedom of choice. Serious leisure has distinct characteristics that distinguish it from casual or relaxing leisure. It demands perseverance, personal effort in the development of specially acquired knowledge and skill, the development of a career in the activity, and strong attachment to or identification with the activity. Serious leisure often involves membership in or identification with a group of participants with distinct beliefs, norms, values, traditions, and performance standards. According to Stebbins, this type of leisure can also be distinguished on the basis of the important psychological benefits that are derived from participation.

If leisure is to make a significant contribution to the quality of life of the individual, Stebbins (1992) feels it is likely characterized by "necessity, obligation, seriousness, and commitment as expressed by regimentation (e.g., rehearsals and practice) and systematization (e.g., schedules and organization)" (p. 9). In the short term, leisure may be no fun. The hard work and perseverance by amateurs, hobbyists, and volunteers to meet the challenges of their leisure is predicted to engender feelings of accomplishment and provide psychological benefits that include self-enrichment, self-gratification, self-actualization, self-expression, positive social identity, re-creation, escape from personal problems, social belonging, and a feeling of contributing to a group (Stebbins, 1992, p. 17). Stebbins also speculates that serious leisure can be important to the quality of older retired adults' lives by providing worklike activity, offering a link with former work associates, current friends, and relatives, expanding one's social circle, promoting transcendence, constituting a theme in the life review, fostering responsibility, and creating the opportunity to feel needed by other people (p. 127).

The argument that serious leisure plays an important role in the individual's quality of life is persuasive, yet it remains untested. While Stebbins's conclusions are based on the self-reports of his respondents about the impact of their serious leisure on the quality of their lives, no research has been undertaken to compare the quality of life of people whose life-styles are characterized by this type of activity with those whose lives are dominated by casual or relaxing leisure. Shamir (1988), in discussing both committed and serious leisure, has cautioned against generalizing too broadly from "those relatively rare cases of leisure involvement where compensations or substitution is evident" (p. 239).

Flow

As with the development of the constructs of committed and serious leisure, the development of the flow model by Csikszentmihalyi (1975) reflects a concern with why and how activities become meaningful to the individual. Unlike these other constructs, however, the flow model focuses more on the phenomenological experience of high levels of commitment or involvement in an activity and the identification and explanation of the conditions and features of activities that lead to optimal experiences or flow. While the flow model allows that some activities have greater potential for being high-investment activities, the source of "high investment" is as much in the mind of the individual as it is in the activity. Consequently, the flow model provides some insight into how the activities of everyday life come to be invested with meaning and experienced as optimal.

On the basis of a series of in-depth qualitative interviews with participants in a variety of active leisure pursuits, Csikszentmihalyi (1975) proposed that the characteristics and conditions of the flow experience that distinguish it from the rest of experience include a centering or focusing of the participant's attention on the task at hand, a loss of self-consciousness, unambiguous feedback about her or his actions, feelings of control over her or his actions and their environment, a momentary loss of anxiety and constraint, and enjoyment (pp. 38-48). The best indicator and the most critical condition for the occurrence of flow is the perception by the individual that his or her personal skills and the challenge provided by an activity match. The idea that flow both reflects and is a consequence of high personal investment in an activity is clear in Csikszentmihalyi's work. Flow experiences are "the best moments of our lives, are not the passive, receptive, relaxing times" and they "occur when a person's body or mind is stretched to its limits in a voluntary effort to accomplish something difficult and worthwhile" (Csikszentmihalyi, 1990, p. 3).

Stebbins (1992, p. 112) has observed that the conditions outlined by Csikszentmihalyi to produce flow are highly similar to those provided by serious leisure. While Csikszentmihalyi does not refer to serious leisure specifically, he has recognized that activities requiring commitment, discipline, and effort are more likely to provide the conditions for flow experiences (Csikszentmihalyi, 1990, pp. 162-163). In a recent study, he and a colleague concluded that it appeared easier for people to enjoy and experience flow in their jobs than their free time because work activities are more likely to have built-in goals, feedback, rules, and challenges, all of which encourage involvement in the activity (Csikszentmihalyi & LeFevre, 1989).

In subsequent work, Csikszentmihalyi has theorized about the link between flow experiences and well-being. While some activities, such as sports, games, art, and hobbies, appear to consistently produce flow, he theorizes that well-being results from how people experience all their day-to-day activities (Csikszentmihalyi & Larson, 1984). Consequently, to improve quality of life, one must learn to transform one's daily pursuits into flow-producing activity. "When a person is able to organize his or her consciousness so as to experience flow as often as possible, the quality of life is inevitably going to improve" (Csikszentmihalyi, 1990, p. 52). The regular experience of flow translates into a sense of mastery and control "that comes as close to what is usually meant by happiness as anything else we can conceivably imagine" (Csikszentmihalyi, 1990, p. 4).

Csikszentmihalyi and his colleagues have reported a considerable amount of research dealing with how people experience their everyday lives and the conditions in which they report flow. To aid in this research, they have developed the *experiential sampling method* (ESM; Larson & Csikszentmihalyi, 1983). Their respondents typically carry electronic pagers with them for a period of several days, usually one week. In response to a random signal, respondents take out a booklet of brief questionnaires and complete a series of questions indicating their current activity, psychological state, and the social and physical context of their activity.

Some evidence for the relationship between involvement in flow activities and, at least, short-term subjective well-being can be inferred from a study of 107 full-time working men and women who reported on 4,971 moments in their daily lives during the course of a week (Graef, Csikszentmihalyi, & McManama Gianinno, 1983). The researchers found some evidence to suggest that the more frequently respondents experienced their skills matching the challenges provided by their daily activities, the happier and less tense they were over the course of the week.

In an ESM study of a week in the life of a group of 75 adolescents, Kleiber, Larson, and Csikszentmihalyi (1986) found that watching television, listening to music, reading, and resting activities, while freely chosen, were experienced as requiring little effort or challenge. They argued that this set of activities would appear to reflect a category of "relaxed leisure" (p. 175), a type of experience that may restore one's energy but not requiring the exertion of effort. In contrast, the activities of sports, games, arts, and hobbies were experienced not only as freely chosen but as challenging and requiring concentration. They interpreted their results to suggest that, when the adolescents were working toward a goal in a structured activity, whether leisure or not, they felt at their best.

Notwithstanding the persuasiveness of this argument and evidence that activities in which skills and challenges match lead people to feel more active and happy during participation, little empirical evidence is available to suggest that people who experience more of these high-investment flow activities in their daily lives are also likely to be more satisfied in general with their lives.

High-Investment Activities and Life Satisfaction Among Retired Older Adults

The psychological link between participation in high-investment activities and quality of life common to the commitment, serious leisure, and flow constructs is "competence." Activities that require an investment of effort are seen to provide opportunities to maintain and further develop the sense of competence that allows people to frequently experience enjoyment and develop positive feelings about themselves. The notion of competence is an important element in a number of social psychological theories that attempt to explain effective human functioning and mental health—for example, learned helplessness (Seligman, 1975), self-efficacy (Bandura, 1982), and intrinsic motivation (Deci & Ryan, 1985). The competence construct has also been seen as extremely important for understanding a wide range of leisure behaviors (see Iso-Ahola, 1989; Iso-Ahola & Mannell, 1985).

Little research has been reported that allows us to single out the importance of high-investment activities in the life-styles and quality of life of older adults or explore the processes involved. The findings of two recent studies reported by Kelly and his colleagues (Kelly & Ross, 1989; Kelly et al., 1987), however, begin to shed some light on this issue. With the use of telephone and mail surveys of random samples of 400 and 380 older adults residing in Peoria, Illinois, the researchers found that those people reporting higher levels of life satisfaction as measured by Neugarten's life satisfaction scale (Neugarten, Havighurst, & Tobin, 1961) were also more likely to participate in cultural, travel, sports, and constructive home activities. As previously mentioned, they labeled these activities "high-investment" activities. While these results provide tentative support, the researchers had no independent evidence available to corroborate that the respondents who reported participating in these activities were committed and heavily invested in them.

My colleague Jiri Zuzanek and I have been conducting a series of studies using the experience sampling method. The subjects of one of these studies were retired older adults. We recently reported a set of analyses examining the experience of freedom and intrinsic motivation in the daily lives of our study group that are relevant to the issue of high-investment activity (Mannell et al., 1988). In the remainder of the chapter, I will report some additional analyses of these data that allow a closer look at the occurrence and the experiences and conditions associated with high investment in the freely chosen activities engaged in by retired older adults in the course of their daily lives. Analyses will also be presented to determine if those respondents who were more satisfied with their lives were highly invested (experienced flow) in a greater proportion of their daily activities.

Sample

The subjects were 92 retired older adults comprising 40 men and 52 women between the ages of 55 and 88, with a mean age of 69. Of the participants, 71% lived in their own homes, 24% lived in their own apartments, and 5% lived with relatives. The majority (66%) were married, 23% were widowed or separated, and 11% had never been married. The respondents' occupations had varied from upper management and professional (21.1%), white collar and semiprofessional (49.1%), to sales/service and blue collar (23.9%), and 42% had some college or university-level education. Few reported physical disabilities, and no respondents were confined to their homes due to health-related problems; 83% of these older adults rated their health as good or very good.

Method

The data were gathered using the experience sampling method (ESM) and personal interviews to study a variety of life-style issues. The participants carried electronic pagers for 1 week. Radio signals emitted from a central location caused the pagers to make an audible beep, which served as the stimulus for subjects to complete an experience sampling form (ESF) that they carried with them. The pager signals were sent between 8:00 a.m. and 10:00 p.m. with one signal occurring at a random time within every 2-hour block. The participants responded to an average 37 of the 49 signals for the week (76%) and provided a total of 3,412 self-reports on random moments during their daily lives.

Flow in Extrinsically Motivated and Committed Activity

It is generally assumed that true, meaningful, and involving leisure occurs in activities that are freely chosen and engaged in for intrinsic reasons (Mannell & Bradley, 1986). Typically, commitment or obligation are considered sources of extrinsic motivation. In the leisure and psychological literatures, intrinsic reasons are often characterized as participation in an activity for its own sake and immediate enjoyment (e.g., Deci & Ryan, 1985; Neulinger, 1974). In intrinsic motivation theory as well as in its application to leisure theory, it is assumed that, when people are free to choose what they wish to do and their choices are not influenced by anything except their own internal psychological needs, they will make good choices that are beneficial to themselves. Consequently, in a recent study (Mannell et al., 1988) we predicted that our retired older adult respondents would be more likely to experience flow in freely chosen and intrinsically motivated activities. We classified the activities each respondent reported over the course of the study week into four types on the basis of whether they were freely chosen or constrained and intrinsically or extrinsically motivated. We found, as expected, that flow occurred more frequently and the respondents showed higher levels of psychological investment in freely chosen activities; however, flow was experienced to a much greater extent in freely chosen extrinsically motivated activities than in freely chosen intrinsically motivated activities.

We argued that this unexpected finding could be considered consistent with the notions of commitment and serious leisure. The items on the ESF that the respondents checked to indicate extrinsic motivation reflected choosing to participate due to a sense of obligation or commitment (that is, they could check that they were doing the activity primarily for others, for their own long-term benefit, or for both these reasons). Intrinsic motivation was indicated by checking that they had chosen to become involved in the activity for its own sake or immediate enjoyment. For the purposes of this discussion, I have provided a reanalysis of the data comparing the experience of flow or degree of psychological investment in only those activities that were freely chosen but differing in the extent to which the respondents chose to participate because of a sense of commitment or obligation (see Figure 10.1).

Freedom of choice was assessed by the participants responding to the question on the ESF, "How much choice did you have in selecting this activity?" on a 10-point scale ranging from *none* (0) to *very much* (9). The individual's freedom of choice for each activity reported was defined as "constrained" if his or her rating on the scale fell below the mean for all activities he or she reported during the study week and as "free" if the rating was above his or her own mean.

Flow was operationalized by measuring the levels of affect, potency, concentration, and relaxation experienced at the time of participation in the activity as well as the perception of a skill-challenge match accompanying participation. Affect was assessed with two 7-point semantic differential items (happy-sad, cheerful-irritable). Potency, a measure of feelings of mental and physical activation, provided some indication of the feelings accompanying the perception of being

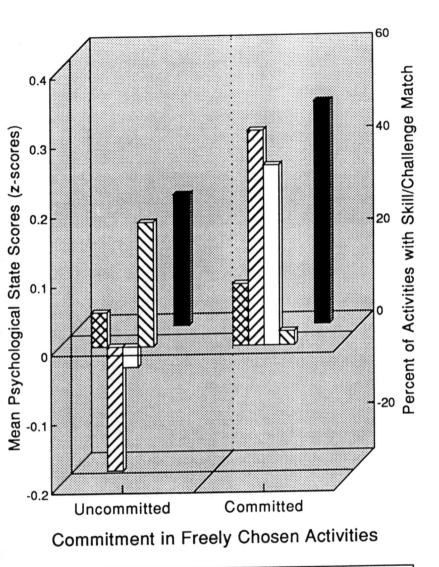

Figure 10.1. Experience of Flow (high investment) in Freely Chosen Uncommitted and Committed Activities

NOTE: Experience of flow in activities measured by mean affect, potency, concentration, relaxation, and percentage of activities in which skills matched challenges.

in control of one's actions and the environment (Csikszentmihalyi, 1975, p. 44) and it was a composite measure of four items (alert-drowsy, active-passive, energetic-tired, excited-bored). One item was used to measure the level of relaxation experienced (relaxed-tense). Csikszentmihalyi (1975, p. 48) has suggested that the centering of attention will be experienced as greater concentration. Participants responded to the question, "How well were you concentrating?" on a 10-point Likert scale. Responses to all these scales were converted to individual z-scores. To assess whether personal skills matched the challenges provided by the activity, respondents were asked to rate the "challenges of the activity" and their "skills in the activity" also using 10-point scales. Following Csikszentmihalyi and LeFevre's (1989) recommendation for operationalizing flow with the experiential sampling method data, those activities in which both challenges and skills were rated as greater than the respondent's own mean scores across all his or her skill and challenge ratings for the week were classified as flow. Nonflow experiences comprised situations where challenge or skill levels or both skill and challenge levels were below the individual's mean level. The flow scores for each respondent were calculated as the percentage of their weekly activities rated as above average in both challenge and the demand for skill when freely chosen and engaged in for intrinsic reasons (uncommitted leisure) versus extrinsic reasons (committed leisure). The data were analyzed using repeated measures analysis of variance.

As can be seen from Figure 10.1, when the respondents had the freedom to choose an activity, when they felt no external commitment or obligation to engage in the activity for others or for their own long-term benefit, and when participation was simply for their own immediate enjoyment, the activities they selected were more likely to be experienced as relaxing and less likely to be challenging of their skills or psychologically involving. All indicators of flow differed significantly ($p < .05$) for the two conditions with the exception of affect. It could be argued that the freely chosen and extrinsically motivated activities are the experiential analogue of committed and serious leisure and, as we would expect, participation in them was more likely to result in the experience of high-investment flow.

The Nature of Freely Chosen and Committed Activities

Were certain types of activities more likely to constitute committed leisure and high-investment activity in the daily lives of these retired older adults? Activity profiles for the freely chosen uncommitted and committed conditions were created (see Figure 10.2). To the question on the ESF, "What was the main thing you were doing?" the participants reported the activity in which they were currently involved. Each response was coded into 1 of 57 activity categories. For the current analysis, the number was reduced to four broad categories, which included (a) volunteer/home/family care activity (e.g., voluntary work, housework, child care), (b) self-care (e.g., personal maintenance, using medical services), (c) passive leisure (e.g., relaxing, reading, watching television, socializing), and (d) active leisure (e.g., exercising, hobbies, games). As can be seen in Figure 10.2, the proportions of each type of activity comprising the uncommitted and committed conditions were different (p < .001).

The largest constituent of the freely chosen and uncommitted activities was passive leisure. For the committed activities, volunteer/home/family care contributed the largest proportion of activities, and a higher proportion of active leisure activities occurred in this condition as well. It would appear that the difference in the types of activities dominating the two conditions is consistent with our ideas of what constitutes high-investment pursuits. It should be noted, however, that all types of activity when freely chosen can be experienced as committed or serious and demanding of effort and skill.

High-Investment Activities, Flow, and Life Satisfaction

To return to our original question, we can ask: "Do people who are more satisfied with their lives also participate in more high-investment activities in the course of their daily lives?" Over 95% of the respondents indicated that the week in which they participated in the study was a typical week for them. Consequently, I am assuming that the ESM data reflect relatively typical activity and experiential patterns in the lives of the respondents. A path analysis was conducted to examine the relationship between the percentage of each respondent's week of activities that were volunteer/home/family care and active leisure activities (what I will call "potential high-investment activities"), the percentage that were freely chosen and motivated by a sense of commitment or obligation (freely chosen-committed activities), the percentage in which flow was experienced (flow activities), and the level of life satisfaction reported by the respondents.

Life satisfaction was measured during the interview portion of the study with a six-item version of the Neugarten et al. (1961) life satis-

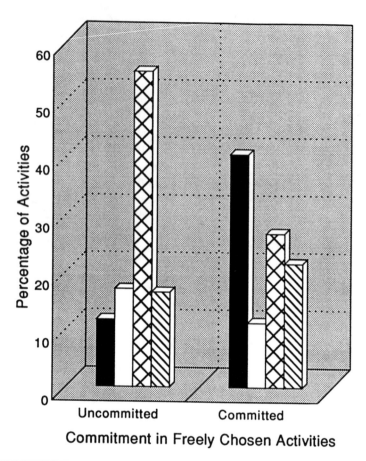

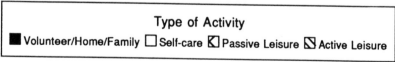

Figure 10.2. Proportion (in percentage) of the Four Major Types of Activity Experienced as Freely Chosen Uncommitted and Freely Chosen Committed

faction scale. As a whole, these older adults were highly satisfied with their lives. The study group was very homogeneous not only in terms of sociodemographic background but in how satisfied the participants were with their lives. On a scale ranging from a low of 6 to a high of 30, actual scores ranged from 15 to 30 with a mean of 24.2. Coefficient alpha in the current study was .67. In spite of this homogeneity, the path analysis (see Figure 10.3) suggests that those respondents who experienced flow in more of their activities, what we have argued is an indicator of high investment in an activity, reported higher levels of life satisfaction. The beta weights reported in Figure 10.3 are all significant ($p < .05$). The proportion of the respondents' daily activities that were classified as potential high investment and freely chosen-committed were not directly related to life satisfaction. The analysis suggests, however, that respondents who engaged in a greater number of potential high-investment activities were more likely to experience more of their activities as freely chosen and committed. In turn, those respondents who were more likely to participate in activities they freely chose but in which they also felt some commitment or obligation were more likely to experience flow or be highly invested in the activity at the moment signaled.

When the amount of flow experienced by the bottom 30% of respondents (mean life satisfaction = 20.3) in their daily lives was compared with that experienced by the top 30% (mean life satisfaction = 28.2), the high-satisfaction group experienced significantly ($F[1,48] = 6.8, p < .01$) more of their activities as flow (mean = 36.6%) than the low satisfaction group (mean = 28.0%).

Conclusion

If we assume that the week reported was a typical week in the lives of our respondents as was the level of investment in their activities, these analyses provide support for the hypothesis that those older adults who are more satisfied with their lives invest greater effort (indicated by their experiencing flow) in more of their daily activities than those who report less satisfaction with their lives. This high investment in more of the activities of everyday life, however, was not guaranteed simply by participating in more potentially high-investment activities such as volunteer work, sport and exercise, home maintenance, hobbies, travel, and cultural pursuits. When participation was voluntary, the occurrence of flow in these activities was mediated by the presence or absence of a sense of commitment or obligation to participate. As we have seen, this notion of commitment in freely chosen activities is

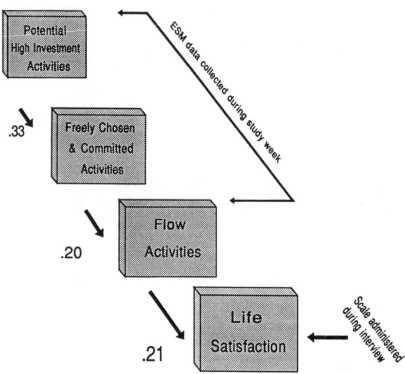

Figure 10.3. Path Analysis of the Relationship Between the Number of Potential High-Investment Activities, Freely Chosen Committed Activities, and Flow Activities Reported During the Study Week and Life Satisfaction

central to understanding the potential role of committed, serious leisure and flow in the quality of life.

Given the freedom to choose, which for many older adults expands at retirement and is more of an issue at this stage in life than during the working years, some people may need the feeling of external compulsion, obligation to self or others, or long-term commitment to overcome the "psychological inertia" or resistance to engage in activities that require an investment of effort. In the context of daily life, this "psychological inertia principle of leisure" makes some sense. For example, when faced with making a choice of how to use our free time, we likely often feel, at the moment of decision, a lack of motivation to engage in something that requires a substantial investment of effort or that might involve short-term psychological or physical costs. Consequently, the choice to engage in casual or relaxing activities, such as sitting and watching television or curling up with a book, may be made. This choice and these activities would likely be perceived as intrinsically motivated by the relatively immediate pleasure anticipated. In contrast, a sense of obligation or commitment to an activity that requires a greater investment of energy, such as playing with one's children or grandchildren or exercising for health reasons, may cause the individual to forgo the anticipated short-term pleasure of these less demanding activities. While having freedom of choice, the obligation or commitment wins over immediate personal enjoyment. Once one is engaged in these freely chosen committed activities, however, the activities may have greater potential for challenging one's skills and, consequently, producing powerful feelings of flow that would not have resulted from more passive activities like watching television or reading a book.

Csikszentmihalyi and Larson (1984) speculate that what we have called high-investment activities can contribute to the successful transition from adolescence to adulthood by providing "structured systems of participation" that require discipline and lay the "groundwork" for experiencing enjoyment in more constrained and obligatory adult activities (p. 175). It could also be argued that this transition is only the first of two in the life cycle. The second occurs at retirement. Having a repertoire of serious leisure activities that have the potential to challenge one's skills, and feeling committed to them, may contribute to the successful negotiation of the transition required of older adults as they move from a life-style dominated by constrained and obligated work activities to a life-style characterized by freedom of choice.

References

Backman, S. J. (1991). An investigation of the relationship between activity loyalty and perceived constraints. *Journal of Leisure Research, 23*, 332-344.

Bandura, A. (1982). Self-efficacy mechanisms in human agency. *American Psychologist, 37*, 127-147.

Becker, H. S. (1960). Notes on the concept of commitment. *American Journal of Sociology, 66*, 32-40.

Bryan, H. (1977). Leisure value systems and recreational specialization: The case of trout fishermen. *Journal of Leisure Research, 9*, 174-187.

Buchanan, T. (1985). Commitment and leisure behavior: A theoretical perspective. *Leisure Sciences, 7*, 401-420.

Csikszentmihalyi, M. (1975). *Beyond boredom and anxiety.* San Francisco: Jossey-Bass.

Csikszentmihalyi, M. (1990). *Flow: The psychology of optimal experience.* New York: Harper Perennial.

Csikszentmihalyi, M., & Kleiber, D. A. (1991). Leisure and self-actualization. In B. L. Driver, P. J. Brown, & G. L. Peterson (Eds.), *Benefits of leisure* (pp. 91-102). State College, PA: Venture.

Csikszentmihalyi, M., & Larson, R. (1984). *Being adolescent.* New York: Basic Books.

Csikszentmihalyi, M., & LeFevre, J. (1989). Optimal experience in work and leisure. *Journal of Personality and Social Psychology, 56,* 815-822.

Deci, E. L., & Ryan, R. M. (1985). *Intrinsic motivation and self-determination in human behavior.* New York: Plenum.

Graef, R., Csikszentmihalyi, M., & McManama Gianinno, S. (1983). Measuring intrinsic motivation in everyday life. *Leisure Studies, 2,* 155-168.

Havitz, M. E., & Dimanche, F. (1990). Propositions for testing the involvement construct in recreational and tourism contexts. *Leisure Sciences, 12,* 179-195.

Haworth, J. T. (1984). The perceived nature of meaningful pursuits and the social psychology of commitment. *Society and Leisure, 7,* 197-216.

Haworth, J. T. (1986). Meaningful activity and psychological models of non-employment. *Leisure Studies, 5,* 281-297.

Iso-Ahola, S. E. (1989). Motivation for leisure. In E. L. Jackson & T. L. Burton (Eds.), *Understanding leisure and recreation: Mapping the past, charting the future.* State College, PA: Venture.

Iso-Ahola, S. E., & Mannell, R. C. (1985). Social and psychological constraints on leisure. In M. G. Wade (Ed.), *Constraints on leisure.* Springfield, IL: Charles C Thomas.

Kando, T. M. (1980). *Leisure and popular culture in transition.* Toronto: C. V. Mosby.

Kelly, J. R., & Ross, J. (1989). Later-life leisure: Beginning a new agenda. *Leisure Sciences, 11,* 47-59.

Kelly, J. R., Steinkamp, M. W., & Kelly, J. R. (1987). Later-life satisfaction: Does leisure contribute? *Leisure Sciences, 9,* 189-200.

Kleiber, D., Larson, R., & Csikszentmihalyi, M. (1986). The experience of leisure in adolescence. *Journal of Leisure Research, 18,* 169-176.

Larson, R., & Csikszentmihalyi, M. (1983). The experience sampling method. In H. T. Reis (Ed.), *Naturalistic approaches to study social interaction.* San Francisco: Jossey-Bass.

Lawton, M. P. (1987). Activities and leisure. In M. P. Lawton & G. Maddox (Eds.), *Annual review of gerontology and geriatrics* (Vol. 5). New York: Springer.

Mannell, R. C., & Bradley, W. (1986). Does greater freedom always lead to greater leisure? Testing a person × environmental model of freedom and leisure. *Journal of Leisure Research, 18,* 215-230.

Mannell, R. C., Zuzanek, J., & Larson, R. W. (1988). Leisure states and "flow" experiences: Testing perceived freedom and intrinsic motivation hypotheses. *Journal of Leisure Research, 20,* 289-304.

McCarville, R. E. (1991). An empirical investigation of the influence of cost information on willingness to pay for public aerobics classes. *Leisure Sciences, 13,* 85-96.

Neugarten, B., Havighurst, R., & Tobin, S. (1961). The measurement of life satisfaction. *Journal of Gerontology, 16,* 134-143.

Neulinger, J. (1974). *The psychology of leisure.* Springfield, IL: Charles C Thomas.

Roberts, K. (1981). *Leisure, work and education*. Bletchley, Britain: Open University Press.

Seligman, M. E. P. (1975). *Helplessness: On depression, development and death*. San Francisco: Freeman.

Shamir, B. (1988). Commitment and leisure. *Sociological Perspectives, 31*, 238-258.

Stebbins, R. A. (1982). Serious leisure: A conceptual statement. *Pacific Sociological Review, 25*, 251-272.

Stebbins, R. A. (1992). *Amateurs, professionals, and serious leisure*. Montreal: McGill-Queen's University Press.

Tinsley, H. E. A., & Tinsley, D. J. (1986). A theory of the attributes, benefits and causes of leisure experience. *Leisure Sciences, 8*, 1-45.

11

Organized Contexts of Activity

STEPHEN J. CUTLER
NICHOLAS L. DANIGELIS

This chapter focuses on the organized contexts in which activity occurs among older persons. The importance of considering these contexts is evident from the fact that a sizable segment of the older population maintains some level of activity in organized settings. Data from 1989, for example, indicate that approximately 17% of persons 65 years of age and older (i.e., close to 5 million elders) had served as unpaid volunteers in the previous year (U.S. Senate Special Committee on Aging, 1991a). Analysis of the combined 1990 and 1991 National Opinion Research Center's General Social Surveys shows that 69% of community-residing elders belong to one or more voluntary associations and that 66% attend religious services once a month or more frequently. Of persons 65+ responding to the 1984 National Health Interview Survey's Supplement on Aging, 15% reported using a senior center in the previous year. Thus, for many older individuals, at least part of their total pattern of activity takes place in organized settings.

Clearly, the organized settings in which activity occurs can assume a variety of forms. By "organized contexts of activity," we refer to activities that are located in a secondary group setting where remuneration is not a major reason for participation, that have some degree of recurrence, and that are not principally solitary in nature. Although activity patterns, levels of involvement, and consequences may differ

AUTHORS' NOTE: We would like to express our appreciation to Sarah Gilmore for her contributions to the preparation of this chapter.

depending on the type of setting, the organized context may be formal (e.g., a religious organization) or informal (e.g., a bridge club), and its purposes may be instrumental (e.g., a political action group), expressive (e.g., a literary group), or some combination. Excluded from consideration are activities that are solitary (e.g., hobbies or leisure pursuits that are done individually), located in family- or kin-based primary groups, and involve gainful employment. Rather, our concern is with activities that are voluntaristic and embedded in extrafamilial, extraoccupational group contexts.

In the remainder of the chapter, we explore four aspects of the organized context of activity. First, we call attention to some of the gerontological and sociological perspectives that speak to the theoretical significance of organized activity. Second, we present relatively recent national data on the extent to which older persons participate in different types of organized activity. Third, we examine some of the major predictors of involvement in various kinds of organized activity. Finally, we provide an overview of what studies have shown about the consequences or outcomes for older persons of participating in organized activity. The chapter concludes with a brief summary and suggested directions for further conceptualization and research.

Theoretical Significance of Organized Activity

Study of the organized voluntary activities of older persons has alternatively focused on the functions such activities play in the larger society, the degree to which organized activity represents continuities or discontinuities in one's life, and the leisure role these activities play in maximizing one's self-growth and freedom. It is not surprising therefore that sociology, gerontology, and leisure studies all have something to say about elders' organized voluntary activities.

The dominant sociological strain emphasizes the importance of association memberships as a stabilizing influence in the larger society that represents important moral and political connecting links among the otherwise disconnected populace (de Tocqueville, 1841). Such links are seen to be an especially important source of integration in complex, industrialized societies where individual alienation is a particular problem (Durkheim, 1893/1960, 1897/1951; Kornhauser, 1959).

While focusing on the societal implications of organized associational memberships, it is also possible to consider the positive effects that such memberships have on the individual: information, a sense of belonging, a sense of order. From de Tocqueville's (1841) assertion that "the heart is enlarged, and the human mind is developed" (p. 117) to Durkheim's arguments that associations serve as protection against the anomie produced by the complex division of labor in contemporary society (1893/1960), belonging to and participating in voluntary organized activity have been asserted to benefit both the society and the individual.

As described in Part I of this book, gerontology has extended its thinking about the activity of older persons beyond the simplistic notion that activity per se is good for older people. As an answer to activity and disengagement theories, the continuity perspective initially offered by Atchley (1971) and recently modified by Atchley (1989) and Covey (1981) may be useful in studying the organized, voluntary activities of elders. In particular, Atchley's (1989) distinction between internal and external psychic continuity and Covey's (1981) analysis of the effects of personal and social contexts on continuity of behavior have direct relevance for understanding both the reasons for and the outcomes from elders' organized activities.

A more structurally based gerontological perspective is found in the age stratification work of Riley and her colleagues (see, e.g., Riley, 1985; Riley, Foner, & Waring, 1988). Closely related are ideas on adult development and the life course (Dannefer, 1984; Featherman & Lerner, 1985). While not explicitly focused on the organized activities of older persons, each of these perspectives emphasizes the interplay among biological, psychological, cultural, structural, and demographic factors in the process of aging. All of these are necessary considerations for any theoretical approach to understanding the variability and constancy in organized activities among elders.

One last gerontological perspective that has clear relevance is Ekerdt's (1986) notion of a "busy ethic" that is postulated to dominate the values and norms of older adults. The basic idea is that the Puritan "work ethic" becomes transformed into a "busy ethic" for elders when they reach retirement age. The key question, according to Ekerdt, is whether the "busy ethic" actually produces a busy, active life-style or whether it merely causes elders to interpret what they do as being busy, whether they are or not.

A final perspective comes from the intersection of disciplines that study leisure. Leisure theorists like Dumazedier (1974), Godbey (1990), and Kaplan (1975) have argued that one's later years are a time to maximize self-growth and freedom through behaviors that would loosely be classified as leisure. Empirical work that operationally defines self-growth and freedom and tests assumptions about them is almost nonexistent (but see Torbert & Rogers, 1973). One possibly fruitful line of inquiry is Kelly's (1978) distinction among unconditional, compensatory, relational, and role-determined leisure activities (see also Chambré, 1991).

Missing from all of the above perspectives is a coherent theoretical framework by which to study the voluntary organized activities of older persons. Ideological prescriptions about the societal and individual benefits of such activity abound (the sociologists and leisure theorists). So, too, do conceptual frameworks for distinguishing internal and external continuities in aging and for disentangling age, cohort, and period effects from one another (gerontologists). Currently, however, there is no coherent theory by which to explain the causes and consequences of elders' participation in organized activities.

Patterns and Extent of Activity in Organized Settings

To describe elders' activity in organized settings, it would be helpful to have a classification of such activities. Unfortunately, type of organized activity involvement has been classified in a number of different ways. Some of the more enduring are on the basis of the organization's functions (Gordon & Babchuk, 1959; Rose, 1967), the kinds of activities the organization encompasses (Babchuk, Peters, Hoyt, & Kaiser, 1979; S. J. Cutler, 1976; Knoke & Thomson, 1977), and, for those focusing on elders' involvement, whether the organization is age heterogenous or age homogenous (Trela, 1976; Ward, 1979). A recent effort by Fischer, Mueller, and Cooper (1991) approaches the problem jointly from the perspective of the organization and the volunteer, distinguishing simultaneously the nature of the service activity, whether the work is formal or informal, and whether the volunteer works regularly or occasionally.

This section will describe general voluntary organization membership and activity levels by age, using whatever classification schemes are both possible and reasonable given data restrictions. A significant source of information on the organized volunteer activities of the U.S. citizenry are the General Social Surveys conducted by the National

Opinion Research Center (NORC). If one combines the data from the 1990 and 1991 surveys to increase the numbers of respondents in the older age categories and then examines the numbers of adults who are members of at least one kind of voluntary organization, it is clear that age does not appear to matter. Table 11.1 (row 1) shows that around two thirds of the sample are members of at least one organization, regardless of age.

The composite indicator of organization membership in row 1 is based on questions relating to 16 kinds of associations. To classify them, we followed N. E. Cutler's (1981-1982) procedure of correlating organizational membership by age for each of the 16 to distinguish those that older persons are more likely to join (fraternal, service, veterans, political, farm, and other) (hereafter called "senior"), those that younger people are more likely to join (sports, youth, school, and professional) ("junior"), and those that are "age neutral" (union, hobby, school fraternity/sorority, nationality, and literary). Membership in church-affiliated associations, although positively correlated with age, was kept separate because of its particular importance as a source of well-being (to be discussed later).

The second through fifth rows in Table 11.1 show the percentage in each age group that belonged to at least one of each type of organization. There is, of course, a significantly greater likelihood that elders are members of what we have defined as "senior" groups and younger people members of "junior" groups because of the way the types of organizations were defined. More interesting is the indication that a greater percentage of both young and old belong to "senior" groups than they do to either "junior" groups or "age neutral" groups.

When one looks at church-affiliated group memberships, twice the percentage of oldest respondents (42.9% and 41.3%) are members when compared with the youngest age group (20.9%). To obtain a rough idea as to involvement beyond religious group membership (something not possible with the other types of organizations), we examined religious service attendance, distinguishing those who attend nearly every week ("regularly") from those who attend less often (Table 11.1, row 6). While only 35.0% of the sample attends regularly, the percentages range from a low of 20.6% among those under 25 to highs of 55.7% and 51.6% among those 65-74 and 75 and older.

Volunteering may be seen as conceptually distinct from participation in voluntary associations (Payne, 1977). The older person who volunteers his or her time at a local hospital or library is not necessarily doing

Table 11.1 Voluntary Organization Membership and Activity Profiles by Type of Organization and Age of Respondent

					Age			
	Total	<25	25-34	35-44	45-54	55-64	65-74	75+
Percentage belonging to								
at least one organization[a]	65.7	58.2	62.5	67.8	68.2	67.9	70.2	64.0
at least one "senior" organization[a]	51.5	32.9	44.4	49.6	55.7	61.2	64.7	62.6***
at least one "junior" organization[a]	36.8	47.1	44.7	46.0	39.9	25.1	17.7	12.4 ***
at least one "neutral" organization[a]	30.5	27.8	29.8	34.9	32.0	26.0	29.2	27.7
Percentage belonging to a religious								
organization[a]	33.4	20.9	30.4	29.9	36.4	39.2	42.9	41.3***
(N)	(1,912)	(189)	(435)	(460)	(236)	(218)	(235)	(139)
Percentage attending religious service								
regularly[a]	35.0	20.6	26.5	31.2	34.1	40.3	55.7	51.6
(N)	(2,823)	(296)	(630)	(660)	(367)	(308)	(341)	(221)
Percentage volunteering some hours								
in past year[b]	44.6		46.3	55.2	44.9	36.7	39.7	26.4***
Percentage volunteering at different								
levels in past year[b]								
low	25.1		30.9	30.2	21.5	19.9	19.2	13.3
medium	12.9		11.4	16.6	14.7	11.1	11.8	8.4
high	6.6		4.0	8.5	8.8	5.7	8.7	4.8***
(N)	(3,618)		(1,050)	(841)	(526)	(498)	(451)	(253)

a. Data from National Opinion Research Center, General Social Surveys (1990 and 1991, combined).
b. Americans' Changing Lives Survey (1986).
*p ≤ .05; **p ≤ .01; ***p ≤ .001.

151

so as a member of a voluntary association. The same may be said for the approximately 400,000 older Americans who provide various types of community services through the Retired Senior Volunteer Program (U.S. Senate Special Committee on Aging, 1991b).

Information on actual volunteering activity comes from the 1986 Americans' Changing Lives national survey of American adults 25 years old and over. While no breakdown by type of volunteering activity is possible, estimates of the amount of actual volunteering time given by respondents were obtained. Table 11.1 (row 7) shows that there is a significant difference between age groups regarding actual volunteering activities. About one half of those 25-44 actually put in some volunteering hours in an organized context, while only 26.4% of those 75 and older volunteered. It is noteworthy that far less of a difference exists between the youngest age groups (46.3% and 55.2%) and those 65-74 (39.7%). In the final comparison in Table 11.1, it is clear that the discrepancy in volunteering effort between young and old derives from the larger percentage of the former who do a low amount of volunteering (operationalized as under 30 hours per year). At the upper levels of activity (at least 200 hours per year), older persons are volunteering at least as much as younger ones.

A final source of information comes from Current Population Survey data reported by the U.S. Senate Special Committee on Aging (1991a), where the focus is on the volunteers themselves. In 1989 they note that about one in five Americans over the age of 15 (20.4%) were doing some kind of unpaid volunteer work. This includes 16.9% of those 65 and over. The most popular formal context for volunteering in the whole population and among elders as well was religious organizations (37.4% and 43.3%, respectively). Next in popularity for the total population were school kinds of activities (15.1%) and civic or political organizations (13.2%). For those 65 and over, the next most popular were hospital or other health organizations (17.8%) and social and welfare organizations (14.5%). Finally, data on the amount of hours spent volunteering averaged out to about 4.3 hours per week for the whole sample and 4.7 hours per week for those 65 years old and over. Median weeks per year spent volunteering were 25.2 for the whole sample and 34.9 for elders.

It should be noted that the level of volunteerism found in the ACL study appears to be much higher than that found in the Current Population Survey data. Part of the reason may be attributable to the different target populations (25+ and 16+, respectively), but most of it probably stems from the different question wording and different kinds of probes used. In any event, in both studies the older population appears to be as active as the rest of the population, especially when amount of actual effort expended is compared.

Overall, these data show that membership in at least one voluntary organization does not differ significantly by age but that significant membership differences arise when organizational types are distinguished. Further, in terms of religious group memberships and attendance at religious services, there is a clear, positive association between age and such religious involvement. Finally, regardless of which source one consults, those 65-74 are nearly as likely to volunteer as those who are younger, and the amount of volunteer work those 65 and over do is at least as much as the volunteer work done by the rest of the population. By some measures, it is substantially more.

Predictors of Organized Activity

Numerous studies have examined the question of which elders participate in the types of organized activity that are the focus of this chapter. Comprehensive reviews may be found in Danigelis (1985) for voluntary association memberships, in Chambré (1987) for volunteering, in Koenig (1988) for religion, and in Krout (1989) for senior center participation.

In this section, we present information on the predictors of activity in organized settings among persons 65 years of age and older, again using data from several recent, nationally representative samples of community-residing adults. For participation in voluntary associations and church attendance, we use the combined 1990 and 1991 NORC General Social Surveys. Membership in voluntary associations is the dichotomized indicator measuring whether the older person belongs to any of the 16 types of associations included in the General Social Surveys. Number of memberships is a composite measure of the sum of the number of types to which a person belongs. Frequency of church attendance is based on a 9-point scale, ranging from "never" to "more than once a week," reflecting how often the respondent attends church services.

We use two measures of volunteer activity drawn from the 1986 Americans' Changing Lives Survey. The first is the summary measure of whether the respondent engaged in any volunteer work during the past year, while the second is a measure of the number of hours spent on volunteer activity. Finally, we include a measure of whether persons had used a senior center in the past year that is drawn from the 1984 Supplement on Aging to the National Health Interview Survey.

The six predictors that will be examined include age (measured in single years of age), sex (females = 0, males = 1), race (blacks = 0, whites = 1), education (measured by years of educational attainment), family income (based on multicategory variables, with higher scores representing higher incomes), and subjective health (based on 4- and 5-point scales, ranging from excellent to poor, with higher scores reflecting better health).

Due caution must be exercised in interpreting the results of these analyses. All are based on subsets of respondents 65 years of age and older, and each of the surveys is broadly representative of the national, community-residing population. The surveys vary, however, in their recency, sample sizes, and measures. Perhaps most important is the variation in sample sizes, which affects the significance levels of the correlation coefficients. The analyses based on the General Social Surveys range from Ns of 196 to 562, depending on the rotational, split-sample patterns employed in asking questions in each of the respective years. The sample size for persons 65 years of age and older in the Americans' Changing Lives Survey is approximately 700 (de-pending on the number of missing data cases), while that for the Supplement on Aging data is over 11,000.

Even with these differences, the data on predictors of involvement in organized activities presented in Table 11.2 show important patterns. Among these samples of the older population, age is negatively related to most of the activity measures. With increasing age, older persons are less likely to belong to voluntary associations and to have volunteered at all during the past year. The number of hours of volunteer activity declines with increasing age as does frequency of church attendance. In contrast, there is a very weak but positive and significant relationship between age and use of senior centers.

Sex does not appear to be a major predictor of either voluntary association activity or volunteer activity. Consistent with the results of previous studies, however, women attend church more frequently than men, and they are significantly more likely than men to make use of senior centers. With the exception of church attendance, the data in Table 11.2 also show that race is not a major predictor of these types of

Table 11.2 Predictors of Involvement in Organized Activities (Pearson correlation coefficients)

	Age	Sex	Race	Education	Family Income	Subjective Health
Membership in voluntary associations[a]	−.139**	.094	.025	.188***	.218***	.104
Number of voluntary association memberships[a]	−.073	.100	.085	.377***	.343***	.150*
Volunteered in the past year[b]	−.159***	−.014	.068	.300***	.179***	.225***
Number of hours of volunteer work[b]	−.096*	−.025	.053	.219***	.106**	.179***
Frequency of church attendance[a]	−.088*	−.172***	−.102*	.013	−.022	.062
Used a senior center in the past year[c]	.027**	−.060***	.013	.027**	−.078***	.037***

a. Data from National Opinion Research Center, General Social Surveys (1990 and 1991, combined).
b. Americans' Changing Lives Survey (1986).
c. National Health Interview Survey, Supplement on Aging (1984).
*p ≤ .05; **p ≤ .01; ***p ≤ .001.

organized activity. Older blacks do attend church more frequently than older whites, a finding that has been noted frequently in the literature.

The two socioeconomic variables used in these analyses prove to be strong predictors of organized activity. Higher levels of education and income are associated with a greater likelihood of belonging to voluntary associations and to volunteering in the past year. Older persons of higher socioeconomic status also belong to more associations and contribute more of their time to volunteering. Neither education nor income is significantly related to frequency of church attendance, but education is weakly and positively associated with use of a senior center while income is negatively related to senior center use.

Finally, there is a clear relationship between subjective health and most of these forms of organized activity. All of the correlations indicate that better health is associated with activity, and the relationships are significant for number of association memberships, having volunteered and number of hours spent volunteering, and use of a senior center.

Although these data are cross-sectional and therefore do not speak directly to the question of change, the overall picture suggested by the results is one of declining participation in organized activities with advancing age. Higher socioeconomic status and better health are associated with greater activity. Exceptions to these patterns occur in the case of senior center use, where lower income and, albeit weakly, advanced age are related to greater use. There are no major gender or racial differences in voluntary association activity or in volunteering, but women are more likely than men to attend church and use senior centers and blacks are more frequent church attenders than whites.

Consequences and Outcomes of Organized Activity

Our earlier discussion of theoretical perspectives implies positive consequences for those who participate in organized activities. Chief among the outcomes that have been of interest to gerontologists is the multidimensional domain of psychological well-being. Because the wide variety of organized contexts in which activity occurs makes blanket statements impossible, it is desirable to disaggregate settings of organized activity into some broad groupings, even while acknowledging the diversity that exists within these groupings. Thus we again focus on voluntary association participation, volunteering, participation in religious groups, and participation in senior centers.

Voluntary Association Participation

A number of studies have examined the effects of participation in voluntary associations on the psychological well-being of older adults. The findings present neither a clear nor a consistent picture of how activity in the context of voluntary associations is associated with psychological well-being.

Some research has shown that participation in formal associations is related to higher levels of psychological well-being. In research reported by Graney (1975), both number of memberships and frequency of attendance in voluntary associations were related to happiness, and changes in attendance and membership levels were also associated with changes in levels of happiness. Hoyt, Kaiser, Peters, and Babchuk (1980) also found that the number of association memberships was related to overall life satisfaction.

Other studies, however, have failed to replicate this finding. Lemon, Bengtson, and Peterson (1972) find that life satisfaction is not significantly associated with level of formal activity, and S. J. Cutler (1973) and Ward (1979) report nonsignificant effects of association participation on life satisfaction after the effects of health and socioeconomic status are controlled. These results suggest that self-selection is operating: Healthier and higher socioeconomic status older persons are more likely to be involved in voluntary associations (as we have seen in the previous section), and it is the characteristics the participants bring with them, rather than the association activity per se, that result in higher levels of psychological well-being.

Another pattern of findings suggests that the effects of activity in the context of voluntary associations are limited to certain types of associations and to participants with certain characteristics. After examining the relationship between membership in 16 different types of associations and psychological well-being, S. J. Cutler (1976) noted that only membership in church-affiliated groups was significantly related to life satisfaction and happiness. N. E. Cutler (1981-1982) has shown that membership in associations is more strongly related to life satisfaction for a subset of association types to which older persons are most likely to belong, while Kearney, Plax, and Lentz (1985) noted that life satisfaction was highest among active, high socioeconomic status participants.

Volunteering

As with voluntary associations, and despite the fact that significant proportions of elders report having done volunteer work (see, for example, Herzog & Morgan, 1993), relatively little systematic research has been conducted on the outcomes of volunteer activity. On the positive side, Payne (1977) suggests that the low dropout rate among members of one volunteer program reflects the internalization of a positive self-concept as a volunteer; Hunter and Linn (1980-1981) note in a small study of another volunteer program that the older volunteers had higher life satisfaction, a stronger will to live, and fewer somatic, anxious, and depressive symptoms than did nonvolunteers; and Fogelman (1981) reports higher levels of well-being among Senior Companion Program volunteers than among those on a waiting list to become volunteers. Dye, Goodman, Roth, Bley, and Jensen (1973), on the other hand, found no significant differences between volunteers and nonvolunteers on life satisfaction and morale in still another program, and national data presented in Chambré (1987, Table 9-1) show a nonsignificant relationship between life satisfaction and volunteering after appropriate multivariate controls had been introduced.

Participation in Religious Groups

Fortunately, renewed interest in the role of religiosity in the lives of elders provides evidence from several studies about the consequences of religious activity. In the context of participation in voluntary associations, we have already noted one study that indicates that beneficial effects on psychological well-being are restricted to membership in church-related groups (S. J. Cutler, 1976). Research on other dimensions of religious activity suggests similar positive outcomes for older persons.

Using data from the Duke Longitudinal Study of Aging, Blazer and Palmore (1976) found that religious activity was correlated with happiness, usefulness, and personal adjustment. Furthermore, the strength of these correlations increased over time, leading the authors to conclude that "religion tends to become increasingly important in the adjustment of older persons as they age" (p. 85). Because Blazer and Palmore's measure of religious activity combines church attendance, listening to religious services on radio or TV, and reading the Bible and/or devotional books, this composite indicator of religious activity makes it impossible to separate out the effects of organized activity. Other studies with more clearly delineated measures of organized religious activity, however, reach a similar conclusion.

Markides (1983), for example, examined the relationship between church attendance and life satisfaction among Anglos and Mexican Americans at two times over a 4-year period. For both waves and both groups, life satisfaction was significantly related to church attendance independent of the effects of health and other correlates of life satisfaction. Among blacks, Krause and Tran (1989) have shown that higher levels of organizational religious involvement are associated with higher levels of self-esteem, and Taylor and Chatters (1986) have found that frequency of attendance is associated with the frequency and amount of church-based social support received by church members. Finally, Idler (1987) has shown that higher levels of religious involvement are associated with lower levels of depressive symptomatology, and Koenig, Kvale, and Ferrel (1988) found that organized religious activity (i.e., church attendance and other religious group-related activities) was significantly associated with morale net of the effects of several potentially confounding variables.

Participation in Senior Centers

Very few studies have systematically examined the consequences for psychological well-being of activity in senior centers, and the extant research is generally based on small samples and yields inconsistent results. Thus Toseland and Sykes (1977) find no relationship between senior center participation and life satisfaction. On the other hand, Hanssen et al. (1978) found senior center participants to be less depressed than nonusers, and Krout (1989) found current senior center users having higher levels of life satisfaction than former users. It is not clear from these latter studies, however, whether the differences in well-being would have held up with appropriate controls.

Summary

This overview of research on the consequences of activity in organized settings suggests that voluntary association participation, taken globally, does not necessarily result in heightened psychological well-being. Some members of some types of associations may benefit, but further work is needed on this topic. There is no lack of research on predictors of volunteering and senior center use, but there are fewer systematic studies of outcomes, and these yield inconsistent conclusions. Given the extent of voluntaristic activity and senior center use, research on their consequences for older individuals is also needed. It is in the area of religious activity where the evidence is both more abundant and consistent, indicating that religious activity plays an important role in enhancing the psychological well-being of older adults. Also clear from this review is that most studies have been limited to life satisfaction. Other indicators of psychological well-being—such as depression, self-esteem, sense of control—as well as other outcomes—such as social support—ought to be examined to derive a clearer picture of what types of organized activity benefit what types of persons in what ways.

Conclusion

In this chapter we have examined the organized contexts in which older persons carry out their activities. Clearly, activity occurs within such settings for significant numbers of community-residing elders: about one in six had used a senior center in the past year; still larger percentages (between one sixth and one third, depending on the data source) volunteer their time; and approximately two out of three seniors attend church monthly or more regularly and belong to voluntary associations. Further, the research literature provides detailed descriptions of those whose activities occur in these settings. We know, for example, that age, socioeconomic status, and health are among the most consistent and significant predictors of organized activity.

In contrast to the relative richness of descriptive information about the extent of participation and about the characteristics of older persons who are active in organized settings, there is a paucity of material on a number of other important aspects of organized activity. First, there is no systematically articulated theory or set of theories providing a framework for understanding organized activity. We have briefly mentioned some of the prominent theoretical strands that currently exist, but the task of weaving them into a more integrated perspective remains to be accomplished. Second, with the exception of religiosity, gerontology is far from a definitive understanding of the many possible effects that participation in organized settings might have for older persons. To meet this need will require the use and testing of theoretically grounded, multivariate models based on reasonably large and representative samples with appropriate attention given to a wider range of outcome variables than has been the case to this time. Finally, quantitative studies could profitably be supplemented by programs of qualitative research (for a notable example, see Myerhoff, 1978) directed at achieving a fuller understanding and appreciation of the subjective meaning organized activity has for older persons and of its place in the larger constellation of roles and activities that constitute their lives.

References

Atchley, R. C. (1971). Retirement and leisure participation: Continuity or crisis? *The Gerontologist, 11*, 13-17.

Atchley, R. C. (1989). A continuity theory of normal aging. *The Gerontologist, 29*, 183-190.

Babchuk, N., Peters, G. R., Hoyt, D. R., & Kaiser, M. A. (1979). The voluntary associations of the aged. *Journal of Gerontology, 34*, 579-587.

Blazer, D., & Palmore, E. (1976). Religion and aging in a longitudinal panel. *The Gerontologist, 16*, 82-85.

Chambré, S. M. (1987). *Good deeds in old age: Volunteering by the new leisure class.* Lexington, MA: Lexington.

Chambré, S. M. (1991). Volunteerism by elders: Demographic and policy trends, past and present. In *Resourceful aging: Today and tomorrow: Vol. 2. Volunteerism* (pp. 33-36). Washington, DC: American Association of Retired Persons.

Covey, H. C. (1981). A reconceptualization of continuity theory: Some preliminary thoughts. *The Gerontologist, 21*, 628-633.

Cutler, N. E. (1981-1982). Voluntary association participation and life satisfaction: Replication, revision, and extension. *International Journal of Aging and Human Development, 14*, 127-137.

Cutler, S. J. (1973). Voluntary association participation and life satisfaction: A cautionary research note. *Journal of Gerontology, 28*, 96-100.

Cutler, S. J. (1976). Membership in different types of voluntary associations and psychological well-being. *The Gerontologist, 16*, 335-339.

Danigelis, N. L. (1985). Social support for elders through community ties: The role of voluntary associations. In W. J. Sauer & R. T. Coward (Eds.), *Social support networks and the care of the elderly* (pp. 159-177). New York: Springer.

Dannefer, D. (1984). Adult development and social theory: A paradigmatic reappraisal. *American Sociological Review, 49*, 100-116.

de Tocqueville, A. (1841). *Democracy in America* (Vol. 2; M. Reeve, Trans.). New York: J. and H. G. Langley.

Dumazedier, J. (1974). *Sociology of leisure* (M. A. McKenzie, Trans.). Amsterdam: Elsevier.

Durkheim, É. (1951). *Suicide* (G. Simpson, Ed.; J. A. Spaulding & G. Simpson, Trans.). New York: Free Press. (Original work published 1897)

Durkheim, É. (1960). *The division of labor in society* (G. Simpson, Trans.). New York: Free Press. (Original work published 1893)

Dye, D., Goodman, M., Roth, M., Bley, N., & Jensen, K. (1973). The older adult volunteer compared to the nonvolunteer. *The Gerontologist, 13*, 215-218.

Ekerdt, D. J. (1986). The busy ethic: Moral continuity between work and retirement. *The Gerontologist, 26*, 239-244.

Featherman, D. L., & Lerner, R. M. (1985). Ontogenesis and sociogenesis: Problematics for theory and research about development and socialization across the lifespan. *American Sociological Review, 50*, 659-676.

Fischer, L. R., Mueller, D. P., & Cooper, P. W. (1991). Older volunteers: A discussion of the Minnesota Senior Study. *The Gerontologist, 31*, 183-194.

Fogelman, C. J. (1981). Being a volunteer: Some effects on older people. *Generations, 5*, 24-25, 49.

Godbey, G. (1990). *Leisure in your life: An exploration* (3rd ed.). State College, PA: Venture.

Gordon, C. W., & Babchuk, N. A. (1959). A typology of voluntary associations. *American Sociological Review, 24*, 22-29.

Graney, M. J. (1975). Happiness and social participation in aging. *Journal of Gerontology, 30*, 701-706.

Hanssen, A. M., Meima, N. J., Buckspan, L. M., Henderson, B. E., Helbig, T. L., & Zarit, S. H. (1978). Correlates of senior center participation. *The Gerontologist, 18*, 193-199.

Herzog, A. R., & Morgan, J. N. (1993). Formal volunteer work among older Americans. In S. Bass, F. Caro, & Y-P. Chen (Eds.), *Achieving a productive aging society* (pp. 119-142). Westport, CT: Auburn House.

Hoyt, D. R., Kaiser, M. A., Peters, G. R., & Babchuk, N. (1980). Life satisfaction and activity theory: A multidimensional approach. *Journal of Gerontology, 35*, 935-941.

Hunter, K. I., & Linn, M. W. (1980-1981). Psychosocial differences between elderly volunteers and non-volunteers. *International Journal of Aging and Human Development, 12*, 205-213.

Idler, E. L. (1987). Religious involvement and the health of the elderly: Some hypotheses and an initial test. *Religion and Health, 66*, 226-238.

Kaplan, M. (1975). *Leisure: Theory and policy*. New York: John Wiley.

Kearney, P., Plax, T. G., & Lentz, P. S. (1985). Participation in community organizations and socioeconomic status as determinants of seniors' life satisfaction. *Activities, Adaptation & Aging, 6*, 31-37.

Kelly, J. (1978). Leisure styles and choices in three environments. *Pacific Sociological Review, 21*, 187-207.

Knoke, D., & Thomson, R. (1977). Voluntary association membership trends and the family life cycle. *Social Forces, 56*, 48-65.

Koenig, H. G. (1988). *Religion, health, and aging: A review and theoretical integration*. New York: Greenwood.

Koenig, H. G., Kvale, J. N., & Ferrel, C. (1988). Religion and well-being in later life. *The Gerontologist, 28*, 18-28.

Kornhauser, W. (1959). *The politics of mass society*. New York: Free Press.

Krause, N., & Tran, T. V. (1989). Stress and religious involvement among older blacks. *Journal of Gerontology: Social Sciences, 44*, S4-S13.

Krout, J. A. (1989). *Senior centers in America*. New York: Greenwood.

Lemon, B. W., Bengtson, V. L., & Peterson, J. A. (1972). An exploration of the activity theory of aging: Activity types and life satisfaction among in-movers to a retirement community. *Journal of Gerontology, 27*, 511-523.

Markides, K. S. (1983). Aging, religiosity, and adjustment: A longitudinal analysis. *Journal of Gerontology, 38*, 621-625.

Myerhoff, B. (1978). *Number our days.* New York: Simon & Schuster.

Payne, B. P. (1977). The older volunteer: Social role continuity and development. *The Gerontologist, 17*, 355-361.

Riley, M. W. (1985). Age strata in social systems. In R. Binstock & E. Shanas (Eds.), *Handbook of aging and the social sciences* (2nd ed.; pp. 369-411). New York: Van Nostrand Reinhold.

Riley, M. W., Foner, A., & Waring, J. (1988). Sociology of age. In N. J. Smelser (Ed.), *Handbook of sociology* (pp. 243-290). Newbury Park, CA: Sage.

Rose, A. (1967). *The power structure.* London: Oxford University Press.

Taylor, R. J., & Chatters, L. M. (1986). Church-based informal support among elderly blacks. *The Gerontologist, 26*, 637-642.

Torbert, W. R. (with Rogers, M. P.). (1973). *Being for the most part puppets: Interactions among men's labor, leisure and politics.* Cambridge, MA: Schenkman.

Toseland, R., & Sykes, J. (1977). Senior citizens center participation and other correlates of life satisfaction. *The Gerontologist, 17*, 235-241.

Trela, J. (1976). Social class and association memberships: An analysis of age-graded and non-age-graded voluntary association participation. *Journal of Gerontology, 31*, 198-203.

U.S. Senate Special Committee on Aging. (1991a). *Aging America: Trends and projections.* Washington, DC: U.S. Department of Health and Human Services.

U.S. Senate Special Committee on Aging. (1991b). *Developments in aging: 1990* (Vol. 1). Washington, DC: Government Printing Office.

Ward, R. A. (1979). The meaning of voluntary association participation to older people. *Journal of Gerontology, 34*, 438-445.

12

The Role of Humor in Enhancing the Quality of Later Life

FRANCIS A. McGUIRE

ROSANGELA K. BOYD

Humor and laughter are daily occurrences in the lives of most individuals. Although laughter may not be the *best* medicine, it certainly is therapeutic for many individuals. It has both a preventive and a maintenance function. According to Levine (1977), laughter can be effective in developing ego mastery and relieving anxiety. He also viewed humor as capable of enabling individuals to face their fears, whether they originate from internal or external factors. Indeed, laughter has been identified as having the potential to influence both physical and mental health (Ewers, Jacobson, Powers, & McConney, 1983).

The study of humor in later life has received little attention. Nahemow's (1986, p. xv) statement that "much of the literature in gerontology has been devoted either to detailing the myriad problems of aging or to giving assurances that aging can be fun" remains true today. Even less research has focused on the benefits of humor in later life. The body of knowledge in areas such as the development of humor across the life span and the examination of aging as reflected in humor have received much greater attention. In Nahemow, McClusky-Fawcett, and McGhee's (1986) landmark work, only one chapter was devoted primarily to the

AUTHORS' NOTE: The work that provided the foundation of this chapter would not have been possible without support from the AARP-Andrus Foundation.

therapeutic role of humor. The dearth of humor-related materials is surprising because laughter and humor are enduring factors that are present throughout the life span. The absence of work related to humor as a beneficial activity in later life is an oversight that should be of concern to activity professionals. This chapter will focus on humor and its role in improving the quality of life.

Benefits of Humor

A benefit of humor that has been largely unexplored is the extent to which it can provide a link to the past. According to Kelly (n.d.), continuity "is associated with resources that enable those whose abilities and social circles are being reduced, to stay engaged, to act in ways to continue to express what they are and what they intend to be." Humor can be a way to remain engaged. It can be a link to the past and a bridge to the future. Humorous anecdotes about earlier life, reminiscing about favorite stories read in the past, rereading, or reading for the first time a P. G. Wodehouse story, or viewing old *I Love Lucy* shows can reaffirm the pleasures of life. Laughing with others is a natural event that provides a message of vitality and communion.

Stimulation and variety in life are important. There is evidence that, the less stimulation one receives, the less resistant to external pressures one becomes (Nahemow & Lawton, 1976). Individuals seek arousal and variety in life (Duellman, Borris, & Kielhofer, 1986; Walt, 1978) and act to achieve it. The frail elderly, however, particularly in long-term care facilities, may be denied opportunities for challenge and stimulation. In fact, these individuals may need assistance in identifying and achieving optimum arousal. Nahemow (1986) identified the use of humor as one method for increasing arousal and complexity in the nursing home environment. It provides this function by allowing individuals to see the "flip side" of a situation. According to Nahemow, an environment with a flip side is less intimidating while being more complex. Humor stimuli may effectively activate physical and psychological responses that will benefit the individual. Finally, according to Nahemow, dormant interests may be reawakened by humor, which provides a bridge between the past and the present.

The quality of life issue has been a focus of a great deal of gerontological literature. Identifying approaches to improving the quality of life of older individuals has been a major thrust of researchers and practitioners. Stimulation, brought about by a variety of means, can be an effective tool in improving the quality of life of residents in long-term care facilities.

According to Simon (1988), a sense of well-being depends on an individual's ability to accept her or his situation and focus on growth and development. This involves developing a positive attitude toward life that is sustained even in the presence of loss and disability. According to Robinson (1977), humor can help sustain such an outlook because it is "first and foremost an attitude towards life; a willingness to accept life and accept ourselves with a shrug and a smile, with certain light-heartedness . . . this is not a sense of resignation or indifference, but rather a sense of mastery over life" (p. 134). Humor allows us to view life from a different perspective and allows a person to "defuse anger and/or frustration associated with a distressful event by focusing on its comical elements" (p. 20). Humor can also generate pleasure and potentially elevate mood and morale (Ewers et al., 1983; Napora, 1984; Simon, 1988). The following section reviews some research related to the benefits of humor.

Physical and Mental Health

Much of the interest in the therapeutic values of humor can be traced to Norman Cousins (1979) and his book *Anatomy of an Illness* in which he reported the use of humor as part of his self-imposed therapy for ankylosing spondylitis. Cousins did not conclude that laughter was the direct cause of his "cure" but suggested that the positive frame of mind he developed was at least partly responsible for the successful health outcomes he experienced.

Research into the physical effects of laughter has documented the existence of physiological benefits. A variety of publications (Cogan, Cogan, Waltz, & McCue, 1987; Fry, 1986; Fry & Savin, 1982; Tennant, 1986) have documented benefits to the musculoskeletal system, circulatory system, and respiratory system. One of the best known authors in the area of physiological benefits of humor is William Fry. He (1986) simply but elegantly summed up the literature in this area when he wrote: "People can be emotionally and physically vitalized through humor. Physical deterioration can be made to have less consequence for life quality" (p. 89).

Williams (1986) and Robinson (1977) provide information on ways humor may be an effective intervention in the lives of older people. They view it as providing an outlet of escape, a means of communication, opportunity for insight into the self, an opportunity to release anger, hostility, and stress, a way to deal with frightening feelings, a way to assist in adjustment to new environments and circumstances, and an aid in developing new relationships. When this list of benefits is juxtaposed with Neugarten's (1974) indicators of positive well-being, there is further evidence of the benefits of humor. According to Neugarten, psychological well-being exists if pleasure is taken from everyday life activities, one's life is evaluated as meaningful and acceptable, there is a feeling of success from achieving life goals, and the individual has a positive self-image and exhibits happy and optimistic moods and attitudes. It appears humor can play a role in developing, or maintaining, these characteristics.

A variety of authors have identified humor as an effective tool in adapting to life's stresses and anxieties (Fry, 1982; Goodman, 1983; Peter & Dana, 1982) and as a coping mechanism (Lefcourt & Martin, 1986; Robinson, 1977; Simon, 1988). The relationship of stress to illness has been well established. Therefore the role of humor as a stress mediator has implications for wellness in the later years. Martin and Lefcourt (1983) have completed some of the most significant work in this area. They conducted a series of three studies to examine the moderating effect of humor on the impact of stressful events on mood. Their findings indicated that the ability to use humor and having a good sense of humor reduced the negative effects of stress. Although their studies were conducted using university students as subjects, the work of Martin and Lefcourt may have implications for older individuals. If humor serves the same mediating function between stress and negative affect in the old as in the young, then it can be used as a tool to lessen the psychological impact of life's stressors. Further research is needed in this area, however, before such a claim can be made.

Nemeth (1979) supported the use of humor in clinical settings. A three-group pretest-posttest design was used to examine the efficacy of humor in reducing anxiety in individuals awaiting medical treatment. One group viewed silent films with humorous content, a second group watched silent nonhumorous films, and a third group watched no movies while remaining in the waiting room. Nemeth found the group viewing humorous films had significantly lower levels of anxiety than either of the other two groups. Although these findings only deal with short-term anxiety, Nemeth (1979) speculated about the long-term effects of humor by asking: "Would more exposure to nonthreatening humor on a regular basis provide the individual with enough insights to help him overcome high anxieties and be able to better cope with his daily life?" (p. 43). The question is an intriguing one. Anecdotal evidence from sources such as Cousins (1979) and folk wisdom would indicate humor is an effective umbrella to ward off anxiety. More empirical work is needed, however, to document the effect of humor as a means of reducing chronic anxiety.

Social Interaction

Another benefit of humor is its ability to facilitate social interaction and communication (Blumenfield & Alpern, 1986; Peter & Dana, 1982; Williams, 1986). The importance of continued interaction with significant others has been well documented. Humor provides a realm where communication can occur. Robinson (1970) described humor as "a form of indirect communication that covers messages that are usually emotionally tinged, and might be unacceptable if expressed or acknowledged directly." The facilitation of communication through humor indicates it may be an effective vehicle to assist in the development of friendships in the later years. The importance of humor in fostering communication may be particularly important in long-term care facilities. According to Kaakinen (1992), residents of nursing homes do not talk much. She views silence as "one of the hallmarks of life in a nursing home" and identified the informal communication system as being primary in bringing about this silence. Kaakinen went on to identify nursing homes as "communication-impaired environments" marked by isolation and desocialization. As a result, residents are deprived of a powerful mechanism for adapting to their environment. It is worth noting that Kaakinen specifically identified recreation as a vehicle to reestablish communication. In her view "recreational activities that focus on events that foster interpersonal communication create a communication ambience and invite conversation" (p. 263). While activities such as bingo, viewing entertainment such as movies, and craft projects are inadequate as approaches to facilitating communication, small group activities based on "sharing ideas or experiences" are suggested. Humor can be an effective tool in encouraging interaction in small groups.

Studies of Humor

Simon (1988) conducted one of the few empirical examinations of older adults and their use of humor. She subjected 24 individuals, aged 61 to 89, to a variety of scales related to perceived health, coping, life satisfaction, and affect. Simon found a positive relationship between situational humor, defined as the frequency with which an individual displays humor in a variety of situations, and self-perceived health. In addition, Simon found a negative relationship between coping through humor, the degree to which an individual reported using humor to cope with stress, and health perception. The author's explanation for this finding was that humor may be used as a coping strategy only when there are health problems. Unfortunately, Simon's small sample precludes making generalizations based on her data. In addition, her correlational design makes implications related to causality impossible. The results are, however, intriguing and suggest humor may have a role in physical well-being.

A more recent study by Miles (1988) also examined the relationship between humor and quality of life measures, including life satisfaction and functional health. Miles failed to replicate the findings of the Simon's study. No significant relationships were found between humor, defined as appreciation of humor, and the quality of life measures.

Although the work of Miles did not confirm Simon's findings related to the benefits of humor in later life, several studies have supported the benefits of humor. Peter and Dana (1982) used an experimental design to examine the benefits of a humor group that met over the course of 3 months in a long-term care facility. Each time the group met, a different member was responsible for the selection of humorous material. At the conclusion of the study, the participants in the humor group exhibited more mirth, more interaction, less complaining, more sociability, more alertness, and more interest in personal appearance than they had at the beginning of the program. Although the results are encouraging, they must be viewed with caution. Because residents were given responsibility for bringing humorous materials to the sessions, it may be that this involvement with and control over the program have contributed to the results. Nevertheless, Peter and Dana's work provides additional evidence that humor may have a positive impact in the later years.

A study conducted by the Andrus Gerontology Center at the University of Southern California (Ewers et al., 1983) had similar results. A program called "Life Enrichment Through Humor in Long Term Care Facilities" incorporated a variety of approaches, including showing old comedies, sing-alongs, and thematic parties, to introduce humor into the long-term care environment. Volunteers ran the program for 60 residents. Although difficulties in data gathering precluded scientific evaluation of the program, observations kept of participants' behavior revealed promising benefits for participants. Among the behavioral changes observed were greater awareness among participants of each other, appreciation of the program, enjoyment in discussing the program, expression of more outgoing attitudes, increased socialization, initiation of programs by participants, increased sense of humor in interactions with others, greater openness to participation, and warm responses to volunteers.

Other research efforts (Adams & McGuire, 1986; McGuire, Boyd, & James, 1992; Napora, 1984) have supported the efficacy of humor in improving the quality of life of older individuals. There does appear to be sufficient empirical support for the development of humor programs for older individuals. Several efforts have already been made that will be useful to anyone interested in this area.

Programmatic Interventions

Humor interventions can have two distinct purposes. The first is humor generation. The research above supports the benefits of involvement in humor. The physical act of laughing, the social act of joke telling, the involvement in movies may all result in feeling better. The other approach to humor is helping individuals understand their own sense of humor and possibly improve it. Being able to see the humor in a situation is an effective way to defuse it. Older individuals will benefit from being able to develop a laughter perspective on life. The following section will briefly identify some programs designed to achieve these twin goals.

Joel Goodman (1983) founded the HUMOR Project as a mechanism to

(1) explore the nature and nurture of humor by helping people learn, practice and apply skills for tapping their own sense of humor; (2) to develop and disseminate practical uses of humor that managers, teachers, parents, helping professionals, business people, and young people could integrate into their own work and life-style. (p. 2)

These goals are accomplished through a variety of workshops, publications, training sessions, and speeches.

In his book titled *The Healing Power of Humor: Techniques For Getting Through Loss, Setbacks, Upsets, Disappointments, Difficulties, Trials, Tribulations, and All That Not So Funny Stuff*, Klein (1989) provided 14 techniques for using humor in life. Although the techniques were not designed as an intervention with older individuals, they do suggest ways in which humor may be useful. For example, Klein suggests using humor to turn difficult situations into humorous ones. He recommends structuring an exercise around developing "I have bad news and good news for you" scenarios. Such an approach allows individuals to see the positive in what may be primarily negative events. Another suggestion is to use exaggeration to make the difficult less painful. He recommends exaggerating feelings and overemphasizing the negative until they become so absurd as to be funny. Klein sees the value in finding joy in life. Finding the things that make us happy is a way to retain a positive attitude. Keeping a "joy journal" identifying the positive things that happen is one way to retain such perspective. A good meal, enjoyable conversation, an unexpected visitor, or a particularly pleasurable activity may be entries in such a journal. Reviewing such a journal can be an affirmation of what is positive in life. Another technique identified by Klein is developing "a beginner's mind" to look at things from a new perspective. This will permit a fresh look at life in which things may not be as negative as they appeared at first. Finally, Klein recommends people develop the ability to laugh at themselves. This will not only result in increased acceptance of disabilities and loss but will also make it easier to talk about them with others.

Summary: Humor in Later Life

The literature related to humor and aging is limited. When viewed in conjunction with the general humor literature, however, it is suggestive of the powerful role humor can play in later life. As additional work is done in this area, techniques to take advantage of the potential benefits of humor will be developed. At this time, the literature indicates the major role of humor will be in the long-term care environment. The use of humor can introduce stimulation, communication, and hope into such settings. Humor, however, can also be an important factor in the lives of older individuals residing in the community. Humor can provide a link to the past and a bridge to the future.

References

Adams, E., & McGuire, F. (1986). Is laughter the best medicine? A study of the effects of humor on perceived pain and affect. *Activities, Adaptation & Aging, 8*, 157-175.

Blumenfield, E., & Alpern, L. (1986). *The smile connection: How to use humor in dealing with people*. New York: Prentice-Hall.

Cogan, R., Cogan, D., Waltz, W., & McCue, M. (1987). Effects of laughter and relaxation on discomfort thresholds. *Journal of Behavioral Medicine, 10*, 139-143.

Cousins, N. (1979). *Anatomy of an illness*. New York: Bantam.

Duellman, M., Borris, R., & Kielhofer, G. (1986). Organized activity and adaptive status of nursing home residents. *The American Journal of Occupational Therapy, 40*, 618-622.

Ewers, M., Jacobson, S., Powers, V., & McConney, P. (1983). *Humor, the tonic you can afford: A handbook of ways of using humor in long-term care*. Los Angeles: Ethel Percy Andrus Gerontological Center.

Fry, W. (1982). *The psychology of humor*. Abstract from an address at the Psychobiology of Health and Healing Conference, Brigham Young University.

Fry, W. (1986). Humor physiology and the aging process. In L. Nahemow, K. McClusky-Fawcett, & P. McGhee (Eds.), *Humor and aging*. Orlando, FL: Academic Press.

Fry, W., & Savin, M. (1982). *Mirthful laughter and blood pressure*. Paper presented at the Third International Conference on Humor, Washington, DC.

Goodman, J. (1983). How to get more smileage out of your life: Making sense of humor, then serving it. In P. McGhee & J. Goldstein (Eds.), *Handbook of humor research*. New York: Springer-Verlag.

Kaakinen, J. A. (1992). Living with silence. *The Gerontologist, 32*, 258-264.

Kelly, J. (n.d.). *Life in between: Continuity and constriction*. Unpublished manuscript.

Klein, A. (1989). *The healing power of humor: Techniques for getting through loss, setbacks, upsets, disappointments, difficulties, trial, tribulations, and all that not so funny stuff*. Los Angeles: Jeremy Tarcher.

Lefcourt, H., & Martin, R. (1986). *Humor and life stress: Antidote to adversity*. New York: Springer-Verlag.

Levine, J. (1977). Humor as a form of therapy: Introduction to symposium. In A. Chapman & H. Foot (Eds.), *It's a funny thing, humor*. Oxford: Pergamon.

Martin, R., & Lefcourt, H. (1983). Sense of humor as a moderator of the relationship between stressors and moods. *Journal of Personality and Social Psychology, 45,* 1313-1324.

McGuire, F., Boyd, R., & James, A. (1992). *Therapeutic humor with the elderly.* New York: Haworth.

Miles, E. (1988). *The relationship of sense of humor to life satisfaction, functional health, death anxiety, and self-esteem.* Unpublished doctoral dissertation, California School of Professional Psychology, Irvine, CA.

Nahemow, L. (1986). Humor as a database for the study of aging. In L. Nahemow, K. McClusky-Fawcett, & P. McGhee (Eds.), *Humor and aging.* Orlando, FL: Academic Press.

Nahemow, L., & Lawton, P. (1976). Toward an ecological theory of adaptation and aging. In H. Proansky, W. Ittleson, & L. Rivlin (Eds.), *Environmental psychology: People and their physical settings.* New York: Rinehart & Winston.

Nahemow, L., McClusky-Fawcett, K., & McGhee, P. (1986). *Humor and aging.* Orlando, FL: Academic Press.

Napora, J. (1984). *A study of the effects of a program of humorous activity on subjective well-being of senior adults.* Unpublished doctoral dissertation, University of Maryland, College Park.

Nemeth, P. (1979). *An investigation into the relationship between humor and anxiety.* Unpublished doctoral dissertation, University of Maryland, College Park.

Neugarten, B. (1974). *Successful aging: A conference report.* Durham, NC: Center for the Study of Aging and Human Development.

Peter, L., & Dana, B. (1982). *The laughter prescription: The tool of humor and how to use it.* New York: Ballantine.

Robinson, V. (1970). Humor in nursing. In C. Carlson & B. Blackwell (Eds.), *Behavioral concepts and nursing interventions.* Philadelphia: J. B. Lippincott.

Robinson, V. (1977). *Humor and the health professions.* Thorofare, NJ: Charles B. Slack.

Simon, J. (1988). Humor and the older adult: Implications for nursing. *Journal of Advanced Nursing, 13,* 441-446.

Tennant, K. F. (1986). The effect of humor on the recovery rate of cataract patients. In L. Nahemow, K. McClusky-Fawcett, & P. McGhee (Eds.), *Humor and aging.* Orlando, FL: Academic Press.

Walt, K. (1978). Preferred environments. In S. Kaplan & R. Kaplan (Eds.), *Humanscape: Environments for people.* North Scituate, MA: Duxbury.

Williams, H. (1986). Humor and healing. *Gerontion: Canadian Review of Geriatric Care, 1,* 14-17.

13

Creative Activity and the Arts

Possibilities and Programs

NANCY J. OSGOOD

To successfully cope with the many age-related changes and problems, older adults must be offered leisure opportunities that promote physical and mental health and functioning and that provide them with choice to build a sense of power and control, mastery, and self-esteem. Kelly (1982) suggests that through leisure the elderly can achieve a sense of personal integration—"a drawing together of various strands of the life course into a whole with meaning and coherence" (p. 281). The elderly must "integrate life's meanings, accomplishments, and failures into an acceptance of life with meaning and worth" (p. 282). Leisure activities that incorporate reminiscence and life review, socialization, physical activity, and fun are vital for older adults. Activities that allow for creative expression, personal exploration and growth, and release of tension in a safe environment are important. Creative arts activities— art, creative writing, music, drama, and dance—offer all of these and more to older adults. This chapter focuses on the value of creative arts programs for the elderly.

AUTHOR'S NOTE: Portions of this chapter were previously published in N. J. Osgood, *Suicide in the Elderly* (Rockville, MD: Aspen, 1985), and N. J. Osgood, *Suicide in Later Life* (New York: Macmillan, 1992).

Values of Creative Expression and Creative Arts Activities

Values of Creative Expression

The creative arts have been used in healing since prehistoric times. The shaman, acting as artist and healer, activated the creative imagination and facilitated transcendence from reality or ordinary consciousness into another world or another plane of consciousness. Visualization for healing was also used by the Babylonians, Greeks, East Indians, and ancient Oriental civilizations.

During the twentieth century there has been dramatic growth in and acceptance of the use of creative arts or expressive therapy. Involvement in creative activities provides the necessary opportunity to discover interests, to self-actualize, and to choose a posture toward life. Jung (1971) regarded imagination and creativity as healing forces. Jung felt that deep-seated feelings could be symbolically represented and cathartically released through the creative act, which is basically nonrational.

Humanistic psychology—which emphasizes the importance of creativity, personal growth, and self-actualization and the attainment of one's full potential as a human being—provided additional impetus to the development and use of creative therapeutic intervention techniques. Maslow (1968), who developed a hierarchy of human needs, placed the need for self-actualization at the top of the pyramid. In defining self-actualization, he emphasized self-discovery and realization and noted the strong connection between creativity and self-actualization.

The arts provide a means of expanding the consciousness, of naturally becoming more aware of one's self, particularly of the connection between mind and body. Participation in the arts forces us to become more in tune with our senses (sight, hearing, touch) and our bodies. The arts also provide a means to achieve an identity. Nowhere can one find a better opportunity to develop and express one's unique individuality and identity than through participation in drawing, painting, sculpting, writing, music, drama, or dance. Creative activities are fun. They provide a necessary balance to the strains and tensions and mundane tasks of day-to-day living. We temporarily forget our troubles and cares and relax. Creative involvement can almost magically restore, refresh, revitalize, and re-create an individual. We all have a need for freedom, joy, pleasure, beauty, aesthetics, and passion—these the arts can fulfill.

High-level wellness is a condition of feeling alive, vibrant, and energetic and possessing a true sense of joy and a real zest for living. Participation in the arts stimulates the imagination and provides an avenue to high-level wellness for older adults.

Creative Arts and the Aging

Creativity may be arrested in older individuals by their inhibitions, habits, and expectations or by the lack of opportunities provided by the social and environmental conditions in which they live. Until fairly recently, little attention has been given to the role of creative expression and arts activities as a means of providing life-enriching experiences and enhancing positive mental and physical health in older adults. Practitioners working with older individuals are increasingly recognizing that their clients/patients have creative ability.

Ulysses, the hero of the classical Greek world, who was in his seventies when he began his last set of adventures on the high seas, represents the epitome of the creative adventurer of late life. Creative oldsters have made many creative contributions in various fields. In the field of music, among the many creative older composers, conductors, and performers are Johann Sebastian Bach, Giuseppe Verdi, Arthur Rubinstein, César Auguste Franck, Claudio Monteverdi, and Arthur Fiedler. Creative writers who have continued to produce creative work into their later years include Sophocles, John Milton, William Butler Yeats, Bertrand Russell, Cervantes, Goethe, Tolstoy, Sandburg, and Robert Frost. Well-known artists who have made major contributions in late life include Claude Monet, Rembrandt, Titian, Tintoretto, Michelangelo, Frank Lloyd Wright, and Grandma Moses.

McLeish (1976) developed a concept of the Ulyssean adult, which represents an older adult who remains creative into the late years or who develops and expresses his or her creativity for the first time in later life. The Ulyssean life is possible for older individuals because in many ways the conditions required for the creative life are more available in the later years of adulthood than earlier. Older people have more time to rest and to think; they also possess a rich storehouse of experiences accumulated through life and are more free to adapt unorthodox concepts, one of the recognized patterns of creativity.

Creativity and creative expression can be stimulated and nurtured in older adults through their involvement in creative arts activities. Participation in creative arts activities is therapeutic for older people. Older adults who suffer many physical, cognitive, social, and economic losses often come to view themselves as progressively handicapped, physically and mentally, declining and dependent. Their self-esteem may plummet. Individuality and independence become difficult to achieve in late life. Creative arts provide one way to successfully meet the challenges of aging. Creative arts offer the older adult a choice, which builds pride, confidence, self-esteem, and a sense of control to offset the negative psychological effects of losses.

Creative arts spark the imagination and transport the older individual to a magical world of symbols and images. In that fantasy world, problems can be solved in creative and imaginative ways. That experience equips the older person to deal creatively with the real problems of late life. Through participating in creative activities, the older adult comes to view him- or herself as an active, vital, useful human being.

The arts are inspirational, infusing the older adult with a spirit or zest. Older individuals can be liberated in spirit from poverty, pain, and loneliness and lifted out of the doldrums of depression when they find creative powers in themselves. The role of creative arts activities is significant as a potential contributor to life satisfaction and psychological health for the elderly.

Today there is a need for more leisure programs that build for older adults an atmosphere of creativity and belonging. In recent years many such programs have been implemented across the country. Some of these will be highlighted in the next section.

Creative Arts Programs

Creative Writing

Older adults who are literate can express themselves creatively through writing. The published writings of May Sarton and Florida Scott-Maxwell, two women who write about the experience of growing old, offer examples of the depth and breadth of creative expression that are possible through the medium of creative writing. Older adults can participate in a variety of different writing experiences including letter writing, essay writing, poetry writing, group poetry, journal writing, autobiographical accounts, and production of short stories, plays, and novels.

Creative writing is a form of personal expression and social communication. The activity of writing involves mental play with ideas and concepts, logical thought processes, and memory. The creative writer must be a keen observer of human nature and natural phenomenon and is always aware of the world around him or her, gathering ideas and information to write about. Personal experiences and memories gathered from a lifetime of living provide the raw material for creative writing. As such, the activity naturally encourages personal reflection and reminiscence.

Older adults can be encouraged to write their thoughts, experiences, ideas, and feelings in a personal journal. Keeping a personal journal is similar to writing in a diary every day. Many older people kept diaries as children or possibly into their adult years. The personal journal allows for free expression of ideas and feelings and, as such, provides a cathartic experience. The journal also serves as a concrete record, validating the experiences of the last years of life. In addition, the journal provides a lasting memory in tangible form for family members and friends. Finally, the journal is a historical document in its own right, preserving the history of one individual in one family in one community in one historical time.

Older adults can also be encouraged to write their own autobiographies. Such an activity encourages reminiscence. Like the personal journal, the recorded life story provides a lasting memory for family and friends and a historical document. If writing is very difficult or impossible for the older adult due to loss of vision, serious health impairments, or problems with writing, the older adult can speak into a tape recorder. A family member or friend can then type notes from the tapes.

Poetry is a medium of communication particularly well suited to elders. Elders can participate in poetry listening groups, or they can learn to write poetry as individuals or group poetry. *Haiku* can also be written by older adults.

Reminiscent poetry groups have been conducted successfully with Navajo Americans residing in a nursing home (Lyman & Edwards, 1989). In these sessions each member is encouraged to reminisce about his or her early life as a Navajo. Group sessions begin with the reading of a poem written by the group the week before or a poem written by a well-known poet. Each week a certain theme is developed by the group. Group members share their ideas and feelings for possible inclusion in the poem. Themes include elderly Navajo adventures, Navajo rules of life, Navajo good times, Navajo changes, and challenges facing Navajo elders today. Each person in the poetry group contributes an idea or sentence. No attempt is made to rhyme lines. All contributions are recorded. Then the group facilitator types up the group poem for discussion at the next session. Most poems address directly or indirectly experiences group members have had with "sheepherding." This experience encourages reminiscence and results in a group remembrance. Poetry scrapbooks are created for members to keep and share with family members and friends.

The Scotia-Glenville Central School District and the Schenectady County Council on the Arts have sponsored an intergenerational writing project in New York called Community Creative Writing Class. Older adults and high school students attend a lecture given by an English teacher and then during the week complete a writing assignment. At the end of the week the students and older adults return to class to share their writings and to discuss them together. The program aims to enable students to acquire knowledge and understanding of and respect for elders, and enables elders to have a purpose and make a meaningful contribution.

Art

Creative arts programs for older adults include drawing, painting, clay modeling, sculpting, metal art, and other forms of visual, graphic, or plastic art. Ceramics, folk arts, and other crafts are also included.

The nonverbal form of communication in painting or drawing allows one to express thoughts, feelings, and emotions vividly and personally in images and symbols. The free choice of colors and types of paper or materials further enhances expression, uniqueness, and individuality. One can draw anger or rage, pain or sadness, choosing appropriate lines and strokes or colors that signify these moods and feelings. Working with clay or finger paints is particularly effective. One can actually squeeze, push, and physically manipulate the substance. The senses are aroused and stimulated as one sees and touches.

The expression of pain and the accompanying feelings of anger, rage, guilt, or sorrow through artwork permits catharsis and leads to successful management of the feeling (Landgarten, 1981). Many elderly experience feelings of depression, and art work is one method of working through such feelings. Such feelings expressed through art can be shared and discussed with positive results.

Older adults who participate in creative arts' programs derive three types of benefits: psychoanalytic, creative, and existential/humanistic. Art permits the direct expression of dreams, fantasies, and other inner experiences; and the pictured projections of unconscious material serve psychoanalytic purposes. Through art an individual creates a product that uniquely expresses his or her ideas and feelings. The artwork serves as a tangible symbol of some aspect of the self. Artwork encourages the development of spontaneity, self-expression, flexibility, and originality and of relationships with others through group or family art sessions. Art is viewed as a way of expressing feelings about self, the world, and human relationships.

Intergenerational arts programs have been developed across the country. One innovative program implemented in a community in North Georgia brought "latchkey" teens and elders together. Teens and Elderly for the Arts (TEA) Time was an innovative program of older people sharing folk arts and crafts with latchkey teenagers. Older adults at a local community recreation and parks senior center taught latchkey teenagers candle making, weaving, quilting, and whittling 4 days a week from 2:30 p.m. until 4:30 p.m. A survey of participants—teenagers and "keenagers," as the older participants were called—revealed that the program was beneficial—for both age groups (Keller, 1990).

The Institute for the Study of Developmental Disabilities at Indiana University recently initiated a pilot art therapy program at a group home for mentally retarded adults. Participants ranged in age from 57 to 71. Art sessions were held once a week for 7 months. The art groups were open ended and participants could choose their own subject matter and materials. Harlan (1991) reported that the program had a positive effect on staff and residents. Improved self-esteem, increased social interaction, and more group cohesion were observed.

Music

Participation in music may involve observation, participation, or creation. Observation involves listening to music or watching a musical performance. The listening or watching is active, involving the mind and senses, requiring attention, concentration, and involvement of the participant. For example, the music of Mahler has been effectively used to evoke certain emotions and moods, such as sadness and somberness (Wells, 1977). Music listening appreciation groups are appropriate for older adults. Any type of music may be played—classical, jazz, popular, instrumental, vocal. Listening to live performances is also very stimulating for elders.

For frail older persons, music participation may be through humming, singing, foot tapping, clapping, swaying, or rocking to the music, dancing, or engaging in other body movements. Many elders are interested in learning to play an instrument. The playing of musical instruments or involvement in a rhythm band, using cymbals, bells, tambourines, drums, or other percussion instruments, is also participatory. Most participation occurs in a group situation. Group singing and dancing with others are common favorites. Music games like "Name That Tune" and music sing-alongs encourage another type of enjoyable participation in music activities. Performance groups can perform before friends, family, and community members. Barbershop quartets and rhythm bands are popular performance groups.

Music creation involves writing, composing, or otherwise making music. Music is rhythmic and structured, a natural form of organization. An excellent creative outlet is the composing of original music and lyrics.

Musical participation evokes powerful associations and moods and encourages nonverbal expression of thought, feelings, and emotions. Through participation in or creation of one's own song, dance, or melody, self-expression, self-awareness, and creativity are enhanced. Music is the most mathematical of the expressive arts and can stimulate mental alertness, cognitive function, and awareness of present and self. Music can also restore self-care and positive involvement and independence of the old.

Of all the creative arts, music has the greatest power to invoke memories, thoughts, and feelings from the past. It is a wonderful tool for stimulating reminiscence in elders. Music has soothing, healing properties that promote relaxation, unblock the mind, and encourage free association. Music is a means of expressing tender emotions, such as love; can aid in combatting feelings of loneliness, fear, helplessness, depression, and despair; and can aid the individual in his or her grief work and in the process of dying. Music naturally encourages group participation and verbal and nonverbal social interactions and communication. Finally, music participation in some forms results in improvements in breathing, circulation, posture, muscle tone, sensory processes, and physical health.

Some elderly particularly enjoy group singing, piano and guitar music, rhythm bands, and the music of an earlier era that invokes pleasant reminiscences of childhood days, early courtship experiences, and other significant life events. But other music activities are also appropriate for older adults. These include attendance at recitals, concerts, operas, musical plays, or other musical events and in-depth study of music history, the lives of musical composers, the history of opera, or comprehensive instruction about various instruments or performers. All types of music may be explored—folk, ethnic, classical, jazz, popular.

Beckie Karass (1985), a music therapist in Maryland, has organized reminiscence groups and used music, photos, clothes, scrapbooks, and props to encourage reminiscence. Topics used for reminiscence groups include weddings, vacations, fashions, and romance. Songs about each topic are played and discussed in the group. If the topic is love and romance, for example, the following songs can be played, sung, and discussed: "Heart of My Heart," "I Left My Heart in San Francisco," "Let Me Call You Sweetheart," "Heart and Soul," "Zing! Went The Strings of My Heart," and "With a Song in My Heart." Some songs can be played and residents encouraged to "Name That Tune" or "name the singer." The music serves to set the stage for group discussion of the topic. Questions can be asked to stimulate discussion. Some appropriate ones for the topic of love and romance might be as follows: Tell us about your first romance. Do you remember your first date with your husband? How did you react when your first child fell in love for the first time?

Ruth Bright (1985), a music therapist in Australia, has successfully used music activities with physically ill and dying individuals. Bright presents several examples of how to use music therapy to renew interest in life and bring people out of their shells. Music can also encourage learning. For example, after brain damage, the sense of position is lost. Music can be used to help the individual rebuild sensations of personal and extrapersonal space. Music accompaniment gives a sense of rhythm and helps a patient learn new techniques of breathing more easily. Music can be used to help the brain damaged, those suffering from respiratory disease, depressed individuals, the confused and psychotic, the blind, and the terminally ill in pain.

Drama

Dramatics encourages thought and personal self-reflection as seriousness and humor are used to explore life's meaning. Experiencing emotions—positive and negative—is paramount. Character, story, and meaning are the essential components of dramatic performance. Dramatic effect results from the manner of performance. In dramatics the individual actor is free to express him- or herself in any manner he or she chooses. Each dramatic act is a unique self-expression.

Most people think of formal dramatics when they think about drama. Formal dramatics involves memorization of lines, rehearsal, and performance before an audience. Standard techniques are used. Activities are fairly well structured. Participation in formal dramatics can be very demanding. Formal dramatics encompasses performance of plays as well as play writing. Greenblatt (1985) has successfully used formal dramatics with older adults.

Another type of dramatics frequently used with seniors is informal dramatics, also referred to as creative dramatics, improvisational drama, or applied theater. A relatively new form of dramatic art, creative dramatics is a form of spontaneous creation and expression of feelings drawing upon both past life experiences and feelings and emotions of the moment. No particular skills or talents are required to participate in creative dramatics. All that is required is imagination and a wealth of life experiences and feelings. Applied theater is participatory drama that is spontaneous and expressive, created by the members of a group. Dialogue rather than a polished, memorized final play characterizes creative dramatics.

Many types of formal and informal dramatics activities are appropriate for older adults. The following are some examples: play writing, pageants, puppetry, reader's theater, storytelling, radio drama, clowning, mime or pantomime, improvisation, oral history theater, intergenerational theater, talking book series, and formal performance of a musical or play on a stage before an audience.

Elders Share the Arts (ESTA) is a New York City drama project that has received recognition for "developing the uses of life review as a creative, therapeutic, empowering tool for working with elders and intergenerational groups" (Perlstein, 1991, p. 55). Older adults in ESTA participate in living history workshops where they learn to "shape their recollections into evocative living-history plays, journals, dance, songs, collages, and multimedia works" (Perlstein, 1991, p. 55). Oral history and storytelling form the basis of the workshops. Themes include immigrating to America, love and romance, struggling with discrimination and poverty, racism and sexism, and life during the depression. ESTA holds Annual Living History Festivals where seniors from diverse ethnic and cultural backgrounds share their life experiences through drama and storytelling. In 1991 the program initiated a 3-year multicultural intergenerational project called "Rediscovering America." Fifth graders learn oral history interviewing techniques and work with seniors to learn about America from a different time perspective.

Dance

Dance and music are intricately related; dance is music set to motion. Predating the spoken word, dance is thought to be the very first means of human communication. Primitive people attributed mystical and magical powers to dance, engaging in war dances, rain dances, ghost dances, and religious or ritualistic dances. Joy, fear, hope, and awe were all expressed through dance. We can trace the roots of modern dance therapy to ancient times when the peoples of pretechnological societies engaged in tribal rituals to express communal joy or fear, to heal the sick, or to communicate with their gods.

Dance activities are appropriate for older adults in the community as well as for institutionalized elders. Most dance activities can be adapted for those in wheelchairs. The variety of dance activities that can be offered to elders is endless. According to Wapner (1981), a successful program of dance should include the following movements of a dance repertoire: walking, sliding, gliding, hopping, jumping, jogging, turning, crawling, and rolling. Bending and stretching, the use of stylized and creative movements, expressions of all sorts, exercises, and rhythmic movement are all encouraged. Folk dancing, tap dancing, square dancing, and ballroom dancing may also be used. The elderly particularly enjoy dances from their young adult days; many have participated in folk- or square-dance clubs during their lives. Also appropriate are aerobic dance, social dances such as line and circle dances, African dance, jazz, rhythmic dance, and creative dance.

Participation in dance activities offers many benefits to older adults. Dance activities offer all of the same benefits provided by other forms of physical exercise: improved cardiovascular fitness; improved posture, balance, strength, joint flexibility, endurance, and coordination; effective weight control; improved body image and self-image; greater confidence and greater feelings of power and mastery; and improved sleep, digestion, and circulation. Like other forms of physical exercise, dance decreases depression and anxiety and improves memory and alertness. Dance is an excellent way to release tension and stress and relax. After dancing, older adults feel relaxed and calm; at the same time, they feel vibrant, alive, and energized. Dance is a social activity. Through dance, older adults explore, express, and share feelings with others. They develop mutual trust and understanding. They touch and are touched, a stimulating experience many older adults are lacking. Dance is one way to build community among people.

In 1975 Liz Lerman (1984) started a senior dance troupe known as the Dancers of the Third Age as part of the Dance Exchange in Washington, D.C. The older dancers perform with other dancers in the Dance Exchange. The Dancers of the Third Age perform in senior centers, community centers, and schools. Two innovative dance/fitness programs for seniors in southeastern Connecticut are Dance by the Sea and the Energy Hour. Dance by the Sea began in 1984 in New London, Connecticut.

Summary

Creative arts activities contribute to positive physical and mental health of older adults. They offer an opportunity for creative expression and exploration of personal and aging issues. They contribute to the development of friendships and social interaction and reduce feelings of loneliness, isolation, and depression. They offer older adults enjoyment and fun and help to relieve the burden of day-to-day living. More programs should be developed across the country.

References

Bright, R. (1985). *Music in geriatric care* (2nd ed.). Van Nuys, CA: Alfred.

Greenblatt, F. S. (1985). *Drama with the elderly: Acting at eighty.* Springfield, IL: Charles C Thomas.

Harlan, J. E. (1991). The use of art therapy for older adults with developmental disabilities. In M. J. Leitner & S. F. Leitner (Eds.), *Leisure in later life* (pp. 67-79). New York: Haworth.

Jung, C. (1971). *The portable Jung* (R. F. C. Hull, Trans.). New York: Viking.

Karass, R. (1985). *Down memory lane: Topics and ideas for reminiscence groups.* Wheaton, MD: Circle.

Keller, M. J. (1990). Intergenerational sharing: Teens and elderly for the arts (TEA). *The Journal of Applied Gerontology, 9*(3), 321-324.

Kelly, J. R. (1982). Leisure in later life: Roles and identities. In N. J. Osgood (Ed.), *Life after work: Retirement, leisure, recreation and the elderly.* New York: Praeger.

Landgarten, H. B. (1981). *Clinical art therapy: A comprehensive guide.* New York: Brunner/Mazel.

Lerman, L. (1984). *Teaching dance to senior adults.* Springfield, IL: Charles C Thomas.

Lyman, A. J., & Edwards, M. E. (1989). Reminiscence poetry groups: Sheepherding—a Navajo cultural tie that binds. *Activities, Adaptation, & Aging, 13*(4), 1-9.

Maslow, A. (1968). *Toward a psychology of being.* New York: Van Nostrand Reinhold.

McLeish, J. (1976). *The Ulyssean adult.* Toronto: McGraw-Hill.

Perlstein, S. (1991). Elders share the arts. *Generations, 15*(2), 55-61.

Wapner, E. R. (1981). *Recreation for the elderly.* New York: Todd & Honeywell.

Wells, F. (1977). Psychosonics. In W. Anderson (Ed.), *Therapy and the arts: Tools of consciousness* (pp. 67-82). New York: Harper & Row.

14

Self-Efficacy, Physical Activity, and Aging

EDWARD McAULEY

Adherence to Physical Activity: The Problem

In the past two decades the U.S. Public Health Service (U.S. Department of Health and Human Services, 1980, 1990) has developed a preventive orientation in public health policies, promoting regular participation by children and adults in exercise and physical fitness as a major health objective for the nation and identifying such activity as a behavioral orientation expected to reduce morbidity and mortality. Considerable evidence exists to suggest that habitual physical activity can positively influence a broad range of health conditions, both physiological and psychological. Physical activity and fitness have been linked to risk or symptom reduction in coronary heart disease, cancer, and osteoporosis (see Bouchard, Shephard, Stephens, Sutton, & McPherson, 1990); all-cause mortality (Blair et al., 1989); anxiety (Petruzzello, Landers, Hatfield, Kubitz, & Salazar, 1991); and depression (Camacho, Roberts, Lazarus, Kaplan, & Cohen, 1991).

Although the benefits of exercise in health terms appear to considerably outweigh the risks, the participation rates of North Americans in

AUTHOR'S NOTE: The author was supported by a grant from the National Institute on Aging (#AG07907) while preparing this chapter.

exercise and fitness regimens is not particularly impressive. Best epidemiological estimates report that less than 20% of the 18- to 65-year-old population exercise at sufficient levels of intensity, frequency, and duration to accrue positive health and fitness benefits (Centers for Disease Control, 1987). Furthermore, between 30% and 59% of the adult population is estimated to lead a sedentary life-style (Casperson, Christenson, & Pollard, 1986). More important, many individuals who engage in organized fitness or exercise programs withdraw before any health benefits have been realized. Indeed, the statistics are well documented regarding the alarming attrition rate in exercise programs, which approximates 50% within the first 6 months (Dishman, 1986, 1990). Those who do adhere seldom comply with the prescribed exercise intensity, frequency, and duration necessary to achieve and maintain health benefits. This failure to adhere to exercise regimens parallels the compliance dilemma in modern medicine, one of the most serious problems encountered in disease control and health promotion (Epstein & Cluss, 1982).

The problem of adherence to physical activity regimens is not unique to younger and physically capable individuals. Physical activity is an important component of healthy aging and lack of such activity is in all likelihood the cause of much of the physiological degeneration characteristically found with aging. Casperson (1989) reports that over 40% of individuals 65 and over report no regular physical activity and less than a tenth of this population routinely participate in regular vigorous activity. With cardiovascular disease being the primary cause of death in this country and lack of physical activity being an independent risk factor for coronary heart disease, the large proportion of older Americans who are sedentary is particularly alarming.

Determinants of Physical Activity Participation

A host of determinants have been identified that are either directly or indirectly related to degree of participation in exercise and physical activity, and it is well recognized that the behavior in question is a dynamic, complex, and multiply determined phenomenon (Dishman, 1990; Sallis & Hovell, 1990). As such, the need to examine the interplay between biological, psychological, and environmental variables is acknowledged (Dishman, 1990), as is the necessity of identifying the discrepancies and similarities among the broad array of determinants that are differentially implicated at the various stages (e.g., adoption, maintenance, dropout, resumption) of the exercise process (Sallis & Hovell, 1990). Determinants of physical activity participation are usually grouped in categories that reflect such influences as personal, environmental, programmatic, and cognitive parameters (e.g., Dishman, 1990; Sallis and Hovell, 1990). It should be noted that, whereas the study of exercise patterns in aging populations is not extensive, it appears that older individuals identify very similar factors as reasons for attrition or nonparticipation in exercise and physical activity (McAuley, Poag, Gleason, & Wraith, 1990). Employing an attributional approach to identifying reasons for exercise attrition in older adults, McAuley and his colleagues (1990) reported lack of motivation (including boredom, lack of fun, no interest, and self-discipline) and time management as the most commonly identified categories. Of interest, the majority of the reasons given for dropping out could be classified as being under the control of the individual and subject to change. This interpretation was confirmed when subjects were asked to classify their reason for dropping out along causal dimensions. Results revealed that subjects made predominantly internal, unstable, and personally controllable attributions.

When dealing with these general categories of commonly identified factors, *personal* factors include such variables as demographic characteristics (e.g., education, socioeconomic status), life-style habits (e.g., smoking), activity history (e.g., supervised versus free-living activity, exposure and experience in organized physical activity during youth), and biomedical status (e.g., obesity, exercise tolerance). Such factors have been generally poor predictors of exercise adherence, although they may prove to be useful in specifying factors that are more reliable determinants (Dishman, 1990). *Environmental* factors typically identified as barriers to physical activity participation include inconvenient exercise facilities, intolerance of climate, and lack of time or inability to manage time for exercise. *Programmatic* influences can include aspects of physical activity participation itself (e.g., discomfort, levels of exertion, type of activity) and perceived dissatisfaction with program elements (e.g., instructor, location, time). This latter aspect of adherence has perhaps received the least study. Finally, because many consider exercise adherence to be largely a motivational phenomenon, a number of *cognitive* approaches have been adopted. Such approaches include the study of psychological traits (e.g., locus of control, self-motivation) and states (health beliefs, attitudes, intentions). Although a number of these models (see McAuley & Courneya, 1993; Sonstroem, 1988, for reviews) have met with some success in predicting the maintenance of exercise behavior, it is contended here that Bandura's (1986) self-efficacy-based social cognitive model perhaps holds the most promise for understanding this complex behavior. The remainder of this chapter is devoted to discussion and review of exercise as a means for *enhancing self-efficacy* perceptions in older adults and the role played by such perceptions in *predicting exercise behavior.* In so doing, a brief overview of the theory is first presented, followed by a review of the literature that has specifically attempted to enhance efficacy through physical activity. Finally, the predictive role played by efficacy cognitions in adherence to exercise is examined.

Theoretical Overview

Bandura's self-efficacy theory is a social cognitive model of behavioral causation, which posits that behavior, physiological and cognitive factors, and environmental influences all function as interacting determinants of one another (Bandura, 1986). Efficacy cognitions are directly relevant to the particular behavior of concern and are therefore subject to change as a function of environmental stimuli. That is, positive mastery experiences are likely to facilitate increases in personal efficacy, whereas failures are likely to result in debilitated perceptions of personal capabilities. Broadly defined, self-efficacy cognitions concern the beliefs or convictions that one has in one's capabilities to successfully engage in a course of action sufficient to satisfy the situational demands. Self-efficacy cognitions have consistently been shown to be important determinants of physical activity and exercise behavior as well as social, clinical, and health-related behaviors (Bandura, 1986; O'Leary, 1985; McAuley, 1992a). It is important to realize that self-efficacy is not concerned with the skills an individual has but, instead, with the judgments of what that individual can do with the skills he or she possesses. A colleague working with elderly patients suffering from osteoarthritis of the knee recently relayed a story that emphasizes this point. In testing the physical functioning of these individuals, he asked an older patient who had difficulty walking whether or not he could climb a short flight of stairs. The patient responded positively and, with great difficulty and a few near falls, climbed up and down the stairs twice. For many individuals of similar condition, such a feat would not be perceived as possible. Even when skills are limited, however, belief in personal efficacy can allow one to accomplish objectives that do not appear physically possible.

Individuals with high self-efficacy expectations tend to approach more challenging tasks, put forth more effort, and persist longer in the face of aversive stimuli. When faced with stressful stimuli, low-efficacious individuals tend to give up, attribute failure internally, and experience greater anxiety or depression (Bandura, 1982). Clearly, physical activity can present an array of challenging tasks, requires considerable effort (especially for the sedentary and elderly), necessitates persistence if one is to accrue any of the physical or psychological benefits associated with exercise, and most certainly can be perceived as both aversive and stressful.

Four major sources of efficacy information are commonly identified: mastery accomplishments, social modeling, social persuasion, and physiological states. *Mastery accomplishments* are the most dependable and influential sources of efficacy information with a history of previous successes enhancing efficacy expectations, whereas previous failures will result in lowered perceptions of personal efficacy. In spite of being the most important source of efficacy, mastery experiences are likely to be more debilitated in the elderly. It is argued that this is a product of *perceived* rather than *actual* declining physical abilities in many cases. In essence, declines in the physical capabilities of older individuals may well be reflections of perceived physical efficacy. Thus being unable to physically carry out the tasks one could accomplish some years before serves to lower efficacy expectations, which, in turn, leads to still further decrements in performance. *Social modeling* is a source of efficacy information derived through observation or imagining others engaging in the task to be performed. In modern-day society, the elderly are typically stereotyped as infirm and incapable whereas the young are portrayed far more positively. Efficacy is reduced when aging individuals use younger individuals as the reference for social comparison. Conversely, efficacy cognitions are less likely to be diminished when the reference for social comparison is chronologically similar. *Social persuasion* is a commonly used technique to bolster personal efficacy, but it is less powerful than information based on personal accomplishments. Positive feedback from peers, relatives, and other social supports provides the type of verbal persuasion that serves to enhance beliefs in personal capabilities. Finally, *physiological states* influence behavior through the cognitive evaluation (efficacy expectations) of the information conveyed by the anxiety arousal, fatigue, and muscular strain and tension. That is, somatic sensations are often interpreted as inability to successfully execute the behavior in question (e.g., physical activity). Clearly, as we age, physical functioning becomes more difficult. Those individuals with poor self-efficacy, however, reduce the number and type of physical and social activities they participate in and expend less effort and lack persistence in those endeavors they do undertake.

Bandura (1977, 1986) has argued that the measurement of self-efficacy cognitions should be conducted in a microanalytic fashion by assessing efficacy along three dimensions: level, strength, and generality. *Level* of self-efficacy concerns the individual's expected performance attainment or the number of tasks that he or she can perform leading up to the target behavior. For example, indicating that one can walk/jog a quarter mile in 3 minutes, a half mile in 6 minutes, a mile in 12 minutes, and so on demonstrates successive levels of efficacy. *Strength* of self-efficacy determines the certainty with which the individual expects to successfully attain each of the component tasks or levels. For example, one might feel very confident about being able to successfully complete half a mile in the requisite time period but feel considerably less confident about being able to complete the mile distance, especially in the early stages of exercise regimens for sedentary older individuals. Strength of efficacy is customarily assessed on a 10- to 100-point scale at 10-point intervals. These intervals are representative of the percentage of confidence in the subject's belief that he or she can successfully complete each of the levels (Bandura, 1977). Overall strength of self-efficacy is determined by summing the confidence ratings and dividing by the total number of items (levels) that constitute the target behavior. *Generality* refers to the number of domains in which individuals consider themselves efficacious. Thus someone who has high self-efficacy with respect to exercise may feel quite comfortable about his or her capabilities in jogging, biking, calisthenics, and so on.

Assessments of self-efficacy are generally developed with a view to tapping generative capabilities with respect to a task rather than singular acts that collectively constitute the task. In other words, if one is interested in assessing subjects' efficacy with respect to exercise frequency, it is necessary, for example, to determine their confidence in being able to exercise in the prescribed regimen in the face of potential barriers or obstacles to attendance. Such obstacles might include schedule conflicts, lack of apparent progress, or perceived lack of attention/support from the exercise leader. Simply asking, "How confident are you in attending exercise classes on a regular basis?" is insufficient because it fails to address the many components that are relevant to judging one's efficacy with respect to exercise frequency.

Self-efficacy theory (Bandura, 1986) has generated a considerable literature in multiple domains of behavioral functioning, and the physical activity domain is no exception (see McAuley, 1992a, for a review). Because exercise is a complex behavior, which appears particularly difficult for some individuals to change, it is of little surprise that self-regulatory skills have been consistently implicated in successful adoption and maintenance of this behavior. The presence of a robust sense of self-efficacy and the development and nurturing of skills and strategies to continually enhance such cognitions have been identified as determinants of physical activity in acute exercise bouts in laboratory settings (e.g., Ewart, Taylor, Reese, & Debusk, 1983; Ewart, Stewart, Gillian, Kelemen, Valenti, et al., 1986; McAuley & Courneya, 1992), in long-term exercise participation (e.g., Ewart, Stewart, Gillian, & Kelemen, 1986; Garcia & King, 1991; McAuley, 1992b), and in larger survey population studies (e.g., Sallis, Priski, Grossman, Patterson, & Nader, 1988; Sallis et al., 1986).

Enhancing Self-Efficacy Through Physical Activity

As a psychological variable, self-efficacy cognitions, by and large, either have been studied as determinants of exercise behavior or have been identified as potential mediating mechanisms that might explain the effects of exercise on various aspects of psychological functioning (e.g., Petruzzello et al., 1991). Therefore it is deemed important to determine that exercise and physical activity do indeed enhance perceptions of efficacy as a precursor to suggesting its viability in mediating other physical and psychosocial outcomes. Given the reciprocal deterministic relations proposed by Bandura's (1986) social cognitive theory, perceptions of efficacy are influenced by the information that the individual derives from exercise and physical activity participation. In turn, self-efficacy influences subsequent behavior, affect, and physiological responses.

The majority of the studies in this area have examined physical activity effects on efficacy perceptions in both males and females primarily of middle age and older with approximately half of these studies involving clinical populations. The clear and consistent finding across all studies in this area, however, is that physical activity of both an acute and a chronic nature positively influences perceptions of personal efficacy (McAuley, in press). In the *clinical samples,* older individuals suffering from coronary artery disease (e.g., Ewart et al., 1983; Taylor, Bandura, Ewart, Miller, & DeBusk, 1985) or chronic obstructive pulmonary disease (e.g., Kaplan, Atkins, & Reinsch, 1984) are typically exposed to an acute bout of exercise, generally a physician-supervised, symptom-limited graded exercise test or an exercise-based intervention ranging from 4 to 20 weeks in length. Measures of physical efficacy are taken prior to and following activity and in some rare cases during the program and at follow-up.

One innovative study (Ewart, Stewart, Gillian, & Keleman, 1986) examined the relative merits of adding different components (either weight training or volleyball) to an exercise program (walk/jog) for elderly coronary artery disease patients in an attempt to examine the specificity effects of information on efficacy. Analyses revealed arm and leg *strength* beliefs (lifting, climbing, push-ups) to be enhanced in the weight training group but neither group reported increases in walking/jogging capabilities. As the authors pointed out, patients had been involved in walking/jogging for 35 months and the additional 10 weeks of jogging in the treatment program would be unlikely to provide new information from which to bolster efficacy cognitions. The importance of such findings should be obvious. If we wish to employ exercise and physical activity interventions to enhance aging individuals' sense of efficacy, it is important to provide the necessary information specific to the domain of function that one wishes to enhance.

In studies employing asymptomatic samples, subjects are generally healthy but sedentary individuals exposed to similar acute (e.g., McAuley & Courneya, 1992; McAuley, Courneya, & Lettunich, 1991) or longer-term exercise participation (e.g., McAuley et al., 1991) as the clinical groups. What is quite remarkable about these studies is the relative potency with which acute exercise exposure influences self-efficacy. That is, even a symptom-limited exercise test lasting several minutes is enough to enhance subjects' perceptions of their physical capabilities. Two studies by McAuley and his colleagues illustrate such effects (McAuley et al., 1991; McAuley & Courneya, 1992).

McAuley and Courneya (1992) examined the relationship of preexisting efficacy for exercise with perceptions of effort expenditure and in-task affect during an acute bout of exercise. Subjects comprised sedentary middle-aged adults participating in graded exercise testing. Perceptions of efficacy were assessed prior to and following exercise testing while perceptions of effort expenditure and in-task affect were assessed at 70% of predicted maximum heart rate. Highly efficacious subjects had lower perceptions of effort expenditure and reported more positive affect during exercise than did their less efficacious counterparts. This single bout of exercise, although short in duration, significantly influenced self-efficacy from pre- to posttest, with affective responses during exercise in turn being significant predictors of posttest self-efficacy when statistically controlling for pretest levels of efficacy and physiological conditioning. Such results are entirely in keeping with Bandura's (1986) notion of reciprocal determinism in which efficacy is proposed to influence affective responses and, in turn, be influenced by such responses.

In an attempt to examine both the acute and the long-term effects of exercise exposure on physical efficacy, McAuley et al. (1991) assessed self-efficacy for walking/jogging, bicycling, and abdominal strength prior to and following graded exercise testing at two time points: before the onset of a 20-week walking program and at the conclusion of that program. Subjects were 103 middle-aged (M = 54 years) males and females. Main effects for time were significant with subjects demonstrating a linear increase in efficacy cognitions over time. Given the tenets of self-efficacy theory, these results were entirely expected. There were also significant differences in efficacy responses for males and females, however. Prior to program onset, males were significantly more efficacious than females before and after the initial acute bout of exercise, although both groups demonstrated proportionately equal increases in efficacy. The female subjects made dramatic gains in their efficacy over the course of the 20-week program, however, to the point where they were as efficacious or more so than their male counterparts. Males and females often hold preconceived views of their capabilities (in this case physical) that are based on diverse factors and experiences that may or may not be accurate. Although initial physiological differences between males and females might contribute to such views, it is likely that the different cultural and socialization patterns experienced by males and females of this age group are also contributing factors. That is, older women, in all likelihood, did not participate in physical activity and exercise as young adults. Therefore they would have little physical activity history and experience of past physical accomplishments on which to base their perceptions of physical capabilities.

To our knowledge, this is the only study reporting details regarding such differences in responses between males and females, although another (McAuley & Courneya, 1992) reports initial differences but statistically controls for them in regression analyses. That few studies exist examining gender differences among the aging in psychological responses to and perceptions of exercise is surprising given the traditional lack of data on female subjects in the exercise literature. Because almost half of the studies in this area have been conducted with clinical populations, it is likely or could be argued that both males and females might evidence equally debilitated physical efficacy. Further, many of these studies had disproportionately fewer females (e.g., in coronary artery disease studies) in the sample, thus making statistical comparisons dubious. At any rate, such findings are important and deserve replication and extension.

Exercise and physical activity are often lauded for the supposed effects that they have on psychological outcomes, although the scientific evidence for such effects is equivocal (Plante & Rodin, 1990). McAuley (1991) investigated the mediational role played by efficacy and causal attributions in generating positive affective responses to exercise midway through an exercise program for previously sedentary older males and females. Path analyses of the data demonstrated the consistently reported direct effect of exercise participation on self-efficacy and that such cognitions mediated, along with attributions, exercise effects on affective responses. Subjects who exercised more often had stronger beliefs in their exercise capabilities and made personally controllable attributions for their progress. In turn, these cognitive mediators were more strongly related to positive affect. Thus the individuals' beliefs in their physical capabilities and the degree to which they see outcomes within their personal control both have implications for the generation of positive affect.

As the vast majority of the adult population in North America are either sedentary or intermittently active (Dishman, 1988) and the number of impaired and aging individuals is increasing (Ramlow, Kriska, & LaPorte, 1987), the employment of exercise and physical activity participation to enhance perceptions of personal efficacy appears warranted. Given the consistency with which efficacy is reported as a determinant of *confirmed* exercise and health behavior (McAuley, 1992a; O'Leary, 1985), the reciprocally determining nature of efficacy and behavior appears worthy of future study. Moreover, if exercise is to be championed for its psychological effects, the nature of efficacy as a mechanism influencing psychological health needs to be determined.

Self-Efficacy as a Determinant of Exercise Adherence

As previously noted, self-efficacy has been demonstrated to be a relatively consistent predictor of adherence to exercise regimens (McAuley, 1992a) across a variety of populations. In this section, a brief review of some epidemiological support for this contention in large communities is documented, followed by discussion of empirical efforts that further demonstrate the influence of self-efficacy in this domain.

Sallis and his colleagues (Sallis et al., 1986; Sallis et al., 1988) have conducted two major community studies of social learning correlates of physical activity in the general population and provide evidence that suggests self-efficacy plays an important role in the adoption and maintenance of exercise behavior. Presenting data from the Stanford Community Health Survey, Sallis et al. (1986) reported self-efficacy to be significantly related to exercise behavior at different stages of the natural history of the exercise process. Efficacy cognitions predicted adoption but not maintenance of *vigorous* activity and the maintenance but not adoption of *moderate* activity. Moreover, self-efficacy with respect to vigorous physical activity predicted change in such activity while moderate activity efficacy led to reported changes in moderate activity. It should be noted that this study is one of the few to adopt the perspective that exercise is a dynamic and complex process with different determinants playing more or less important roles at different stages of the exercise process. A further study of the correlates of physical activity in a large (N = 2,053) California community (San Diego) sample reported self-efficacy to be the strongest predictor among a host of social learning variables (Sallis et al., 1988). The epidemiological evidence provides a useful starting point for examining further testimony for the relationship between self-efficacy and exercise adherence that is to be found in a host of empirical studies in both asymptomatic and normal populations.

Perhaps some of the most compelling evidence linking self-efficacy to exercise behavior in older individuals can be found in those studies examining the role played by self-perceptions in recovery from acute myocardial infarction (Ewart, Stewart, Gillian, & Kelemen, 1986; Ewart,

Stewart, Gillian, Kelemen, Valenti, et al., 1986; Ewart et al., 1983; Taylor et al., 1985). Recognizing the importance of restoring perceived physical efficacy following a heart attack, these researchers sought to establish a link between efficacy and physical activities during various stages of coronary artery disease and cardiac rehabilitation. For example, Ewart et al. (1983) demonstrated that self-efficacy predicted treadmill performance in post-myocardial infarction patients and that post-treadmill cognitions were better predictors of subsequent home activity than was actual treadmill performance. This latter finding clearly supports the notion that what one thinks one is capable of is more important than one's actual physical capabilities (Bandura, 1986).

Self-efficacy theory predicts that highly self-efficacious individuals are more likely to adopt or engage in a greater number of like behaviors than are their counterparts whose personal efficacy has been impaired (Bandura, 1986). Where exercise is concerned, those who perceive themselves to be more efficacious with respect to their physical capabilities are more likely to adopt and maintain a life-style in which exercise plays an important role.

Several studies exist that document the mediational role played by perceived efficacy in adhering to prescribed exercise programs and maintaining activity postprogram termination in older healthy populations. Desharnais, Bouillon, and Godin (1986) in predicting adherence to an 11-week adult exercise program demonstrated self-efficacy to be more capable of discriminating between subjects classified as adherers and those classified as dropouts. Similarly, Corbin, Laurie, Gruger, and Smiley (1984), employing a somewhat younger population (M = 30 years), reported general self-confidence in sport and physical activity to influence commitment and involvement in physical activity. Although interesting, both studies elected to examine efficacy by virtue of a single-item question, and in the case of the latter study *general* self-confidence was measured. Assessing subjects' efficacy beliefs regarding exercising in the face of increasingly difficult barriers to participation or beliefs regarding incrementally difficult aspects of exercise prescription represent more appropriate methods for the microanalysis of self-efficacy.

Clearly, the self-efficacy approach to the prediction of physical activity as a health-promoting behavior is governed by situationally dependent information processing. A more traitlike perspective has been espoused by Dishman, Ickes, and Morgan (1980) in which the more general dispositional characteristic of self-motivation is proposed as an important component of activity participation. Supporting (e.g., Heiby, Onorato, & Sato, 1987) and refuting (e.g., Weber & Wertheim, 1989) evidence for this latter proposition exists in the literature and two studies have specifically contrasted the relative predictive utility of the self-motivation and self-efficacy approaches (Garcia & King, 1991; McAuley & Jacobson, 1991). In a clinical trial involving sedentary, healthy, middle-aged males and females (M = 56.4 years), Garcia and King (1991) reported efficacy cognitions but not self-motivation to be positively related to exercise adherence at 6 and 12 months. Moreover, more proximate aspects of the exercise experience (e.g., exertion, enjoyment, and convenience) did not account for significant variance beyond that accounted for by self-efficacy. Similar findings were reported by McAuley and Jacobson (1991) in a study of 58 formerly sedentary, middle-aged females engaged in aerobic activity. Self-efficacy rather than self-motivation predicted both in-class exercise participation and activity outside of class. Both self-efficacy and instructor influence were significant predictors of program attendance. Only self-efficacy, however, was a significant predictor of overall exercise participation (including exercise outside of program participation). Moreover, self-efficacy at program end was significantly correlated with frequency and duration of activity at 2-month follow-up. In both the Garcia and King (1991) and the McAuley and Jacobson (1991) studies, self-efficacy proved to be significantly more influential than self-motivation in predicting exercise participation. These findings are testimony to the wisdom of using state psychological measures rather than omnibus trait measures to predict physical activity.

The previous studies have, by and large, been content to examine the efficacy-adherence literature without considering the relative role that such cognitions might play at different points in what has been referred to as "the natural history of the exercise process" (Sallis & Hovell, 1990). Because exercise is a process in which individuals move from being sedentary to adopting an exercise regimen and either maintaining that regimen or dropping out, it is important to realize that different predictors of exercise participation will have more or less potent influence at different stages. Thus one would expect efficacy expectations to be more influential in those stages of exercise participation where the demands of continued adherence are greater (e.g., early stages of adoption; resumption of activity following dropout, injury). Such a hypothesis was tested in a large prospective study (McAuley, 1992b, 1993) of sedentary older males and females. Subjects participated in a

5-month aerobic exercise program comprised primarily of walking and graduating, in some cases, to jogging (McAuley, 1992b). Subjects were then interviewed at 4 months postprogram (McAuley, 1993). In the first report (McAuley, 1992b), path analysis revealed self-efficacy and body fat to be predictive of exercise frequency (number of sessions attended) and intensity (degree of perceived exertion during each session) at the midpoint of a 5-month program. Exercise participation to that point, however, was the only predictor of subsequent participation over the remaining period of the program. Such findings are consistent with the perspective that cognitive control systems play their most important role in the acquisition of behavioral proficiencies (Bandura, 1989). When behaviors are less demanding and more easily engaged in (in this case, beyond adoption and adaptation), cognitive control systems give way to lower control systems (Bandura & Wood, 1989). Clearly, different mechanisms take on differing degrees of importance at various stages of the exercise process.

In the follow-up study (McAuley, 1993), the self-efficacy-exercise participation relationship was examined in a more demanding context: continued exercise maintenance following termination of the program. Participants were contacted 4 months after program completion, interviewed by telephone, and surveyed by mail as to their exercise participation patterns since program termination. Employing hierarchical regression analyses, it was possible to determine the independent effect of each predictor on exercise participation at follow-up. Results indicated that self-efficacy was a significant predictor of continued exercise participation and shared significant variation with physiological (VO_2max) and behavioral (past exercise frequency and intensity) parameters. Efficacy alone was a significant individual predictor of exercise behavior, however. Thus it appears that, when situations or behaviors become more demanding, efficacy cognitions assume a stronger predictive role. Once again, it is clear that diverse parameters take on varying degrees of predictive importance at different stages of the exercise process (Dishman, 1990; McAuley, 1992b; Sallis & Hovell, 1990).

Other psychological parameters have also been suggested as facilitating adherence with social support being one of the most oft cited (Dishman, 1988; Sonstroem, 1988; Wankel, 1985). The empirical evidence to support such statements has been minimal, however, and whether the relationship is direct or mediated through some other cognitive mechanism has typically not been verified. Duncan (1989;

Duncan & McAuley, in press; Duncan & Stoolmiller, in press) has argued that social support provides a source of efficacy information that, in turn, influences exercise participation. In a cross-sectional model, Duncan and McAuley (in press) used latent growth curve analysis (McArdle, 1986) to show that the social support dimensions of attachment, social integration, and guidance influenced exercise behavior not directly, as many individuals have hypothesized, but *indirectly* through the mediation of exercise efficacy. That is, social support serves to enhance one's sense of exercise capabilities and this, in turn, influences participation. In the longitudinal model (Duncan, 1989; Duncan & Stoolmiller, in press), however, previous exercise behavior was the only significant predictor. Duncan's findings reaffirm the need to assess behavior and possible mediators of that behavior at multiple time points and suggest efficacy to be a significant mediator of social support effects.

The studies documented here provide consistent support for the mediational role played by perceptions of personal efficacy in predicting the adoption and maintenance of exercise regimens among aging populations. If, through appropriate interventions, fitness and exercise leaders can enhance efficacy cognitions and thereby influence adherence to exercise regimens, then self-efficacy should be considered a vital component in the constellation of elements that influence this complex behavior.

Summary

The ability of self-efficacy cognitions to influence a broad range of health behaviors (O'Leary, 1985), including exercise (McAuley, 1992a) and adherence to such regimens, is well established. Moreover, both acute and chronic physical activity participation have been demonstrated to have significant effects on perceptions of personal efficacy and these patterns of relationships have been supported in older populations. In many respects, aging populations may stand to benefit the most from interventions designed to enhance physical efficacy. Declines in physiological functioning are in many individuals *expected* as they age. These expectations result in a reduced sense of physical efficacy and can lead to further reductions in physical repertoires resulting in restricted activities and diminished effort in those activities in which one does engage (Bandura, 1986). It is contended here that older individuals can not only lead longer lives but also lead happier and healthier lives by incorporating physical activity into their lifestyles. Doing so leads to an expansion of activity engagement as well as an enhanced sense of efficacy that, in turn, fuels further activity. Such efficacy cognitions in older adults can be enhanced in several ways, all of which have important implications for how exercise and physical activity programs are structured and implemented. All too often attrition results from negative exercise experiences that stem from lack of success and progress. Program leaders must instill in older adults the realization that mastery experiences can develop every time one exercises. Improvements in duration of activity, distance walked, jogged, or cycled, flexibility, strength, resting heart rate, and so on are all signs that serve to build and maintain perceived efficacy. Therefore placing older individuals in physical activity environments in which they are accorded multiple opportunities for successful physical accomplishments, providing role models of similar age and physical characteristics, offering social support and encouragement, and helping them correctly interpret their physiological responses to exercise participation are all potent strategies for efficacy enhancement. In turn, if we can keep older individuals in exercise programs, the attendant physical and psychological benefits known to result from such participation will be realized.

References

Bandura, A. (1977). Self-efficacy: Toward a unifying theory of behavioral change. *Psychological Review, 84,* 191-215.

Bandura, A. (1982). Self-efficacy in human agency. *American Psychologist, 37,* 122-147.

Bandura, A. (1986). *Social foundations of thought and action.* Englewood Cliffs, NJ: Prentice-Hall.

Bandura, A. (1989). Human agency in social cognitive theory. *American Psychologist, 44,* 1175-1184.

Bandura, A., & Wood, R. (1989). Effect of perceived controllability and performance standards on self-regulation of complex decision making. *Journal of Personality and Social Psychology, 56,* 805-814.

Blair, S. N., Kohl, H. W., III, Paffenberger, R. S., Jr., Clark, D. G., Cooper, K. H., & Gibbons, L. W. (1989). Physical fitness and all-cause mortality: A prospective study of healthy men and women. *Journal of the American Medical Association, 262,* 2395-2401.

Bouchard, C., Shephard, R. J., Stephens, T., Sutton, J. R., & McPherson, B. D. (1990). *Exercise, fitness and health: A consensus of current knowledge.* Champaign, IL: Human Kinetics.

Camacho, T. C., Roberts, R. E., Lazarus, N. B., Kaplan, G. A., & Cohen, R. D. (1991). Physical activity and depression: Evidence from the Alameda County Study. *American Journal of Epidemiology, 134,* 220-231.

Casperson, C. J. (1989). Physical activity epidemiology: Concepts, methods, and applications to exercise science. *Exercise and Sport Science Reviews, 17,* 423-473.

Casperson, C. J., Christenson, G. M., & Pollard, R. A. (1986). Status of the 1990 physical fitness and exercise objectives: Evidence from NHIS 1985. *Public Health Reports, 101,* 587-592.

Centers for Disease Control. (1987). Sex-, age-, and region-specific prevalence for sedentary lifestyle in selected states in 1985: The behavioral risk factor surveillance system. *Morbidity and Mortality Weekly Reports, 36,* 195-198, 203-204.

Corbin, C. B., Laurie, D. R., Gruger, C., & Smiley, B. (1984). Vicarious success experience as a factor influencing self-confidence, attitudes, and physical activity of adult women. *Journal of Teaching in Physical Education, 4,* 17-23.

Desharnais, R., Bouillon, J., & Godin, G. (1986). Self-efficacy and outcome expectations as determinants of exercise adherence. *Psychological Reports, 59,* 1155-1159.

Dishman, R. K. (1986). Exercise compliance: A new view for public health. *The Physician and Sports Medicine, 14,* 127-145.

Dishman, R. K. (1988). *Exercise adherence: Its impact on public health.* Champaign, IL: Human Kinetics.

Dishman, R. K. (1990). Determinants of participation in physical activity. In C. Bouchard, R. J. Shephard, T. Stephens, J. R. Sutton, & B. D. McPherson (Eds.), *Exercise, fitness and health: A consensus of current knowledge* (pp. 78-101). Champaign, IL: Human Kinetics.

Dishman, R. K., Ickes, W. J., & Morgan, W. P. (1980). Self-motivation and adherence to habitual physical activity. *Journal of Applied Social Psychology, 10* 115-137.

Duncan, T. E. (1989). *The influence of social support and efficacy cognitions in the exercise behavior of sedentary adults: An interactional model.* Unpublished doctoral dissertation, University of Oregon.

Duncan, T. E., & McAuley, E. (in press). Social support and efficacy cognitions in exercise adherence: A latent growth curve analysis. *Journal of Behavioral Medicine.*

Duncan, T. E., & Stoolmiller, M. (in press). Modeling social and psychological determinants of exercise behaviors via structural equation modeling. *Research Quarterly for Exercise and Sport.*

Epstein, L., & Cluss, P. A. (1982). A behavioral medicine perspective on adherence to long-term medical regimens. *Journal of Consulting and Clinical Psychology, 50,* 950-971.

Ewart, C. K., Stewart, K. J., Gillian, R. E., & Keleman, M. H. (1986). Self-efficacy mediates strength gains during circuit weight training in men with coronary artery disease. *Medicine and Science in Sports and Exercise, 18,* 531-540.

Ewart, C. K., Stewart, K. J., Gillian, R. E., Keleman, M. H., Valenti, S. A., Manley, J. D., & Keleman, M. D. (1986). Usefulness of self-efficacy in predicting overexertion during programmed exercise in coronary artery disease. *American Journal of Cardiology, 57,* 557-561.

Ewart, C. K., Taylor, C. B., Reese, L. B., & Debusk, R. F. (1983). Effects of early post myocardial infarction exercise testing on self-perception and subsequent physical activity. *American Journal of Cardiology, 57,* 1076-1080.

Garcia, A. W., & King, A. C. (1991). Predicting long-term adherence to aerobic exercise: A comparison of two models. *American Journal of Cardiology, 51*, 394-410.

Heiby, E. M., Onorato, V. A., & Sato, R. A. (1987). Cross-validation of the self-motivation inventory. *Journal of Sport Psychology, 9*, 394-399.

Kaplan, R. M., Atkins, C. J., & Reinsch, S. (1984). Specific efficacy expectations mediate exercise compliance in patients with COPD. *Health Psychology, 3*, 223-242.

McArdle, J. J. (1986). Dynamic but structural equation modeling of repeated measures data. In J. R. Nesselroade & R. B. Cattel (Eds.), *Handbook of multivariate experimental psychology* (2nd ed.). New York: Plenum.

McAuley, E. (1991). Efficacy, attributional, and affective responses to exercise participation. *Journal of Sport and Exercise Psychology, 13*, 382-393.

McAuley, E. (1992a). Understanding exercise behavior: A self-efficacy perspective. In G. C. Roberts (Ed.), *Motivation in sport and exercise* (pp. 107-128). Champaign, IL: Human Kinetics.

McAuley, E. (1992b). The role of efficacy cognitions in the prediction of exercise behavior in middle-aged adults. *Journal of Behavioral Medicine, 15*, 65-88.

McAuley, E. (1993). Self-efficacy and the maintenance of exercise participation in older adults. *Journal of Behavioral Medicine, 16*, 103-113.

McAuley, E. (in press). Physical activity and psychosocial outcomes. In C. Bouchard, T. Stephens, & R. Shephard (Eds.), *Physical activity, fitness, and health.* Champaign, IL: Human Kinetics.

McAuley, E., & Courneya, K. S. (1993). Adherence to exercise and physical activity as health-promoting behaviors: Attitudinal and self-efficacy influences. *Applied and Preventive Psychology, 3*, 65-77.

McAuley, E., & Courneya, K. S. (1992). Self-efficacy relationships with affective and exertion responses to exercise. *Journal of Applied Social Psychology, 22*, 312-326.

McAuley, E., Courneya, K. S., & Lettunich, J. (1991). Effects of acute and long-term exercise on self-efficacy responses in sedentary, middle-aged males and females. *The Gerontologist, 31*, 534-542.

McAuley, E., & Jacobson, L. (1991). Self-efficacy and exercise participation in sedentary adult females. *American Journal of Health Promotion, 5*, 185-191, 207.

McAuley, E., Poag, K., Gleason, A., & Wraith, S. (1990). Attrition from exercise programs: Attributional and affective perspectives. *Journal of Social Behavior and Personality, 5*, 591-602.

O'Leary, A. (1985). Self-efficacy and health. *Behavior and Research Therapy, 23*, 437-451.

Petruzzello, S. J., Landers, D. M., Hatfield, B. D., Kubitz, K. A., & Salazar, W. (1991). A meta-analysis on the anxiety-reducing effects of acute and chronic exercise. *Sports Medicine, 11*, 143-182.

Plante, T. G., & Rodin, J. (1990). Physical fitness and enhanced psychological health. *Current Psychology: Research and Reviews, 9*, 3-24.

Ramlow, J., Kriska, A., & LaPorte, R. A. (1987). Physical activity in the population: The epidemiologic spectrum. *Research Quarterly for Exercise and Sport, 58*, 111-114.

Sallis, J. F., Haskell, W. L., Fortnam, S. P., Vranizan, M. S., Taylor, C. B., & Solomon, D. S. (1986). Predictors of adoption and maintenance of physical activity in a community sample. *Preventive Medicine, 15*, 331-341.

Sallis, J. F., & Hovell, M. F. (1990). Determinants of exercise behavior. *Exercise and Sport Science Reviews, 18*, 307-330.

Sallis, J. F., Priski, R. B., Grossman, R. M., Patterson, T. L., & Nader, P. R. (1988). The development of self-efficacy scales for health related diet and exercise behaviors. *Health Education Research, 3,* 283-292.

Sonstroem, R. J. (1988). Psychological models. In R. K. Dishman (Ed.), *Exercise adherence.* Champaign, IL: Human Kinetics.

Taylor, C. B., Bandura, A., Ewart, C. K., Miller, N. H., & DeBusk, R. T. (1985). Exercise testing to enhance wives' confidence in their husbands' cardiac capabilities soon after clinically uncomplicated acute myocardial infarction. *American Journal of Cardiology, 55,* 635-638.

U.S. Department of Health and Human Services. (1980). *Promoting health and preventing disease.* Washington, DC: Public Health Services, National Institutes of Health.

U.S. Department of Health and Human Services. (1990). *Healthy people 2000: National health promotion and disease prevention objectives.* Washington, DC: Government Printing Office.

Wankel, L. M. (1985). Personal and situational factors affecting exercise involvement: The importance of enjoyment. *Research Quarterly, 56,* 275-282.

Weber, J., & Wertheim, E. H. (1989). Relationships of self-monitoring, special attention, body fat percent, and self-motivation to attendance at a community gymnasium. *Journal of Sport and Exercise Psychology, 11,* 105-114.

PART IV

Programs and Provisions

As stated previously, this is not intended to be a "how-to" book. The previous part illustrated the variety of kinds of activity that older persons may find attractive and stimulating. In this part a critical set of issues will be addressed followed by analyses of two settings for activity: the long-term care facility and retirement communities. The previous chapters provide a context for approaching particular settings and provisions. A summary of some of the implications follows:

1. Most older persons are not sitting around with nothing to do. Most report being busy and short on time. Their routines of ordinary activity, while not spectacular, usually fill the day and evening.

2. Those most satisfied with their lives, however, are most often involved in activity outside the home that provides regular challenge and engagement with other persons.

3. Such activity, for the most part, does not take place in age-segregated settings or programs. A relatively small percentage of older persons engage regularly in such special activities.

4. Most common is a pattern of continuity with activity that has proved satisfying earlier in the life course. Continuity is demonstrated in self-definitions, styles of behavior, developed skills, relationships with family and friends, and other life investments.

5. As a consequence, programs most likely to attract older persons build on familiarity, established competencies and self-images, communities of interaction, and previous histories of satisfaction.

6. If older persons are to make time for regular and demanding activity in their schedules and routines, they will be attracted by quality.

Most older persons are not sitting around waiting for just anything to do. Images of quality leadership, settings, and resources will tend to attract participants. Programs that will attract older persons who see themselves as relatively busy should be in locales and environments associated with high quality rather than age-segregated centers with negative images.

7. Conversely, programs that require individuals to redefine themselves as "old" or in any way incompetent or inferior are less likely to be attractive. The "ageless self" retains values and self-images of ability and is not redefined by age alone. For the most part, age designation or limitation is both unnecessary and counterproductive in programming. Scheduling and access will tend to shape most constituencies without age-based labels.

8. As a consequence, the potential of activities to be attractive and gain participants is far more inclusive than any stereotypes of "old folks" will admit. Especially the "young old" are able to engage in challenging activity with relatively high levels of skill. It is just such activity that builds community and a sense of worth.

One problem with this approach is that it focuses on the able, those with adequate resources, health, finances, and a network of others with whom to share life. It further presupposes that they have histories of activity investment in which they have gained competence and found satisfaction. They may experience limitations but for the most part are able to develop life patterns with both coherence and diversity. The "good news" approach to aging, partly based on improving financial and health circumstances for a majority, threatens to obscure the realities of life for a significant portion of older adults. There are problems with health policy and access to adequate care. There are problems with long-term care quality and cost. There are problems with those who are socially isolated and cut off from many channels to resources most take for granted. There remain problems of gender in which the current and past circumstances of women are truncated by gender roles and outright economic discrimination.

In Chapter 15 Val Freysinger addresses this enormous and complex issue of inequality and inequity. Some research has taken an accepting functional perspective and begun to identify "differences" by race, gender, and social class. Other research has been more critical in its premises and has found differences that reflect fundamental repression in the social system. In either case, it is evident that sizable proportions of the older population of the United States have "lived conditions" that are far more limited than others take for granted. Further, those limitations are cumulative through the life course and may be based on arbitrary social identification by race, ethnicity, language, gender, sexual orientation, or socioeconomic class. This remains a society with considerable structural discrimination that follows individuals from birth to death. Even what we are taught to enjoy in alleged "free-time activity" varies in access to opportunity and sex role socialization. No emphasis on the relative satisfaction of most older adults should mask the real heterogeneity of life conditions. The "OK world" of the majority is far from universal, not by accident but by political and social policy. It is an issue of relative power to control resources and of self-determination. There is a dialectic between the consequences of socialization and the differential contexts of social structure.

The complexity of this issue requires selection in any single chapter or book. The examples here, however, are not trivial. Gender has had impacts on physical activity for women with consequences for health, self-definitions of competence, safety, and body images. Women do not enter later life with the same histories of opportunity and resources as men. Race remains fundamental to access to opportunity, social interaction settings, and social identities. Histories of racism and denial of access as well as economic exclusion continue to have significance in all aspects of life including later life activity. Social class indexed by economic opportunity and reward determines both work conditions and market opportunity. All sorts of settings and opportunities for leisure activity are provided by upscale markets for the wealthy and near-wealthy. Little is available for the poor. In between, mass leisure can be rented or purchased by the middle mass of wage workers, mostly in services, who are replacing the old white-collar and blue-collar middle and working classes. In fact, market saturation of upscale recreation-based retirement communities has led to a number of bankruptcies in areas where the middle mass and poor have lost former access to water and land. The chapter outlines how race, gender, and class are more than variables in a survey; they are the conditions that open and close options in the lives of real people negotiating their later lives.

Longer life has more implications than just health improvements. One, of course, is that the number of persons in long-term care institutions is expected to grow as the proportionately fastest-growing segment of the population are those 85 and over. Judith Voelkl, in Chapter 16, analyzes the activity possibilities of those whose frailty has led to a loss of independence in living conditions. The frail, especially those in institutions, are limited in both ability and environment. Yet, activity remains important to the quality of life. There are still possibilities of challenge to ability that are the basis for involvement, self-images of worth, and communities of action. Crucial in care settings is the fostering of communication among residents. Activity may provide the major stimulus to communicative exchange, too often rare in institutions. Activity, broadly defined, may be a primary basis for viable adaptation to an institutional environment and to developing a sense of community there. No activity program, however, can overcome the impact of the total environment of a long-term care institution.

Gordon Streib exercises his knowledge of both activity patterns and community development in Chapter 17. As individuals have a life cycle, so do recreation-based retirement communities. They begin by being "leisure oriented" in design, ethos, and marketing. They draw residents who expect to be relatively active. The importance of both access to resources and social expectations is demonstrated by newcomers in such communities. Like any cohort, however, they age. Their abilities and intimate relationships are changed by health decrements and by death. Activity patterns, predominantly social to begin with, have to be revised when companions are lost. Physical, mental, and communicative abilities may decline decrementally or in abrupt trauma. The ability to make new friends may be limited as well by the loss of some skills required for familiar activity. The community itself then changes as the early settlers age in their new place. The leisure-based identities acquired on arrival may be altered through the years. In a parallel process, there is restriction and constriction in the activity patterns of the community and its residents. The community, however, gains some continuity through the replenishing process as frail residents are replaced by a new cohort of settlers.

This part of the book reminds us of limits that occur and recur in the opportunities and abilities of older adults. There is more here than simply a concern for the 20% to 30% who lack adequate financial resources for viable aging in a market-dominated society. We come to later life with continuities that are woven together into sets of values, skills, interests, fears, relationships, and resources that are cumulative through the life course and into old age. Activity is more than just doing things (despite the initial definition). Activity engages and expresses the self in social context. Activity is who we are as well as what we do. It is who we have become and are becoming as well as a set of time allocations. And it is all that has happened in a society that allocates resources and opportunities in every institutional context by arbitrary criteria that include race, ethnicity, gender, and economic placement.

15

The Community, Programs, and Opportunities

Population Diversity

VALERIA J. FREYSINGER

When I do not see plurality stressed in the very structure of a theory, I know that I will have to do lots of acrobatics—of the contortionist and the walk-on-the-tightrope kind—to have this theory speak to me without allowing the theory to distort me in my complexity.
—Maria Lugones (spoken in September 1988)

Research has documented the important role of leisure activity involvement to older adults' psychological and physical well-being. Specifically, this research has shown that activity participation in later life is related to life satisfaction (Dorfman & Moffett, 1987; Kelly, Steinkamp, & Kelly, 1986; Palmore, 1979; Riddick & Daniel, 1984; Russell, 1987), mental health and well-being (George, 1978; Gordon & Gaitz, 1976; Lawton, Moss, & Fulcomer, 1986-1987; Markides & Lee, 1990; Russell, 1990), morale (Freysinger, Alessio, & Mehdizadeh, 1990; Larson, 1978; Lawton, 1985; Teaff, 1992), and self-confidence (Freysinger & Nevius, 1992). In other words, leisure involvement is indicative of the quality of life experienced by the individual and provided by the society of which she or he is a part (Allison & Smith, 1990; Neulinger, 1982). Particularly in later life, when participation in required activity and social roles is changing, opportunity for involvement in informal, social, or leisure activity is deemed important (Allen & Chin-Sang, 1990; Atchley, 1989; Havighurst, 1961). Research suggests that it is the quality, not the quantity, of leisure activity participation that is important to well-being (Larson, Zuzanek, & Mannell, 1985; Lemon, Bengston, & Peterson, 1972; Russell, 1987) and a number of explanations for the positive relationship between these factors have been offered.

Activity theory posits that the social interaction that accompanies activity involvement is the reason well-being is enhanced (Lemon et al., 1972; Longino & Kart, 1982). Based on her analysis of the 1978 Quality of American Life data, Ritchey (1990), however, questions this and contends that social comparison theory may provide a framework for understanding the relationship between activity and well-being. According to this theory, individuals gain a positive or negative sense of themselves through interacting with others who serve as a source of comparison. Leisure activity is a context for social interaction and hence social comparison. Another theory providing an explanation of the activity-well-being link is the attribution theory of aging (Iso-Ahola, MacNeil, & Szymanski, 1977). This theory posits that satisfaction with life in old age is related to individuals' perceptions of personal causation and personal control. Feelings of personal adequacy and competence provide the older individual with the ability to meet or adapt to the demands of later life. Leisure is believed to be a context where such feelings are fostered (Baltes, Wahl, & Schmid-Furstoss, 1990; Mobily, Lemki, & Gisin, 1991; Sneegas, 1986). An integration of these theories is suggested by the research of Kelly et al. (1986). In their study of 400 adults 40 years of age and older, they found engagement in meaningful leisure activity to be both a context for primary relationships (a sense of connectedness and community) and a source of meaning and worth (a sense of purpose and competence). Research also suggests that activity involvement may be indicative of an individual's level of physical and mental functioning or health (though whether an active life leads to increased longevity has been questioned—see Lee & Markides, 1990). Indeed, an interactive relationship may well exist, with better health allowing activity involvement and activity involvement enhancing the older adult's health and sense of well-being.

Given the relationship between leisure activity involvement and well-being in later life, it seems important that older adults are not impeded from, but indeed are supported in, their activity involvement. The major premise of this chapter is that, in a stratified social system such as that which exists in the United States and Western societies generally, opportunities and resources (i.e., time, money, health, skills, and knowledge) for leisure activity systematically vary. While age itself is a factor differentiating the distribution of societal resources, gender, race, and class are also factors that are believed to distinguish leisure provisions and resources in later life. It is necessary to understand just how and why such factors mediate access to and engagement in leisure so that programs and policies facilitative of leisure interests and motivations can be developed.

This chapter focuses on these issues. What is known about the relationship of gender, race, and class to opportunities for leisure in later life is critically examined and issues for future research are proposed. Underlying this discussion is the assumption that the experience of aging and leisure is a political issue and the significance of this is discussed first.

The Politics of Age Heterogeneity and Leisure Opportunity

Despite persistent stereotyping and generalization, the heterogeneity of the older adult population has long been a topic of research and discussion. Life span and life course theorists have characterized aging or development as a process not only of increasing intraindividual but of interindividual differentiation (Nelson & Dannefer, 1992). Maddox (1987) has noted that heterogeneity can be seen in the pursuit of well-being and in a wide range of social, behavioral, and biological processes of aging. Drawing from the work of Pollak (1948), Maddox suggests that age might better be seen as a dependent variable. That is, "the social meaning of age which is relevant to our understanding of the life course is not determined solely by biological processes indexed by chronological age" (p. 561). Specifically, indicators of social status (such as occupation, income, and level of education), because of their relationship to the allocation of societal resources, predict not only mental and physical health but also cognitive functioning, patterns of social and activity involvement, retirement decisions and options—that is, the experience of old age (George, 1978; Lawton, 1985; Maddox, 1987; Markides & Lee, 1990; Palmore, Nowlin, & Wang, 1985). And social status factors in Western societies are stratified by age, gender, race, and/or class (Dressel, 1986; J. S. Jackson, 1988; Minkler & Stone, 1985; Rodeheaver & Datan, 1988; Taylor & Chatters, 1988; Thomas & Hughes, 1986). Based on their research on the retirement experience of elderly Mexican Americans, Zsembik and Singer (1990) indeed concluded that there is a need "not just for a reconceptualization of retirement and working life, but also for a reconceptualization of the later years of the life cycle. This research should directly confront the issues of race, ethnicity, gender, and social class to highlight the often overlooked diversity among older persons in the U.S." (p. 757). Further, heterogeneity must be explored not only among the recognized subgroups of elderly (i.e., different ethnic/racial, class, and gender groups) but within these subgroups as well (J. J. Jackson, 1988; Ralston & Griggs, 1985).

Similarly, leisure is a political issue. That is, what individuals are allowed to pursue for leisure and what they are able to pursue given their time, money, skills, and opportunities is an issue of power; and power is dependent on one's age, gender, race, and class. Further, power and privilege are perpetuated and contested in leisure; that is, not only are notions of age, gender, race, and class produced and reproduced in leisure, such notions are challenged and resisted as well (Clarke & Critcher, 1985; Freysinger & Flannery, 1992; Wearing, 1990; J. Wilson, 1988). Indeed, the intersection of these factors is critical to any understanding of health, well-being, and leisure opportunity and resources in later life.

Finally, scholars of gender, race, and class are increasingly pointing to how the complex factors of gender, race, and class are interlocked with one another in the United States (Dressel, 1991; Spelman, 1988). That is, gender issues are not simply parallel to, but intertwined with, race and class issues. Gender, race, and class are not variables of identity independent of one another. What it means to be a woman or man depends not only on one's ethnicity or race but also on one's class. Similarly, it may be argued that age is not an aspect of identity separate from gender, race, and class. Hence what it means to be an older person and the access one does or does not have to resources and opportunities for leisure will depend on such factors.

Most research treats these factors discretely, however, assuming that, by holding them constant or "controlling for" them, they have no effect. As Spelman (1988) points out,

> To talk about gender differences where race and class are constants is to talk about gender differences in the context of race and class similarity; but far from freeing us from the context of race and class, keeping them constant means they are constantly there. The same point applies when we are talking about race or class differences where gender is the same. (p. 104)

The vast majority of both gerontological and leisure research on gender differences in activity participation has used Euro-American or unidentified ethnic/racial samples. Similarly, much research on the activity participation of ethnic/racial minority elderly has not addressed the intersection of gender and race. In her discussion of aging black women, Jacqueline J. Jackson (1988) notes that

> the characterization of older black women in the literature and by aging organizations reveals the problem of "artificial dissection" of black women, as if they sometimes are black and sometimes female, but not simultaneously so. [Yet] black women are a group which, unlike black men and white women, has been simultaneously affected by both racism and sexism. (p. 33)

Indeed, the research of Allen and Chin-Sang (1990) on the meaning of leisure for aging black women offers support for this contention. Hence the literature on the impact of gender, race, and class on leisure opportunity and resources should be read and interpreted with these caveats in mind.

Gender

Research indicates that the activities of the majority of older women and men are quite ordinary (Kelly & Westcott, 1991). Further, research suggests that those older adults who have maintained an active and diverse leisure life-style (and have relative health and wealth), may be among the least constrained subgroups of the population (E. L. Jackson, 1990). Research also indicates that, while meanings of leisure are consistent across gender (Donald & Havighurst, 1959; Shaw, 1985), women and men differ in leisure time, participation, and interests. For example, research has shown that, in general, women have less leisure time than men. This is particularly true for women who are employed outside the home and married and/or have children living at home (Deem, 1982; Henderson, Bialeschki, Shaw, & Freysinger, 1989). As for the later years of life, some have found that women, more than men, perceive increased freedom and free time (Harris, Begay, & Page, 1989). Others, however, contend that, if a woman is married in later life, domestic and family responsibilities continue to dominate, structuring a woman's day and leisure involvements and limiting her time for self (Mason, 1987; McGuire, 1982). Indeed, in a study of barriers to leisure and family stage, Witt and Goodale (1981) found that the barrier "limitation of family's and friends' expectations" increased in prevalence over family stage (i.e., the older the children). For men, these expectations were of a much lower order and more constant. Further, while both men and women showed an increase in the barrier "feelings of daily stress," men's feelings of increased stress over time appeared to have less to do with family expectations than was the case for women. This is quite similar to the results of a study reported 20 years earlier; Havighurst (1961), in the Kansas City Study of Adult Life, found women's leisure, to "fit in" with their housework but was seldom seen as a relief or contrast from work. Men, on the other hand, indicated their leisure was used as either a relief from or contrast to work or that it had no relation to it.

Quite a bit of research has been conducted comparing the activity participation of older women and men. Because of their mandate to serve the entire older adult population and underserved groups in particular, a number of recent studies have focused on involvement in senior citizen centers. This research reveals that, while the overall rate of participation in senior citizen centers is low (Kelly & Reis, 1991), women have higher rates of participation than men (Krout, Cutler, & Coward, 1990); this is so despite the fact that wives are more likely to support and encourage their husbands' involvement in such activity than are husbands their wives' activity (Ralston & Griggs, 1985). Other research has found tremendous variance among senior centers in attendance and participation and suggests that participant characteristics are influenced by the variability of senior centers themselves (Ralston, 1991a). Still, women in general tend to have higher rates of participation in formal or organized programs, though this involvement is mediated by health and class (George, 1978; Havighurst, 1961) and the type of program (Fischer, Mueller, & Cooper, 1991). According to Deem (1982), women's engagement in voluntary, church, and other organized programs does not just reflect women's "charitable nature." It is also a reflection of the fact that involvement in such organizations is an accepted leisure pursuit for females. Further, personal safety is typically not a concern in such settings (Henderson et al., 1989; Mason, 1987).

Research has found that, when marital status is controlled, the time spent alone by older women and men does not differ (Larson et al., 1985). Research has also found that the leisure of both women and men is increasingly family and home centered with advancing age and that older women participate more in social interaction with family and friends than men do (Gordon & Gaitz, 1976; Kelly et al., 1986; Mac-Neil, Teague, McGuire, & O'Leary, 1986; Mason, 1987). Again, researchers contend that gender differences in such activity are consistent with sex role expectations and reflect both socialization and lifelong patterns of opportunity (Deem, 1982; Henderson et al., 1989; McGuire, 1982).

Similar explanations are offered for the gender difference found in involvement in physical activity, sport, and outdoor recreation. While, in general, participation in such activity is lowest in old age (Kaplan, 1986; Kelly et al., 1986; MacPherson, 1984; McGuire, O'Leary, Mihalik, & Dottavio, 1985), across history, as well as the life span, women have been found to have lower levels of physical activity and outdoor recreation involvement than men (Freysinger, 1990; Henderson et al., 1989; Unkel, 1981). For example, in their study of 1,441 persons 20 years of age and older, Gordon and Gaitz (1976) found that older men had higher levels of involvement in external, high-intensity activity (e.g., sport, physical activity, and exercise) while older women were more involved in internal, low-intensity activity (e.g., watching TV, visiting friends, reading). Kelly et al. (1986) in their study of 400 adults aged 40 and older also report higher levels of involvement of men in exercise, sport, and outdoor recreation, at least until advanced old age (i.e., 75 years or older). And in a review of the research on participation in outdoor recreation and sport, Smith (1980) also documented gender differences and concluded that such differences were more a matter of normative expectations than of physical differences between women and men.

Race/Ethnicity

Relatively little research has investigated the activity participation of ethnic/racial minority aged. Ralston (1991b) has recently noted the paucity of research and stated that this situation exists despite the fact that "demographic trends show that the number of minority elderly is growing at a faster rate than white elderly . . . by 2025, it is projected that 15% of the older population will be nonwhite" (p. 325).

The research that does exist tends to be comparative; that is, ethnic/racial minority aged are compared with older adults from the dominant culture (nonminority whites or Euro-Americans). Woodard (1988) contends that there are at least two related problems with such comparative research. First, the "unique social order" of the minority group is lost or ignored. Second, such research tends to view the behavior of the dominant culture as the norm and any differences exhibited by the minority group are seen as deviant or in some way abnormal or pathological.

The extent to which, as well as how and why, ethnicity/race affects the activity participation of older adults has been the topic of much discussion. According to Barresi (1987), the extent to which race and ethnicity affect the experience of aging depends upon the ethnic/racial group's assimilation into the "host culture." This is consistent with one of the dominant explanations of ethnic/racial differences in leisure behavior—the ethnicity perspective. According to this perspective, "leisure is an integral reflection of culture" (Washburne, 1978, p. 177). Leisure patterns are based on subcultural styles. Differences in participation patterns are attributed to subcultural variations in norms, values, and expectations (Allison, 1988). Washburne (1978) contends that this perspective challenges two traditional assumptions about African Americans in particular in the United States: (a) that African Americans do not possess a true and distinct culture and (b) that African Americans' assimilation into a mass "omniculture" is an inevitable and desirable societal goal. At the same time, this perspective has been criticized for lumping ethnic/racial groups together and assuming a shared set of subcultural norms and values without consideration of the variety of factors (e.g., age, nativity, class, gender, acculturation) that influence one's cultural identification and activity participation (Antunes & Gaitz, 1972; Newton, 1980). For example, in their study of the outdoor recreation preferences and constraints of Euro- and African-American elderly, McGuire, O'Leary, Alexander, and Dottavio (1987) found few significant differences. They concluded that "the presumption of homogeneity in individuals sharing one trait, such as race, is not a valid one when designing programs and services" (p. 103).

There is some research, specifically on the activity participation of older adults, that supports the ethnicity perspective. For example, examinations of senior center participation suggest that older adults' perception of congruence between their cultural identity and that provided for and exhibited by the center—in terms of staffing, programs/activities, or members—is a factor influencing involvement (Allison & Smith, 1990; Ralston, 1984; Ralston & Griggs, 1985; Yearwood & Dressel, 1983; Yeatts, Crow, & Folts, 1992). Further, while organized activity programs such as those provided by senior centers and church have been identified as important contexts for social and recreational activity participation for ethnic/racial minority elderly, it has been suggested that such settings may also be exploitive of these individuals (Allen & Chin-Sang, 1990; Grant, 1982; Ralston, 1991b).

Another common explanation of racial differences in leisure behavior—the economic marginality perspective—has also been supported. According to this perspective, differences in the leisure activities of various ethnic/racial groups are a function of differences in the experience of poverty and/or discrimination. Participation is a function of economic resources and the various consequences of socioeconomic discrimination, including a lack of opportunity (Allison, 1988; Washburne, 1978; Woodard, 1988). The criticism of this perspective is that lack of variation in the economic resources of ethnic/racial minority groups is often assumed.

Several studies have been conducted to examine the effect of income, education, or occupation (social class) on leisure within and between racial groups. Brown and Tedrick (1991) used the 1988 Nationwide Recreation Survey to compare the outdoor leisure involvements of older black and white Americans. They found that overall older blacks had significantly lower rates of participation in 31 outdoor activities than older whites. Older black females had the lowest involvement in any group and participation among blacks in general was negatively related to income and education. Other research examining the outdoor recreation activities of African and Euro-Americans suggest that the barriers perceived vary by race and that socioeconomic factors underlie these differences (Allison, 1988; McDonald & Hutchinson, 1986).

The economic marginality perspective has also been tested in research on senior center participation. In a study of center participation among black elderly, Ralston and Griggs (1985) found that, in contrast to white senior center participants who tend to be blue collar in background, older blacks who were female and had white-collar backgrounds were more likely to attend such centers. This may be a reflection of the tendency senior centers have traditionally had not to target groups such as minority, low-income elderly in an effort to maintain their clientele (Ralston, 1991b).

Gibson (1988) presents a number of limitations of minority aging research, including the type of data analyses that are conducted and the data interpretations offered. Gibson contends that too little attention has been given to the concomitants of multiple causation. The ethnicity and economic marginality perspectives are one example. Gibson notes that few researchers have attempted to separate the effects that are due to race or minority group membership from those that are due to class. Those studies that have examined this interaction suggest that it is important. For example, in their study of race, sex, and socioeconomic status differences in senior center use, Ralston and Griggs (1985) found that white-collar black women differed from other subgroupings in the study on a number of factors, including commitment to become involved in a senior center and social support for such involvement. Antunes and Gaitz (1972), in an examination of the ethnicity and marginality hypotheses, compared the political and social participation of Mexican Americans, blacks, and whites. They found that ethnicity accounted for more variance in these three groups' level of activity participation than either socioeconomic status or age. Ethnicity, socioeconomic status, and age showed different interactions among the three groups, however, leading Antunes and Gaitz to conclude that the concept of ethnicity must be further explored. In addition, research suggests that different variables explain participation in different activities and multiple variables must be combined for a complete explanation of participation in specific activities (Kelly, 1989; Woodard, 1988).

Other omissions from analyses, according to Gibson (1988), are structural factors, such as discrimination, that may well be central to individual interest in, as well as community opportunities for, activity participation (see also Yeatts et al., 1992). Again, there is some research available supporting the importance of this factor. In his study of the leisure of African Americans living in Chicago, Woodard (1988) found that fear of prejudice was positively related to respondents' participation in home and neighborhood-based activities. Whether or not fear of racism is particularly relevant to current cohorts of older African Americans who were raised in the pre-civil rights United States is not known. What is known is that there is much continuity in leisure activity participation across the life span and that older African Americans today were legally, directly and indirectly, denied many opportunities to develop leisure interests and skills.

Further, much research on racial/ethnic minority elderly treats all minority groups as the same, inferring the characteristics of one minority group to another or the characteristics of some members of a minority group to all members of the group (Gibson, 1988; J. J. Jackson, 1988; Ralston, 1991b). Again, the literature has documented the diversity of ethnic identification within any given racial group (Ego & Shiramizu, 1992; J. J. Jackson, 1988). As noted by Kelly (1989), "Leisure, like all domains of life, is thoroughly ethnic, *in* and *of* particular cultures" (p. 103). While older adults have old age in common, they differ on ethnicity/race, social class, and a variety of other factors that structure their life opportunities.

Social Class

As noted above, social class mediates the impact of gender and race on activity resources and opportunities in old age just as it does at any other point in the life span. In fact, W. J. Wilson (1980) has argued that, with the growth of white-collar employment and the passing and enforcement of affirmative action measures, life chances (access to quality jobs, housing, recreational opportunities, and so on) are more a function of skills than of race. While such "deracialization" is the topic of much debate, the fact remains that older adults' social class (income, education, occupation, and power) does stratify their resources and opportunities (Cutler & Hendricks, 1990). Yet, class in the United States is an issue that many reject or want to ignore (DeMott, 1990; Ehrenreich, 1989). Still, research over the years indicates that leisure is not only affected by one's social class but that leisure is also a means of expressing or distinguishing one's social status or class (Cutler & Hendricks, 1990; Dawson, 1985; Noe, 1974; Wilensky, 1964).

The most obvious effect social class has on leisure is economic; individuals are more or less able to afford participation in different recreational activities. But class also is reflective of educational and occupational background and hence one's skills, abilities, interests, expectations, time, energy, opportunities, and associations (Dawson, 1985; Kelly, 1989). For example, in an investigation of the impact of race, sex, and class on use of senior centers, Ralston and Griggs (1984) found that only one obstacle—lack of interesting activities—showed a significant difference. White-collar respondents were more likely to perceive this as an obstacle to participation than blue collar. In general, working- and lower-middle-class whites have been found to dominate the current membership of senior citizen centers (Krout, Cutler, & Coward, 1990; Ralston, 1991). Yet, Tissue (1971) claimed that senior centers are middle class in orientation, impeding the participation of working- and lower-class individuals. The results of this study may be indicative of a change that has taken place in the membership of these centers or the tremendous variation in senior center characteristics and client populations (Kelly & Reis, 1991; Ralston, 1991a).

As has been noted previously, the effects of social class on activity participation will vary by activity (as well as a variety of other factors). In general it has been found that middle- and upper-middle-class individuals are more likely to be involved in a greater number and range of activities, specifically, cultural events, voluntary association membership, travel and interaction outside immediate neighborhoods, and sport and outdoor activities that require equipment, memberships, and extended investments of time (Kelly, 1989; Reitzes, Mutran, & Pope, 1991; Tissue, 1971). In the Kansas City Study of Adult Life, Donald and Havighurst (1959) found a number of significant relations between meanings of leisure and occupational status. For example, upper-middle-class individuals tended to stress achievement and benefits to society and lower-middle-class individuals, contact with friends. Havighurst (1961) concluded, however, that the context or form of activities are more closely related to social class than are the meanings.

According to Cutler and Hendricks (1990), with the availability of installment purchasing, distinctions in the leisure activities of upper- and lower-income groups may have blurred somewhat but differential preferences still exist. Indeed, some would argue that leisure is a realm of life in which class is increasingly expressed or displayed (Ehrenreich, 1989). A lack of consideration of ethnicity/race, gender, and age in most previous research, however, limits any conclusions made about social class and recreation participation in later adulthood.

Future Research

Throughout the discussion thus far, a number of issues raised by and limitations of existing research on the recreational opportunities of older adults have been presented. While any of these can be the basis of future research, three issues are highlighted.

1. Goodale and Witt (1990) state:

We have come to recognize that although the direct provision of services and facilities may help overcome some barriers for some people, the simple provision of more opportunities is usually not enough. The dynamics of participation or nonparticipation are complex, encompassing psychological, health-related, and other *personal* factors. Too, there are both philosophical and practical—social, political and economic—limitations to multiplying facilities and programs. (p. 422, emphasis added)

While personal factors certainly are important mediators of activity participation, the contention of this chapter is that social factors also influence activity participation and both personal and social factors have political meaning. In particular, gender, race, class, and age—personal factors that are socially constructed—stratify opportunities and resources for leisure.

For example, in studying the relationship of ethnicity and race to older adults' leisure participation, a sophisticated understanding of the concepts of ethnicity, race, and dominant and minority status is needed (J. J. Jackson, 1985). Thought must be given to how these concepts can be operationalized, particularly in survey research. It is not sufficient to treat race or ethnicity as categorical data. In a racist society, ethnicity and race have both personal and social/political meanings. Our research must reflect this awareness.

Further, a particularly glaring lack in the research on aging and recreational activity is research focusing on older Asian/Pacific Americans (Ego & Shiramizu, 1992) and Native Americans. In this literature review, not one study was found exploring the activities of these elderly. They are indeed neglected minority groups (Ralston, 1991b).

2. The assimilation of ethnic/racial minorities into the dominant culture as a goal or expectation is increasingly questioned and criticized today. For example, Allison (1988) contends that, while the concept of assimilation may convey the notion of the blending of two or more cultures, in reality the assumption is that the subordinate culture will adopt and blend into the majority because the beliefs, norms, and practices of the majority culture are valued. Further, a lack of willingness to assimilate is often interpreted as ungratefulness and recalcitrance on the part of the ethnic/racial minority. Research suggests, however, that cultural pluralism is not only a more accurate description of the population of the United States today but also of the outcome of interethnic contact (Allison, 1988; McDonald & Hutchinson, 1986).

Leisure and recreation activities are often promoted as a site for the expression, development, and celebration of cultural identity and the crossing and bridging of cultural differences. Research on the role of leisure in both creating and transcending ethnic/racial boundaries in later adulthood would enhance our understanding of leisure interests and constraints.

3. Explanations for gender relations and sex differences in leisure behavior and activity participation typically extend from one of two theories: what Connell (1985) identifies as sex role theory and power analysis. According to sex role theory, sex differences stem from socialization and stereotypes. Gender is a role we learn to enact. Individuals learn to be female or male by patterning themselves after existing same-sex role models (e.g., parents, teachers, figures in the media) and they do this because of social norms and sanctions. In principle, sex inequalities can be eliminated by taking measures to break down stereotypes and redefine the roles. This explanation has dominated and continues to dominate much of our understanding of gender differences and inequalities in leisure activity participation, particularly in later adulthood (e.g., Gordon & Gaitz, 1976; Havighurst, 1961; Kelly, 1983) when birth cohort is seen as a factor influencing the activity patterns of current generations of older women and men (Freysinger, 1990; Kelly et al., 1986).

The analysis of power is a more recent and increasingly frequent explanation of gender differences and inequalities in leisure activity participation. These analyses focus on the system and processes of patriarchy and the sexual domination of females by males (Connell, 1985). The economic, domestic, and political power men exercise over women is the starting point. Gender inequalities are discussed in terms of the sexual division of labor, vocabularies of gender derogation, the violence in male sexuality, or the structure and dynamics of capitalism. Gender differences in leisure behavior are attributed to the relationships of power and privilege that exist between women and men; to women's lack of power and privilege; to their subjugation to men, particularly in the functioning of home, family, and everyday life; and their lack of access to resources (time, money, training; e.g., Deem, 1982; Mason, 1987).

Because of weaknesses with both of these explanations, Connell (1985) suggests a third theory of gender—one that recognizes the nonstatic, complex, dialectic process of power and the extent to which gender relations are about the interweaving of personal lives and social structure, one that may be useful when exploring the leisure activities of older women and men. According to Connell, "There must be, first, a really thorough rejection of the notion that natural difference is a 'basis' of gender, that the social patterns are somehow an elaboration of natural difference. . . . Social gender relations do not express natural patterns: they negate the biological statute. . . . The social is radically un-natural, and its structure can never be deduced from natural struc- tures" (pp. 268-269). There must also be a rejection of the notion that all men have power over all women in all realms of life. While gender (and class and race) relations are constraining, they are constantly being worked on, "and—in ways pleasant and unpleasant—transformed" (p. 267). Recent research on women and leisure has begun to explore leisure not only as a site of the reproduction of gender relations but also as a site of resistance and empowerment (Freysinger & Flannery, 1992; Henderson & Bialeschki, 1991; Wearing, 1990). Similarly, leisure as a context of class struggles and the transformation of class relations has also been explored (Clarke & Critcher, 1985; Dawson, 1985; J. Wilson, 1988). Less attention has been given to race relations in the context of leisure, though the role of sport in reproducing and transforming images of race has been addressed (Messner & Sabo, 1990).

The later years of life have never been the focus of these studies, however. Missing is an examination of the intersection of gender, race, and class in later adulthood as well as an examination of leisure as a site of both oppression and resistance. Research has shown that what older adults do is not necessarily what they prefer to do (McGuire, 1985; Ralston, 1991a), that age and sex norms influence individuals' (including older adults') perceptions of appropriate activity (Ostrow & Dzewaltowski, 1986), and that gender, race, and class do distinguish both opportunities and resources for leisure in later life. What is now needed is an exploration of why this is so, based on an understanding (a) of the politics of age, gender, race, class, health, and leisure in the United States, (b) that age, gender, race, and class interact in the construction of human identity, and (c) that relations of power and privilege are fluid and hence constantly renegotiated and reimposed. Research on the organization of the practices (such as recreation and leisure) through which gender, race, and class relations are sustained and transformed in later adulthood would provide tremendous insight into the experience of aging and older adults' participation in leisure.

References

Allen, K. R., & Chin-Sang, V. (1990). A lifetime of work: The context and meanings of leisure for aging black women. *The Gerontologist, 30,* 734-740.

Allison, M. T. (1988). Breaking boundaries and barriers: Future directions in cross-cultural research. *Journal of Leisure Research, 10,* 247-259.

Allison, M. T., & Smith, S. (1990). Leisure and the quality of life: Issues facing racial and ethnic minority elderly. *Therapeutic Recreation Journal, 24,* 50-63.

Antunes, G., & Gaitz, C. M. (1972). Ethnicity and participation: A study of Mexican-Americans, blacks, and whites. *American Journal of Sociology, 80,* 1192-1211.

Atchley, R. (1989). A continuity theory of normal aging. *The Gerontologist, 29,* 183-189.

Baltes, M. M., Wahl, H. W., & Schmid-Furstoss, U. (1990). The daily life of elderly Germans: Activity patterns, personal control and functional health. *Journal of Gerontology, 45,* P173-P179.

Barresi, C. M. (1987). Ethnic aging and the life course. In D. E. Gelfand & C. M. Barresi (Eds.), *Ethnic dimensions of aging* (pp. 18-34). New York: Springer.

Brown, M. B., & Tedrick, T. (1991, October). *An identification of the outdoor leisure involvements of older black Americans.* Paper presented at the Leisure Research Symposium, Baltimore, MD.

Clarke, J., & Critcher, C. (1985). *The devil makes work: Leisure in capitalist Britain.* London: Macmillan.

Connell, R. W. (1985). Theorising gender. *Sociology, 19,* 260-272.

Cutler, S. J., & Hendricks, J. (1990). Leisure and time use across the life course. In R. Binstock & L. George (Eds.), *Handbook of aging the social sciences* (3rd ed., pp. 169-185). New York: Academic Press.

Dawson, D. (1985). On the analysis of class and leisure. *Society and Leisure, 8,* 563-572.

Deem, R. (1982). Women, leisure and inequality. *Leisure Studies, 1,* 29-46.

DeMott, B. (1990). *The imperial middle: Why Americans can't think straight about class.* New York: Morrow.

Donald, M. M., & Havighurst, R. J. (1959). The meanings of leisure. *Social Forces, 37,* 355-360.

Dorfman, L. T., & Moffett, M. M. (1987). Retirement satisfaction in married and widowed rural women. *The Gerontologist, 27,* 215-221.

Dressel, P. (1986). Civil rights, affirmative action, and the aged of the future: Will life chances be different for blacks, Hispanics, and women? An overview of the issues. *The Gerontologist, 26,* 128-131.

Dressel, P. (1991). Gender, race and class: Beyond the feminization of poverty in later life. In M. Minkler & C. L. Estes (Eds.), *Critical perspectives on aging: The political and moral economy of growing old* (pp. 245-252). Amityville, NY: Baywood.

Ego, M. M., & Shiramizu, B. (1992). Older Asian/Pacific Americans: Provision of responsive leisure programming and research paradigms. In *Proceedings from the Sandra Modisett Symposium on Aging and Leisure* (pp. 77-84). Reston, VA: AAHPERD.

Ehrenreich, B. (1989). *Fear of falling: The inner life of the middle class.* New York: Pantheon.

Fischer, L. R., Mueller, D. P., & Cooper, P. W. (1991). Older volunteers: A discussion of the Minnesota Senior Study. *The Gerontologist, 31,* 183-194.

Freysinger, V. J. (1990). A lifespan perspective on women and physical recreation. *Journal of Physical Education, Recreation and Dance, 61,* 48-51.

Freysinger, V. J., Alessio, H., & Mehdizadeh, S. (1990, November). *Change and sex differences in morale in later adulthood: A panel study.* Paper presented at the annual Scientific Meeting of the Gerontological Society of America, Boston.

Freysinger, V. J., & Flannery, D. (1992). Women and leisure: Empowerment and resistance. *Society and Leisure, 15,* 305-324.

Freysinger, V. J., & Nevius, C. (1992). Activity involvement and self confidence in later adulthood: A descriptive study. In *Proceedings of the Sandra A. Modisett Symposium on Aging and Leisure in the 1990s* (pp. 41-46). Reston, VA: AAHPERD.

George, L. K. (1978). The impact of personality and social status factors upon levels of activity and psychological well-being. *Journal of Gerontology, 33,* 840-847.

Gibson, R. C. (1988). Minority aging research: Opportunity and challenge. *The Gerontologist, 28,* 559-560.

Goodale, T. L., & Witt, P. A. (1990). Recreation nonparticipation and barriers to leisure. In E. L. Jackson & T. L. Burgon (Eds.), *Understanding leisure and recreation: Mapping the past and charting the future.* State College, PA: Venture.

Gordon, C., & Gaitz, C. M. (1976). Leisure and lives: Personal expressivity across the lifespan. In R. H. Binstock & E. Shanas (Eds.), *Handbook of aging and the social sciences* (pp. 310-341). New York: Van Nostrand Reinhold.

Grant, J. (1982). Black women and the church. In G. T. Hull, P. B. Scott, & B. Smith (Eds.), *Black women's studies* (pp. 141-152). Old Westbury, NY: Feminist Press.

Harris, M. B., Begay, C., & Page, P. (1989). Activities, family relationships, and feelings about aging in a multicultural elderly sample. *International Journal of Aging and Human Development, 29,* 103-117.

Havighurst, R. (1961). The nature and value of meaningful free time activity. In R. Kleemeier (Ed.), *Aging and leisure* (pp. 309-344). New York: Oxford University Press.

Henderson, K. A., & Bialeschki, M. D. (1991). A sense of entitlement to leisure as constraint and empowerment for women. *Leisure Sciences, 13,* 51-65.

Henderson, K. A., Bialeschki, M. D., Shaw, S., & Freysinger, V. J. (1989). *A leisure of one's own: A feminist analysis of women and leisure.* State College, PA: Venture.

Iso-Ahola, S. E., MacNeil, R., & Szymanski, D. (1977, October). *Social psychological foundations of therapeutic recreation: An attributional analysis.* Paper presented at the Leisure Research Symposium, Las Vegas, NV.

Jackson, E. L. (1990). Variations in the desire to begin a leisure activity: Evidence of antecedent constraints? *Journal of Leisure Research, 22,* 55-70.

Jackson, J. J. (1985). Race, national origin, ethnicity and aging. In R. H. Binstock & E. Shanas (Eds.), *Handbook of aging and the social sciences* (pp. 264-303). New York: Van Nostrand Reinhold.

Jackson, J. J. (1988). Aging black women and public policies. *The Black Scholar, 3,* 31-43.

Jackson, J. S. (Ed.). (1988). *The black American elderly: Research on physical and psychosocial health.* New York: Springer.

Kaplan, M. (1986). Elderly and outdoor recreation. In *The President's Commission on Americans Outdoors* (pp. D25-D32). Washington, DC: Government Printing Office.

Kelly, J. R. (1989). Leisure behaviors and styles: Social, economic and cultural factors. In E. L. Jackson & T. L. Burton (Eds.), *Understanding leisure and recreation* (pp. 89-111). State College, PA: Venture.

Kelly, J. R., & Reis, J. (1991). Identifying senior program participants. *Journal of Park and Recreation Administration, 9,* 55-64.

Kelly, J. R., Steinkamp, M., & Kelly, J. (1986). Later life leisure: How they play in Peoria. *The Gerontologist, 26,* 531-537.

Kelly, J. R., & Westcott, G. (1991). Ordinary retirement: Commonalities and continuity. *International Journal of Aging and Human Development, 32,* 81-89.

Krout, J. A., Cutler, S. J., & Coward, R. T. (1990). Correlates of senior center participation: A national analysis. *The Gerontologist, 30,* 72-79.

Larson, R. (1978). Thirty years of research on the subjective well-being of older adults. *Journal of Gerontology, 16,* 134-143.

Larson, R., Zuzanek, J., & Mannell, R. (1985). Being alone vs. being with people: Disengagement in the daily experience of older adults. *Journal of Gerontology, 40,* 375-381.

Lawton, M. P. (1985). Activities and leisure. In M. P. Lawton & G. Maddox (Eds.), *Annual review of gerontology and geriatrics* (Vol. 5, pp. 127-164). New York: Springer.

Lawton, M. P., Moss, M., & Fulcomer, M. (1986-1987). Objective and subjective uses of time by older people. *International Journal of Aging and Human Development, 24,* 171-188.

Lee, D. J., & Markides, K. S. (1990). Activity and mortality among aged persons over an eight-year period. *Journal of Gerontology, 45,* 539-542.

Lemon, B. W., Bengston, V., & Peterson, J. (1972). An exploration of the activity theory of aging. *Journal of Gerontology, 27,* 511-523.

Longino, C., & Kart, C. (1982). Explicating activity theory: A formal replication. *Journal of Gerontology, 37,* 713-722.

MacNeil, R. D., Teague, M. L., McGuire, F. A., & O'Leary, J. T. (1986). Aging and leisure: A literature synthesis. In *The President's Commission on Americans Outdoors* (pp. S103-S113). Washington, DC: Government Printing Office.

MacPherson, B. D. (1984). Sport participation across the life cycle: A review of the literature and suggestions for future research. *Sociology of Sport Journal, 1,* 213-220.

Maddox, G. L. (1987). Aging differently. *The Gerontologist, 27,* 557-564.

Markides, M. S., & Lee, D. J. (1990). Predictors of well-being and functioning in older Mexican-Americans and Anglos: An 8-year follow-up. *Journal of Gerontology, 45,* S69-S73.

Mason, J. (1981). No peace for the wicked: Older married women and leisure. In E. Wimbush & M. Talbot (Eds.), *Relative freedoms* (pp. 75-86). Philadelphia: Milton Keynes.

McDonald, J. M., & Hutchinson, I. J. (1986). Minority and ethnic variations in outdoor recreation participation: Trends and issues. In *The President's Commission on Americans Outdoors* (pp. S41-S51). Washington, DC: Government Printing Office.

McGuire, F. A. (1982). Leisure time, activities and meanings: A comparison of men and women in late life. In N. Osgood (Ed.), *Life after work* (pp. 132-147). New York: Praeger.

McGuire, F. A. (1985). Constraints in later life. In M. G. Wade (Ed.), *Constraints on leisure* (pp. 335-353). Springfield, IL: Charles C Thomas.

McGuire, F. A., O'Leary, J. R., Alexander, P. B., & Dottavio, F. D. (1987). A comparison of outdoor recreation preferences and constraints of black and white elderly. *Activities, Adaptation and Aging, 9,* 95-104.

McGuire, F. A., O'Leary, J. R., Mihalik, B. J., & Dottavio, F. D. (1985, October). *Sport involvement across the lifespan: Expansion and contraction of sports activities.* Paper presented at the Leisure Research Symposium, Dallas, TX.

Messner, M. A., & Sabo, D. F. (Eds.). (1990). *Sport, men and the gender order.* Champaign, IL: Human Kinetics.

Minkler, M., & Stone, R. (1985). The feminization of poverty and older women. *The Gerontologist, 25,* 351-357.

Mobily, K., Lemki, J. H., & Gisin, G. J. (1991). The idea of leisure repertoire. *Journal of Applied Gerontology, 10,* 208-223.

Nelson, E. A., & Dannefer, D. (1992). Aged heterogeneity: Fact or fiction? The fate of diversity in gerontological research. *The Gerontologist, 32,* 17-23.

Neulinger, J. (1982). Leisure lack and the quality of life: The broadening scope of the leisure professional. *Leisure Studies, 1,* 53-63.

Newton, F. C. R. (1980). Issues in research and service delivery among Mexican American elderly: A concise statement with recommendations. *The Gerontologist, 20,* 200-213.

Noe, F. P. (1974). Leisure lifestyles and social class: A trend analysis 1900-1960. *Sociology and Social Research, 58,* 286-295.

Ostrow, A. C., & Dzewaltowski, D. A. (1986). Older adults' perceptions of physical activity participation based on age-role and sex-role appropriateness. *Research Quarterly for Exercise and Sport, 57,* 167-169.

Palmore, E. B. (1979). Predictors of successful aging. *The Gerontologist, 19,* 427-431.

Palmore, E. B., Nowlin, J. B., & Wang, H. S. (1985). Predictors of function among the old-old: A 10-year follow-up. *The Gerontologist, 40,* 244-250.

Pollak, O. (1948). *Social adjustment in old age: A research planning report.* New York: Social Science Research Council.

Ralston, P. A. (1984). Senior center utilization by black elderly adults: Social, attitudinal and knowledge correlates. *Journal of Gerontology, 39,* 224-229.

Ralston, P. A. (1991a). Determinants of senior center attendance and participation. *Journal of Applied Gerontology, 10,* 258-273.

Ralston, P. A. (1991b). Senior centers and minority elders: A critical review. *The Gerontologist, 31,* 325-331.

Ralston, P. A., & Griggs, M. B. (1985). Factors affecting utilization of senior centers: Race, sex and socioeconomic status differences. *Journal of Gerontological Social Work, 9,* 99-111.

Reitzes, D. C., Mutran, E., & Pope, H. (1991). Location and well-being among retired men. *Journal of Gerontology, 46,* S195-S203.

Riddick, C., & Daniel, S. (1984). The relative contributions of leisure activity and other factors to the mental health of older women. *Journal of Leisure Research, 16,* 136-148.

Ritchey, L. H. (1990). *Activity theory: A test of mediating factors between activity and life satisfaction.* Unpublished manuscript, Scripps Gerontology Foundation, Miami University, Oxford, OH.

Rodeheaver, D., & Datan, N. (1988). The challenge of double jeopardy. *American Psychologist, 43,* 648-654.

Russell, R. (1987). The importance of recreation satisfaction and activity participation to the life satisfaction of age-segregated retirees. *Journal of Leisure Research, 19,* 273-283.

Russell, R. (1990). Recreation and quality of life in old age: A causal analysis. *Journal of Applied Gerontology, 9,* 77-89.

Shaw, S. M. (1985). The meaning of leisure in everyday life. *Leisure Sciences, 7,* 1-24.

Smith, D. H. (1980). Participation in outdoor recreation and sports. In D. H. Smith & J. Macauley (Eds.), *Participation in social and political activities* (pp. 177-201). San Francisco: Jossey-Bass.

Sneegas, J. J. (1986). Components of life satisfaction in middle and later life adults: Perceived social competence, leisure participation and leisure satisfaction. *Journal of Leisure Research, 18,* 148-158.

Spelman, E. V. (1988). *Inessential woman.* Boston: Beacon.

Taylor, R. J., & Chatters, L. M. (1988). Correlates of education, income and poverty among aged blacks. *The Gerontologist, 28,* 435-441.

Teaff, J. D. (1992). Leisure and psychological well-being among Mexican-American elderly. In *Proceedings of the Sandra Modisett Symposium on Aging and Leisure* (pp. 85-90). Reston, VA: AAHPERD.

Thomas, M., & Hughes, M. (1986). The continuing significance of race: A study of race, class and quality of life in America, 1972-1985. *American Sociological Review, 51,* 830-841.

Tissue, T. (1971). Social class and the senior citizen center. *The Gerontologist, 11,* 196-200.

Unkel, M. B. (1981). Physical recreation participation of females and males during the adult life cycle. *Leisure Sciences, 4,* 1-27.

Washburne, R. F. (1978). Black under-participation in wildland recreation: Alternative explanations. *Leisure Sciences, 1,* 175-189.

Wearing, B. (1990). Beyond the ideology of motherhood: Leisure as resistance. *Australian and New Zealand Journal of Sociology, 26,* 36-58.

Wilensky, H. (1964). Mass society and mass culture: Interdependence or independence? *American Sociological Review, 29,* 173-197.

Wilson, J. (1988). *Politics and leisure.* Winchester, MA: Allen & Unwin.

Wilson, W. J. (1980). *The declining significance of race: Blacks and changing American institutions.* Chicago: University of Chicago Press.

Witt, P. A., & Goodale, T. L. (1981). The relationship between barriers to leisure enjoyment and family stages. *Leisure Sciences, 4,* 29-49.

Woodard, M. D. (1988). Class, regionality and leisure among urban black Americans: The post-civil rights era. *Journal of Leisure Research, 20,* 87-105.

Yearwood, A. W., & Dressel, P. L. (1983). Interracial dynamics in a southern rural senior center. *The Gerontologist, 23,* 512-517.

Yeatts, D. E., Crow, T., & Folts, E. (1992). Service use among low-income minority elderly: Strategies for overcoming barriers. *The Gerontologist, 32,* 24-32.

Zsembik, B. A., & Singer, A. (1990). The problem of defining retirement among minorities: The Mexican Americans. *The Gerontologist, 30,* 749-757.

16

Activity Among Older Adults in Institutional Settings

JUDITH E. VOELKL

Little is known about the daily activity patterns of older adults residing in nursing homes. Many questions may be asked in regard to residents' activity involvement. For instance, what types of activities do residents engage in during their daily lives? With whom do residents spend their time? When the subjective aspects of daily experiences are considered in relation to the objective factors of residents' time use, the picture of daily life becomes exceedingly difficult to describe. It seems possible that residents are happiest when engaged in certain activities or when spending time with favored companions.

The nursing home environment, which has been depicted as being bound by rules and structured to control residents' time and interests, may strongly influence residents' activity involvement in day-to-day life (Goffman, 1961; Gubrium, 1974; Sommer & Osmond, 1960-1961). Residents of nursing homes are generally expected to follow a predetermined schedule that leaves little individuality in how they spend their time. In spite of the powerful shaping influence of the institutional environment, however, it appears that some residents still have positive experiences in certain freely chosen activities in the nursing home. For instance, Goffman observed that some residents became fully engrossed in "removal activities," which involved the perception of autonomy. A resident looking through a family photo album, who experiences involvement within that recollective time and space, is engaged in a removal activity. Another example is the resident who participates in a crafts group and loses track of time, lets go of the pressing worry of when her scheduled shower will occur, and becomes fully engrossed in a large block needlepoint project.

It seems imperative that we understand the activity involvement of older adults residing in nursing homes because the manner in which people spend their time has been found to be significantly related to well-being (Iso-Ahola, 1980; Lawton, 1985; Lewinsohn, 1976). Further, it seems important to understand the interactions between resident characteristics and aspects of the nursing home environment that may influence activity. For example, do residents who are able to create removal activities in their daily lives differ on variables of physical health, mental status, or perceived control from residents who are unable to create removal activities? How does the nursing home environment, in physical layout or staffing patterns, foster autonomous activity involvement as well as social interaction? The purpose of this chapter is to review the literature pertaining to the activity of older adults residing in institutional environments. Initially, the characteristics of nursing home residents and nursing home environments are presented. They are followed with a discussion of select models guiding inquiry into the activity involvement of nursing home residents and the empirical research stemming from these models. Finally, future directions for research are discussed.

Characteristics of Nursing Home
Residents and Facilities

Nursing Home Residents

According to the National Nursing Home Survey, approximately 1.5 million people resided in nursing homes in the United States in 1985 (National Center for Health Statistics, 1989). Of these residents, 88% were age 65 and older. Almost half of the residents were 85 years of age or older (45%) in comparison with the age groups encompassing the young old (65-74, 16%) and old (75-84, 39%). Further, a majority of the residents were found to be female (75%) and white (93%; Hing, 1987).

Functional abilities. The National Center for Health Statistics (1989) reported that most residents need assistance with activities of daily living: 89% of nursing home residents required assistance with bathing, 75% with dressing, 60% with transferring, 49% with toileting, and 39% with eating. In terms of assistive devices, 64% of the residents used eyeglasses and 6.5% used hearing aids (National Center for Health Statistics, 1989).

Of all residents, 85% received assistance with instrumental activities of daily living. More specifically, 75.3% needed assistance with the handling of money, 73.5% with care of their personal belongings, and 62.7% with using the telephone (National Center for Health Statistics, 1989).

Mental status/mental health. A number of studies report findings on the mental status and mental health of nursing home residents (Hyer & Blazer, 1982; National Center for Health Statistics, 1989; Rovner, Kafonek, Filipp, Lucas, & Folstein, 1986). Results from the National Nursing Home Survey of 1985 indicate that approximately 62% of the residents of nursing homes have memory impairments or problems with disorientation. In addition, 43.3% of the residents had the diagnosis of senile dementia or chronic organic brain syndrome. Rovner and his associates found that 74% of a random sample of 50 residents met the criteria of a DSM-IIIR diagnosis of primary degenerative dementia or multi-infarct dementia.

In terms of mental health, the National Center for Health Statistics (1989) reported that 65.8% of nursing home residents had a mental disorder, 41.8% had a mood disturbance, and 38.4% had behavioral problems. A number of gerontologists have indicated that there is a high prevalence of depression among nursing home residents (Hyer & Blazer, 1982; National Center for Health Statistics, 1989; Rovner et al., 1986). The National Center for Health Statistics (1989) reports that 13.8% of the 65.8% of residents identified as having a mental disorder met the criteria of a depressive disorder. Hyer and Blazer (1982) found that approximately 25% of 149 residents of nursing homes in North Carolina met the criteria for having a major affective disorder.

Nursing Home Facilities

The National Nursing Home Survey reported that there were 19,100 nursing homes in the United States as of 1985 (National Center for Health Statistics, 1989). According to federal standards (U.S. Congress, 1987), nursing home facilities must provide nursing services, pharmaceutical services, dietary services, activity services, and social services.

The 1985 National Nursing Home Survey (National Center for Health Statistics, 1989) found, however, that the number of staff employed in nursing homes varied greatly by discipline. For instance, for every 100 beds, there were .2 registered physical therapists, .6 social workers, and 1.2 activity directors.

Activity and Leisure Behavior

A number of models depicting the interaction between older adults and the environment have emerged from the environmental psychology and gerontology literature (Carp, 1987; Kahana, 1982; Lawton & Nahemow, 1973; Moos & Lemke, 1985). These models have been developed in an attempt to provide a theoretical understanding of older adults' behavior. In particular, it seems that the ecological model (Lawton & Nahemow, 1973), accompanied with empirical research, provides a basis for understanding the activity of older adults residing in nursing homes. In this section the ecological model will be presented, followed by research pertaining to the activity of nursing home residents. (For a comprehensive review of person-environment models, see Carp, 1987.)

The Ecological Model

The ecological model developed by Lawton and Nahemow (1973) indicates that the outcome of positive behavior and affect among older adults is dependent on the relationship between individuals' competence and the demands or press of the environment (see Figure 16.1). Functional abilities, cognitive abilities, and mental health indices are a few of the variables that may be examined in regard to competence. The "press of the environment" refers to social and physical environmental demands. The ecological model suggests that a delicate balance is needed between an older adult's capabilities and environmental demands for positive behavior and affect to result. A mild increase in environmental press may be challenging and demand an individual's attention (i.e., maximum performance potential). A mild decrease in environmental press may be experienced as comfortable and relaxing (i.e., maximum comfort).

The environmental docility hypothesis, a basic tenet of the model, suggests that the environment is seen as "a more potent determinant of

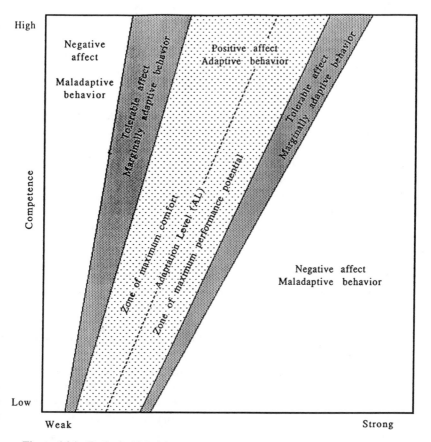

Figure 16.1. Ecological Model
SOURCE: Adapted from Lawton and Nahemow (1973).

behavioral outcomes as personal competence decreases" (Lawton, 1990, p. 639). Lawton has also proposed an environmental proactivity hypothesis, suggesting that, when an individual's competence is commensurate with the demands of the environment, "the variety of environmental resources that can be used in satisfaction of the person's needs increases" (Lawton, 1990, p. 639). An example of environmental proactivity may involve an older adult who has experienced physical decline moving into an assisted living facility that optimally facilitates autonomy and independence in daily activities. This supportive environment may allow the older adult to more readily use resources not only for necessary survival activities but also for freely chosen activities.

Lawton (1985) has identified several similarities between the ecological model and Csikszentmihalyi's (1975) model of optimal experiences. Optimal experiences, also called flow, emerge from moments when an individual perceives that his or her skills match the perceived challenges of the activity (Csikszentmihalyi, 1975, 1982, 1988). A sense of control over the environment, positive affect, a high level of concentration, and intrinsic motivation accompany the moments in daily life when challenges and skills match. Individuals seeking these optimal experiences develop their abilities to channel attention to the activity at hand.

Lawton (1985) has suggested that flow occurs within experiences falling at the outermost edge of the zones of maximum performance potential or maximum comfort. Based on Csikszentmihalyi's (1988, 1990) recent conceptualization of flow, which relates flow experiences to an individual's ability to focus his or her attention to the current task, it seems that flow may also stem from increased opportunity for adaptation-level experiences or when personal competence increases to promote environmental proactivity. When older adults find themselves in environments that provide optimal amounts of adaptation experiences—moments that are free from the distraction of negative environmental press—they may find increased time to focus their attention on activities in which they can become fully involved and experience flow.

Perhaps the most useful conceptualization of these models in relation to activity among older adults in nursing home environments is to consider the ecological model as placing an older adult in an environment that is responsive to his or her competence level and fosters "proactivity." This type of environment would provide a variety of resources that may foster activity choice and participation. An activity-rich environment may heighten a resident's ability to create and experience flow in daily life.

Empirical Findings

A number of empirical studies have been undertaken to examine the activity of older adults residing in nursing homes. A review of these studies will be presented in the following sections: (a) descriptive studies, (b) explanatory studies, and (c) intervention studies.

Descriptive Studies

Activity involvement. An early study by Gottesman and Bourestom (1974) systematically examined the activity involvement of 1,144 residents of nursing homes. The activity of each subject was observed at 24 random times over the course of 2 days. Residents were observed to spend 39% of their time in no observable activity, 17% in passive activity, 23% in personal care, and 20% watching television or socializing. Residents were in contact with another person only 17% of the time. Level of social activity was found to be positively related to level of independence in activities of daily living and mental status.

In a more recent study, Voelkl (1989) used the experience sampling method (ESM) to track the daily experiences of 12 older adults residing in nursing homes. The ESM involved each participant carrying an electronic paging device for 4 to 7 days and completing a self-report form regarding activity involvement, companionship, and subjective aspects of their immediate conscious experience when signaled. In terms of social interaction, the 307 self-reports indicated that residents were alone a majority of the time (62.8%), followed by time spent with other residents (16.3%), "others" (13.3%), and staff (7.6%). The reports also indicated that residents spent approximately 35% of their activity involvement engaged in passive activities, 20% in self-care, 12% watching television, 11% eating, and 22% engaged in independent activities (individual response bias was controlled for). Participants' highest level of affect was experienced while engaged in independent activities (i.e., socializing, crocheting, attending church groups, and so on). The lowest level of affect was experienced while eating.

The findings on activity involvement from these two studies were similar in time spent in independent activities and self-care (Gottesman & Bourestom, 1974; Voelkl, 1989). The findings differed in amount of time spent in passive or null activity, however. This may be due to the fact that all participants in Voelkl's study were alert and oriented, whereas Gottesman and Bourestom included residents who varied on mental status.

Social interactions. Although little is known about the quality of the social interactions of residents, the studies by Gottesman and Bourestom (1974) and Voelkl (1989) suggest that little time is spent with other

Table 16.1 Challenge Skill Channels

Channel	Challenge	Skill	Percentage	Mean Subjective Experience
1	high	moderate	5.5	.6045
2	high	high	14.0	.4115
3	moderate	high	13.4	.4018
4	low	high	11.7	.2055
5	low	moderate	4.2	−.2418
6	low	low	37.1	−.2901
7	moderate	low	3.6	−1.0296
8	high	low	7.5	−.1331
missing			2.9	

NOTE: Mean scores are z-scores.

people. Research by Baltes and colleagues illuminates the potential difficulties associated with social interactions in the nursing home (Baltes, Kindermann, Reisenzein, & Schmid, 1987; Baltes & Reisenzein, 1986). Baltes has reported that residents displaying personal maintenance or constructive behaviors receive little social support. Residents who engage in dependent maintenance behavior receive the greatest amount of support from social partners. It seems possible that residents may learn to seek out the social rewards associated with dependent behaviors rather than the intrinsic rewards associated with more autonomous activities.

Flow experiences. Based on Csikszentmihalyi's model of optimal experiences (i.e., flow), Voelkl (1990) examined the ESM data of 12 older adults residing in nursing homes to discover whether flow experiences occurred in daily life. A basic premise of the flow model is that, when perceived challenges and skills are high and equivalent, an individual will experience flow or positive subjective experiences. Of the 307 reported experiences, 37.1% were found to contain low challenges and low skills (see Table 16.1). High frequencies were also found in the channels containing high skill and varying levels of challenge. Subjective experience was found to be significantly related to the independent variable of challenge/skill ratio. The highest level of subjective experience was reported in relation to high-challenge/moderate-skill experiences, whereas the lowest level of subjective experience was reported in moderate-challenge/low-skill experiences (see Table 16.1).

The type of activity was also significantly related to challenge/skill channel (Voelkl, 1990). Residents reported a high frequency of low-challenge/low-skill experiences when engaged in self-care activities. When residents were engaged in passive activities, nearly one half of their experiences fell within the low-challenge/low-skill channel. Other types of activities (i.e., eating, watching television, and independent activities) were distributed among a number of different challenge-skill ratios. The findings of this exploratory study suggest that a relationship may exist among residents' activity involvement, perceptions of challenge and skill, and subjective experience.

Explanatory Studies

Recently, several studies have been designed to examine the interactions between resident characteristics, the institutional environment, and residents' activity (Lemke & Moos, 1989; Timko & Moos, 1991; Voelkl & Mathieu, 1992). For example, Voelkl and Mathieu (1992) used ESM data from 17 residents to examine the relationship of depression status to frequency of activity participation and accompanying affect. They found that frequency of activity involvement significantly varied in relation to depression status. The nondepressed subjects reported spending more time in self-care and passive activities and less time watching television in comparison with depressed subjects. The level of affect across type of activity was also significantly lower among subjects identified as depressed in comparison with subjects identified as nondepressed.

In another study, Lemke and Moos (1989) found that older adults with high-level functional abilities participated less in facility organized activities and at a greater rate in informal and community activities. They also noted that "residents with high functioning are more likely to participate in facility activities in settings with high autonomy, whereas more impaired individuals are more likely to participate if they are in a setting that has moderate or low autonomy but is high on staff richness, services, and rapport" (p. S146). These findings highlight the importance of incorporating measures of residents' competence level and the environment to understand the activity of residents.

Intervention Studies

A number of researchers have implemented interventions in nursing home environments to examine whether activities can be used to enhance residents' perceptions of control and well-being (Banziger & Roush, 1983; Langer & Rodin, 1976; Schulz, 1976; Shary & Iso-Ahola, 1989). For example, several studies were designed to enhance control by providing residents' choices regarding activity involvement and opportunities to independently care for an object such as a bird feeder or plant (Banziger & Roush, 1983; Langer & Rodin, 1976). These studies found that the experimental groups provided with an opportunity to experience control displayed higher levels of interpersonal activity, physical activity, and life satisfaction than the control groups.

Other investigations have found that the provision of refreshments and activity resources enhance residents' socialization (Gillespie, McLellan, & McGuire, 1984; Quattrochi-Tubin & Jason, 1980). Even though the results are promising in terms of increasing socialization, the findings of a study by Carstensen and Erickson (1986) reported that, when the content of the social interactions was examined, the majority were nonsensical and unreciprocated.

Riddick and Keller (1991) provide a comprehensive review of studies designed to measure the effectiveness of activity interventions. The studies reviewed, as well as several others cited in this section, do not specifically examine interventions designed to enhance involvement in any specific type of activity, such as independent pursuits or recreation. Rather, the studies focus on the effects of activity on variables such as well-being, physical health, and social behavior. Many questions remain regarding the effectiveness of interventions in enhancing activity, the meaningfulness of enhanced activity to residents, and the effect of increased activity levels on quality of life measures.

Summary

The studies reviewed provide a preliminary understanding of the activity of nursing home residents. The descriptive studies provide insights into residents' engagement in daily activities. The findings suggest that a good portion of residents' days are spent in no observable activity and in self-care (Gottesman & Bourestom, 1974; Voelkl, 1989). The explanatory studies assisted in further illuminating understanding of residents' activity behavior by including variables representing competence level and/or environmental factors (Lemke & Moos, 1989; Voelkl & Mathieu, 1992).

The intervention studies indicate that changes in the environment may positively affect the socialization and well-being of residents. These findings are promising as it appears that environments have the potential to be altered to enhance residents' activity and facilitate "proactivity" (Lawton, 1990). Many questions remain, however, as to the quality of the increased behavior (Carstensen & Erickson, 1986), the outcomes related specifically to type and frequency of activity involvement, differential effects of interventions in relation to resident characteristics (Carstensen & Erickson, 1986; Ellis & Yessick, 1989), and the long-term effects of the interventions (Rodin & Langer, 1977; Shary & Iso-Ahola, 1989). While the studies reviewed are informative, it should be kept in mind that they only provide us with an elementary understanding of residents' activity. One of the limitations of the studies reviewed is inconsistency in the conceptualization of activity and the instruments used to measure activity, making it difficult to compare findings and indicating the complexity of fully understanding the activity of residents of nursing homes. Another limitation is the lack of studies including variables pertaining to environmental factors (i.e., staffing patterns, physical layout of the facility) and residents' competence (e.g., functional abilities, mental status). Finally, the findings of the reviewed studies provide little insight into the occurrence of removal and flow activities or how these types of activities may relate to overall well-being among residents.

Future Directions

A number of issues related to nursing home residents and facilities have not been addressed in the research pertaining specifically to activity. To enhance our knowledge of residents' activity, future studies need to address several (a) individual characteristics and (b) environmental factors.

Individual characteristics. Given the incidence of dementia among residents of nursing homes (National Center for Health Statistics, 1989), it seems important to include this factor in future studies addressing activity. The level of orientation or the diagnosis of dementia was mentioned in only a few of the studies reviewed (e.g., Gottesman & Bourestom, 1974).

The complexity of understanding the activity patterns among residents with dementia and the difficulty of planning appropriate interventions is compounded by the recent findings that there is a high prevalence of depression among older adults with dementia and that the observable symptoms of depression may vary with the stage of dementia (Pearson, Teri, Reifler, & Raskind, 1989; Reifler, Larson, Teri, & Poulsen, 1986). Teri and Logsdon (1991) have suggested that interventions include the development of individualized pleasant activity schedules for residents. Scholars are also focusing on the design of the environment to foster optimal daily activity among older adults with dementia (Lawton, 1989).

Environmental factors: Activity programs. The Omnibus Budget Reconciliation Act of 1987 outlines requirements for nursing homes that are aimed at enhancing the quality of care (U.S. Congress, 1987). One is specifically focused on activity programs, requiring that "an on-going program, directed by a qualified professional, of activities designed to meet the interests and the physical, mental, and psychosocial well-being of each resident" (U.S. Congress, 1987, pp. 1330-1163) be conducted in each facility.

Activity professionals commonly believe that activity programs are an important component of the psychosocial services offered in nursing homes (MacNeil & Teague, 1987; Teaff, 1985). Activities may have the potential to foster flow experiences in residents' daily lives (Voelkl & Birkel, 1988) and to assist residents in maintaining important aspects of self-identity (Atchley, 1989; Davis & Teaff, 1980). Previously, a number of studies using the provision of activity opportunities to enhance residents' perceptions of control and well-being were cited (Langer & Rodin, 1976; Shary & Iso-Ahola, 1989). Several studies have also been conducted to examine the impact of specific activity interventions. These include reminiscence (Rattenbury & Stones, 1989), humor (see Chapter 12), and family interventions (Weiss & Thurn, 1990).

Studies examining the effectiveness of activity programs in maintaining or enhancing the well-being of residents are essential in light of current legislation (U.S. Congress, 1987). Stemming from the ecological model, studies should be designed to include variables measuring individual differences among residents and environmental factors in relation to the efficacy of activity interventions.

Another line of future research to be undertaken involves the efficacy of activity programs in facilitating flow experiences in residents' daily lives. Studies need to be designed to evaluate whether residents differ in response to activities engineered to facilitate flow experiences. Residents who perceive a high level of control or those with few physical limitations may respond more readily to flow activity interventions. Another consideration is whether environmental factors in the institution influence residents' response to flow activity interventions. For instance, do staffing patterns or residents' choices in their daily routine facilitate residents' responsiveness to activity programs? If research verifies that activity professionals can provide programs that increase residents' flow experiences in daily life, it will be important to examine the relationships between participation in flow activities and residents' daily activity patterns, well-being, and social interactions.

References

Atchley, R. C. (1989). A continuity theory of normal aging. *The Gerontologist, 29*(2), 183-190.

Baltes, M. M., Kindermann, T., Reisenzein, R., & Schmid, U. (1987). Further observational data on the behavioral and social world or institutions for the aged. *Psychology and Aging, 2*(4), 390-403.

Baltes, M. M., & Reisenzein, R. (1986). The social world in long term care institutions: Psychosocial control toward dependence. In M. M. Baltes & P. Baltes (Eds.), *The psychology of control and aging* (pp. 315-343). Hillsdale, NJ: Lawrence Erlbaum.

Banziger, G., & Roush, S. (1983). Nursing homes for the birds: A control relevant intervention with bird feeders. *The Gerontologist, 23*(5), 527-531.

Carp, F. (1987). Environment and aging. In D. Stokols & I. Altman (Eds.), *Handbook of environmental psychology* (pp. 329-360). New York: John Wiley.

Carstensen, L. L., & Erickson, R. J. (1986). Enhancing the social environments of elderly nursing home residents: Are high rates of interaction enough? *Journal of Applied Behavior Analysis, 19*(4), 349-355.

Csikszentmihalyi, M. (1975). *Beyond boredom and anxiety.* San Francisco: Jossey-Bass.

Csikszentmihalyi, M. (1982). Toward a psychology of optimal experience. (L. Wheeler, Ed.), *Review of Personality and Social Psychology, 3*, 13-36.

Csikszentmihalyi, M. (1988). The flow experience and its significance for human psychology. In M. Csikszentmihalyi & I. Csikszentmihalyi (Eds.), *Optimal experience: Psychological studies of flow in consciousness.* New York: Cambridge University Press.

Csikszentmihalyi, M. (1990). *Flow: The psychology of optimal experience.* New York: Harper & Row.

Davis, N. B., & Teaff, J. D. (1980). Facilitating role continuity of the elderly through recreation programming. *Therapeutic Recreation Journal, 14*(2), 32-36.

Ellis, G. D., & Yessick, T. (1989). Toward person by situation research in therapeutic recreation. *Therapeutic Recreation Journal, 23*(1), 24-35.

Gillespie, K., McLellan, R. W., & McGuire, F. M. (1984). The effect of refreshments on attendance at recreation activities for nursing home residents. *Therapeutic Recreation Journal, 18*(3), 25-29.

Goffman, I. (1961). *Asylums.* New York: Anchor.

Gottesman, L., & Bourestom, N. (1974). Why nursing homes do what they do. *The Gerontologist, 14,* 501-506.

Gubrium, J. (1974). On multiple realities in a nursing home. In J. Gubrium (Ed.), *Late life: Communities and environmental policy* (pp. 61-98). Springfield, IL: Charles C Thomas.

Hing, E. (1987). Use of nursing homes by the elderly: Preliminary data from the 1985 National Nursing Home Survey. In *Advance data from Vital and Health Statistics* (Vol. 135). Washington, DC: Government Printing Office.

Hyer, L., & Blazer, D. G. (1982). Depression in long-term care facilities. In D. G. Blazer (Ed.), *Depression in later life* (pp. 268-295). St. Louis, MO: C. V. Mosby.

Iso-Ahola, S. (1980). *The social psychology of leisure and recreation.* Dubuque, IA: William C. Brown.

Kahana, E. (1982). A congruence model of person-environment interaction. In M. P. Lawton, P. G. Windley, & T. O. Byerts (Eds.), *Aging and the environment: Theoretical approaches* (pp. 97-121). New York: Springer.

Langer, E. J., & Rodin, J. (1976). The effects of choice and enhanced personal responsibility for the aged: A field experiment in an institutional setting. *Journal of Personality and Social Psychology, 34*(2), 191-198.

Lawton, M. P. (1985). Activities and leisure. *Annual Review of Gerontology and Geriatrics, 5,* 127-164.

Lawton, M. P. (1989). Environmental approaches to research and treatment of Alzheimer's disease. In E. Light & B. D. Lebowitz (Eds.), *Alzheimer's disease treatment and family stress: Directions for research* (pp. 340-362; U.S. Department of Health and Human Services, DHHS Pub. No. 89-1567). Washington, DC: Government Printing Office.

Lawton, M. P. (1990). Residential environment and self-directedness among older people. *American Psychologist, 45*(5), 638-640.

Lawton, M. P., & Nahemow, L. (1973). Ecology and the aging process. In C. Eisdorfer & M. P. Lawton (Eds.), *Psychology of adult development and aging* (pp. 657-668). Washington, DC: American Psychological Association.

Lemke, S., & Moos, R. H. (1989). Personal and environmental determinants of activity involvement among elderly residents of congregate facilities. *Journal of Gerontology, 44*(4), S139-S148.

Lewinsohn, P. M. (1976). Activity schedules in the treatment of depression. In C. E. Thoreson & J. Krumboltz (Eds.), *Counseling methods* (pp. 74-83). New York: Holt, Rinehart & Winston.

MacNeil, R., & Teague, M. (1987). *Leisure and aging: Vitality in later life.* Englewood Cliffs, NJ: Prentice-Hall.

Moos, R. H., & Lemke, S. (1985). Specialized living environments for older people. In J. E. Birren & K. W. Schaie (Eds.), *Handbook of the psychology of aging* (pp. 864-889). New York: Van Nostrand Reinhold.

National Center for Health Statistics. (1989). *The National Nursing Home Survey: 1985 summary for the United States* (DHHS Publication No. [PHS] 89-1758). Hyattsville, MD: Author.

Pearson, J. L., Teri, L., Reifler, B. V., & Raskind, M. A. (1989). Functional status and cognitive impairment in Alzheimer's patients with and without depression. *Journal of the American Geriatrics Society, 37*, 1117-1121.

Quattrochi-Tubin, S., & Jason, L. A. (1980). Enhancing social interaction and activity among the elderly through stimulus control. *Journal of Applied Behavior Analysis, 13*, 159-169.

Rattenbury, C., & Stones, M. J. (1989). A controlled evaluation of reminiscence and current topics discussion groups in a nursing home context. *The Gerontologist, 29*(6), 768-778.

Reifler, B. V., Larson, E., Teri, L., & Poulsen, M. (1986). Dementia of the Alzheimer's type and depression. *Journal of the American Geriatrics Society, 34*, 855-859.

Riddick, C., & Keller, J. (1991). The benefits of therapeutic recreation in gerontology. In C. P. Coyle, W. B. Kinney, B. Riley, & J. W. Shank (Eds.), *Benefits of therapeutic recreation: A consensus view* (pp. 151-204). Philadelphia: Temple University Press.

Rodin, J., & Langer, E. (1977). Long-term effects of a control-relevant intervention with the institutionalized aged. *Journal of Personality and Social Psychology, 35*(2), 897-902.

Rovner, B., Kafonek, S., Filipp, L., Lucas, M. J., & Folstein, M. (1986). Prevalence of mental illness in a community nursing home. *American Journal of Psychiatry, 143*(11), 1446-1449.

Schulz, R. (1976). Effects of control and predictability on the physical and psychological well-being of the institutionalized aged. *Journal of Personality and Social Psychology, 33*, 563-573.

Shary, J. M., & Iso-Ahola, S. E. (1989). Effects of a control-relevant intervention on nursing home residents' perceived competence and self esteem. *Therapeutic Recreation Journal, 23*(1), 7-16.

Sommer, R., & Osmond, H. (1960-1961). Symptoms of institutional care. *Social Problems, 8*(3), 254-263.

Teaff, J. (1985). *Leisure services with the elderly.* St. Louis: Times Mirror/Mosby.

Teri, L., & Logsdon, R. G. (1991). Identifying pleasant activities for Alzheimer's disease patients: The Pleasant Events Schedule-AD. *The Gerontologist, 31*(1), 124-127.

Timko, C., & Moos, R. H. (1991). A typology of social climates in group residential facilities for older people. *Journal of Gerontology, 46*(3), S160-S169.

U.S. Congress. (1987). *Omnibus Budget Reconciliation Act of 1987* (100th Congress, 1st Session, Public Law 100-203). Washington, DC: Government Printing Office.

Voelkl, J. E. (1989). *The daily experiences of older adults residing in institutional environments.* Unpublished doctoral dissertation, Pennsylvania State University.

Voelkl, J. E. (1990). The challenge skill ratio of daily experiences among older adults residing in nursing homes. *Therapeutic Recreation Journal, 24*(2), 7-17.

Voelkl, J. E., & Birkel, R. C. (1988). Application of the experience sampling method to assess clients' daily experiences. *Therapeutic Recreation Journal, 24*(3), 23-33.

Voelkl, J. E., & Mathieu, M. A. (1992). *Differences between depressed and non-depressed residents of nursing homes on measures of daily activity involvement and affect.* Unpublished manuscript, University of Illinois, Urbana-Champaign.

Weiss, C. R., & Thurn, J. M. (1990). Perceived effects of a training program to enhance family members' ability to facilitate reminiscing with older disoriented residents. *Therapeutic Recreation Journal, 24*(1), 18-31.

17

The Life Course of Activities and Retirement Communities

GORDON F. STREIB

Activities and roles have been studied in life cycle and life course terms by a number of researchers (Cutler & Hendricks, 1990; Gordon & Gaitz, 1976; Kelly, 1974, 1977, 1983; Kelly, Steinkamp, & Kelly, 1986). In studying the activities of individuals as well as groups, a naturalistic classification of stages includes infancy, childhood, maturity, late adulthood, and old age. The use of stages and cycles has also been employed in the study of families, organizations, economies, and communities. Retirement communities and their stages have been the focus of research by social scientists at the University of Florida (La Greca, Streib, & Folts, 1985). In this chapter, I describe and analyze the activities of postretirement individuals in relation to the stages of the retirement communities in which they live.

Retirement Communities

Retirement communities have been described as "American Originals" (Hunt, Feldt, Marans, Pastalan, & Vakolo, 1984). There are many aspects of retirement communities that make them a uniquely American

AUTHOR'S NOTE: I appreciate the comments and suggestions by W. Edward Folts on an earlier version of this chapter.

type of residential environment. The origins of retirement communities can be traced back to a desire of some older persons to live in a warmer climate with other people of similar age and stage of life. The availability of fairly large tracts of land in Sunbelt states made it possible to create *de novo* communities that were attractive to retirees. In recent decades, many retirement communities have been established in northern states, such as New Jersey and Pennsylvania, because some older adults preferred to remain in familiar surroundings. The mobility of older Americans, the willingness to relocate, and the desire to own a home in a special age-segregated environment was also integral to the social movement that encompassed the acceptance and extraordinary growth of retirement communities. The term *retirement community* includes a wide range of physical characteristics, organization, class level, and amenities. Hunt et al. (1984) present a descriptive typology with six classifications: retirement new towns, retirement villages, retirement subdivisions, retirement residences, and continuing care retirement communities. Researchers at the University of Florida (La Greca et al., 1985) focused specifically on the life stages of retirement communities and the issues of autonomy and decision making. They divided these retirement communities into two broad types: those in which the residents owned their homes and rented the land upon which the homes were located and those in which residents owned both the homes and the land. The Florida researchers studied communities described as leisure-oriented retirement communities (Folts, Streib, & Logan, 1993) in which only social and recreational services were provided.

Descriptive Tools for Studying Activities

How does one describe the changes that occur in individuals and in retirement communities with the passage of time? Are there orderly sequences that one can observe? How can one describe these sequences? Critics of a developmental approach—whether of individuals or of societies—have pointed out there is a tendency to see stages as rigid and linear phases. Another criticism is that the passage of time may seem to create a strong directionality that results in unilineal sequences.

My approach is to employ the stages of the life course as descriptive tools that help us to discern some measure of order in an otherwise very complex set of events and processes. Aging is a time-bound process with considerable variability both for individuals and for retirement communities. Using the concept of a developmental course to study activities provides a first step in attempting to link the functioning older person to particular settings. This chapter offers a tentative beginning toward a more precise understanding of how older individuals, who are undergoing physical changes in late life, carry out a complex variety of activities in one type of sociocultural environment—the leisure-oriented retirement community.

Retirement Communities and Their Stages

The researchers at the University of Florida developed stages so as to study autonomy and decision making in retirement communities. This chapter transforms this stage approach to the studying of activities. Table 17.1 presents a picture of stages that have been developed for many retirement communities. It is difficult, given our limited knowledge, to pinpoint exactly how long a stage may be. I offer the table as a preliminary scheme for understanding the variable temporal element of each stage. For example, the planning and development stages may be rather short, and in other cases these stages may take an extended period of years. The development may be hampered by complications related to zoning, the provision of water and sewer services, the location of roads, and a variety of environmental considerations, not to mention the complex issues related to financing a project. Similarly, marketing may be carried out rather quickly or may involve a long and detailed sales campaign. Early retirement communities, such as those launched in the 1960s, were often started with little attention to marketing. The high levels of demand required little marketing effort. In recent years, because of competition, developers have typically paid more attention to all phases of development, including marketing. Today it is typical for a retirement community to be built in phases. A new section will not be offered for sale until almost all the homes in the preceding one have been sold.

One of the primary factors is whether a retirement community has land on which to expand. In some instances—such as the case study described later in this chapter—a community can reach its mature stage within a few short years. Further expansion can be blocked by the lack of land or available resources. In other cases, the original developers acquired such large tracts of land that expansion has been continuing for over 30 years. In these communities one area is in its mature stage while at the same time other areas within the same community are just being developed.

Table 17.1 Retirement Communities and Their Life Stages

	Life Stages		*Activities*
Stage 1: Establishment	Marketing Initial sales Residents move in		Erection of clubhouse and provision of facilities for recreational activities, sports social programs
Stage 2: Transitions	From developer to new owner	To resident ownership and self- government	Activities added or dropped according to residents' wishes Maintenance and preservation of facilities for marketing to new residents
Stage 3: Maturation	Maintain physical facilities Emergence of new issues and problems Discussion and decision about adding supporting care facilities Replacement of old timers by newcomers		Aging in place of first residents Efforts to secure new leadership for arrival of new cohorts: creation of "newcomer" clubs and "good-neighbor" groups Volunteer support groups

The maturity stage of a retirement community may have a variety of outcomes. For example, one of the earliest planned communities was a subdivision within a small Florida city (Hunt et al., 1984). After about 15 years, the community gradually lost its character as a retirement community because it was a desirable place to live and younger families moved in. Now, another 10 years later, apartment units that are age restricted to older adults have been constructed on the fringe of this retirement subdivision.

In another case, a community that started out for lower-middle-class residents has gradually expanded over a period of 30 years. The original community had a very small community building and all activities had to be organized by the residents themselves because the developer was trying to keep resident costs low for persons of modest income. As each new section has been added, the level of affluence has increased. The latest development is a large, expensive subdivision with an 18-hole golf course and an elaborate clubhouse. Demand for retirement communities with upscale facilities has dramatically changed the character of what began as simply a low-cost place to live.

Life Stages and the Individual

Biologists have generally viewed aging in terms of declines and losses. This perspective has met with strong opposition from social scientists who place emphasis upon the social definition of aging. Social scientists emphasized the need to conceptualize old age in more active terms. Hence the emergence of "activity theory" in contrast to "disengagement theory." (Writers on both sides of the activity continuum acknowledged that it was both inaccurate and pretentious to refer to either of these perspectives as theories.) Table 17.2 illustrates a life stage approach to individuals and their activities. Some caveats are necessary. The table is a descriptive tool designed to help order complex events and processes. Further, it is important to emphasize that, just as the early stages of life are marked by considerable differential development of physical, mental, and social capability, so too the later phases of life have different rates of decline. Dannefer and Sell (1988) have provided an overview of aging and the life course and suggest that there is considerable heterogeneity.

A theoretical orientation that focuses upon the aging individual in relation to time is the much maligned disengagement theory (Cumming & Henry, 1961). Although the critics of disengagement theory offer pertinent and penetrating criticism of the paradigm, there is a heuristic truth in the basic idea underlying disengagement. The original statement, however, was perhaps an oversimplification of the complex aging process.

A modification of disengagement was stated in *Retirement in American Society* (Streib & Schneider, 1971), where we employed the concept of *differential disengagement* by which we meant that disengagement occurs at different rates and in different amounts for the various roles in a person's role set. In other words, disengagement operates unevenly in pace, in role demands, and in the accompanying activities. Differential disengagement is a useful way to see activities over the life course because persons take on and drop activities as they move through life. The pace may be gradual, and in some cases change may be imperceptible. In other persons there may be sudden and dramatic shifts in activities and roles. Differential disengagement is also compatible with the study of how retirement communities provide a benign setting for older persons to become involved in new and perhaps different activities. As they age in place, they tend to shift the emphases of their

Table 17.2 Community Residents and Their Retirement Stages

Age	Work Status	Physical Condition	Activity
55-64	Working or early retirement	High physical function	Active adulthood Participation in many activities of choice, such as sports, clubs, travel Some assume leadership roles
65-74	Normal retirement—"young old"	Medical problems may start to limit activities for some: arthritis, coronary, and respiratory difficulty	Continuation of activities of choice Some persons start the shift from strenuous to spectator or sedentary activities and may phase out leadership and self-governance roles
75-84	Late retirement—"old"	Physical problems continue to appear: decline in sight, hearing, and locomotion may cause limitations	Lower energy levels Decline in physical levels hampering driving, travel Participation in more sedentary activities Continue social activities
85+	"The old old"	Often considerable reduction in physical capacity	Reduction in most physical activities Continue some social activities in and outside home as visiting, card playing, films, attending functions in clubhouse

activities from those that are more demanding of physical, psychological, and social resources to those that are less challenging. Most persons adapt and disengage differentially as they tend to "decline." Some gerontologists stress the importance of activities in general, especially physical activities (Palmore, 1979). The link between participation in activities, multiple role involvement, and "successful aging" among women has been reported by Moen, Dempster-McClain, and Williams (1992). Some 55-year-olds have limited physical, psychological, and social resources, while some 85-year-olds have extraordinary amounts of physical and social energy that can be drawn upon when needed to adapt to environmental demands.

Social Roles in Retirement Communities: A Typology

There is obvious self-selection among persons who choose to live in retirement communities (Longino, 1982, 1990). In general, persons who seek age-segregated living environments tend to have higher levels of health, educational attainment, and economic status. Moreover, retirement communities provide opportunities for the expression of social roles, some of which were enacted in earlier settings. A valuable empirical typology of residents in three retirement communities has been provided by Nancy Osgood (1982, 1983). She observed six types of social roles: organizers, joiners, socializers, recreationalists, humanitarians, and retirees. The organizers devote considerable time and effort to create projects and activities that meet the needs and interests of fellow residents, which include clubs, organizations, projects, classes, study groups, and musicals. These persons constitute about 10% to 15% of the population. The joiners are the persons who join the clubs and organizations and participate in the activities developed and promoted by the organizers. Socializers are friendly persons who enjoy spending their time socializing with friends and neighbors on an informal basis. Humanitarians are the residents who devote a great deal of time helping others in the community, particularly those who are older or sicker. In some communities there is a mutual support group, and in other cases a humanitarian will "adopt" an older resident of a neighborhood as her or his personal responsibility.

Recreationalists are residents whose primary roles and interests are in leisure activities: golf, swimming, card playing, and so on. A considerable proportion of residents who move to leisure-oriented retirement communities do so because they offer easily available and economical leisure activities. The persons that Osgood identifies as retirees are those who have retreated from their available social roles. These residents are usually older or sicker and have withdrawn into the retiree role because of failing health. Many may originally have been organizers, joiners, or recreationalists but after 10 or 12 years in a community are very willing to have younger and healthier residents organize and participate in the myriad activities found in typical retirement communities. There is a life course of social roles with some organizers "burning out."

About 10% to 15% of a community are organizers and about the same are retirees. The majority of the residents are found in the other four types or a combination of types. As residents age in place, the number of retirees tends to increase as the health of residents tends to decline.

If a community does not continue to attract new, younger residents, the organizers may become a smaller proportion and the number of activities and organizations that are available may begin to decline. This is an important example of the way in which the stages of the community intersect and interface with the activities of the residents and the social roles in which they are engaged.

Importance of Activities in Retirement Communities

A significant consideration in the decision of many persons to relocate to retirement communities is the opportunity to occupy themselves in a variety of pleasant and rewarding leisure activities. Many of these activities are those in which persons have engaged earlier in life. Moving to a retirement community, however, also enhances the possibility of exploring new interests and hobbies in a new place.

In general, the activities are carried out in a neighborly and friendly setting in close proximity to residents' homes. It is not necessary to cope with traffic, night driving, parking problems, or fear of crime when one merely has to walk to the clubhouse or drive a golf cart a few blocks to participate in a wide range of activities. The location of a golf course, swimming pool, or tennis court only minutes away is a definite advantage to those who wish to use the sports facilities. All of these factors, plus the security of an age-dense community and the support of new neighbors and friends, has resulted in strong positive evaluations of retirement communities by those who move there (Bultena & Wood, 1969; Osgood, 1982).

The focus on activities in this type of housing environment is particularly important for attracting new residents. The provision of recreational activities such as a golf course may be the prime stimulus for the relocation. Then, too, for people who are free of work responsibilities, there is a desire to fill time with enjoyable activities and to find new self-identities. In typical retirement communities, neighbors do not particularly care about former fame or fortune. More important is an individual's new identity, which is defined by the activities he or she chooses, his or her skill in carrying them out, and his or her sociability and personality. Thus activities become extremely important in socializing individuals to their new environment and facilitating their adaptation to relocation. Activities are more than merely a way to entertain oneself or "fill time," for they set the stage for new friendships and associations. When people have moved to a new location, they have a larger range of choices of new things to try—to develop new competencies and to shed activities they are tired of pursuing. Kelly (1982, p. 288) states: "One issue that remains to be investigated is whether leisure identities can replace those related to other roles in providing meaning and integration to life in the third age. Can leisure become, for some, a central set of role identities around which life can be reoriented?" The answer to this question would be positive for many people who choose to relocate to retirement communities. The rich array of activities offered serves to provide a "new life," and the residents are overwhelmingly positive about their third age.

Another reason activities are important is that the developers of retirement communities emphasize them in their marketing effort to attract new residents. The emphasis on happy, active, engaged older people is highlighted in brochures, videos, and other promotional materials and is usually quite successful in dispelling any notion that the retirement community is a place for old folks to sit in a rocking chair and mark time before moving into a nursing home. Newly retired people are especially attracted by an environment in which everyone is busy pursing interesting individual interests.

Types of Activities Available

The variety of activities offered in many communities is truly staggering. Following is an abbreviated list of the over 100 activities scheduled in one community of only 2,000 residents: (a) *social:* potluck suppers, dances, movies, bridge, pinochle, travel club, state clubs, singles club; (b) *sports:* golf, swimming, tennis, fishing, boating, shuffleboard, and various tournaments; (c) *crafts and hobbies:* ceramics, lapidary, quilting, fabric painting, stamp collecting; (d) *arts, music, and dramatics:* art classes, chamber music, choral groups, concerts; (e) *educational:* lectures, foreign language classes, study clubs, investment groups, book review, library committee; (f) *health and fitness:* exercise groups, hiking clubs, yoga, Weight Watchers; (g) *self-governance:* various committees and activities related to operating the community; (h) *religious:* Bible study, weekly religious services, hymn singing; and (i) *service and philanthropic:* good neighbor groups, money-raising activities for various good causes, either within the community or for broader charitable needs outside the retirement community.

The wide range of activities offered facilitates differential disengagement and differential engagement. There are choices for any stage of old age and any level of energy. Newly retired persons might choose tennis lessons, line dancing, swimming, and the travel club. After 10 years their choices might shift to card playing, hymn singing, movie night, and potluck suppers. But the availability of such a wide range of activities, and their proximity to one's own home, means that it is easier to remain socially engaged in a retirement community than in a "normal" age-integrated neighborhood.

It is significant that in this community, first studied by the Florida researchers 10 years ago, there are now on the activities program an Alzheimer support group, Meals-on-Wheels, Good Neighbors Club Assistance, and Home Health Services. This is a clear example of stages in the adaptation of the community to the phenomenon referred to as "aging in place."

Governance as an Activity

Self-government is an activity more often occurring in retirement communities than in age-integrated neighborhoods. Self-governance occupies considerable time and effort in some retirement communities. In others it consists primarily of organizing the recreational activities, sports competitions, hobby groups, and social functions. Sometimes there is a recreation director, who either organizes the events or serves to stimulate, coordinate, and assist the members in these efforts. In other communities an elected board of directors is responsible for the day-to-day operation of the community. Typically, the board hires a manager, but they may monitor his or her performance closely and be consulted on all decisions.

In studying decision making in 36 retirement communities, Streib, Folts, and La Greca (1985) reported that most residents appear content to allow other residents, or in the case of the larger communities a competent and benign management, to make most of the decisions. When a crisis does develop, however, a substantial number of the residents can be mobilized, and they can act more quickly than the residents of nonretirement communities. While residents typically express a desire not to be constantly involved in self-government, they also want to be involved in decision making if a situation arises that threatens their interests or enjoyment of the life-style. Most residents seek stability, and many are threatened by change. For a small number of residents, however, power and decision making represent a challenging continuation of earlier roles and involve the use of skills and competencies honed and used during their working years. Another interesting finding was that, in all 36 communities studied, a few persons are perceived as instigators of discord. Some were able to create considerable mischief by outwardly opposing the existing power structure and by attempting to escalate trivial issues into "causes" that severely hampered efforts at self-government.

As a community ages and its residents age in place, a shortage of persons able and willing to fill leadership positions emerges. Persons who have leadership skills and are willing to serve eventually feel they have taken "their turn." Thus an inflow of new residents is usually needed for self-government to function effectively.

Activities and the Life Cycle

The way in which life cycle stages of individuals may be studied is found in the large-scale research carried out by Gordon and Gaitz (1976). More than 1,400 persons from age 20 to 94 were interviewed at length about their leisure activities. The study population was divided into five life cycle stages corresponding to five age categories. Seventeen specific leisure activities were the focus of inquiry. These activities were ordered according to increasing "expressive involvement intensity." On the low end were activities such as resting and solitude. Visiting or entertaining were considered to be of medium intensity, and activities such as highly competitive games and sports were regarded as high in intensity. This operationalization of "activity" emphasizes the fact that activities are not only active, busy endeavors but also include passive, informal, and unorganized ways of spending time.

The researchers reported a negative relationship between stage of the life cycle and leisure participation. The youngest group (20 to 29) were about 4 times as likely to report a high level of leisure participation as the oldest (persons over 75 years of age). One of the important conclusions reported by these researchers was that "what may be given up in the later years are the strenuous and outside-the-home activities, not the moderate-intensity and home centered forms of sociability and media-based symbolic interaction" (Gordon & Gaitz, 1976, p. 327).

Bultena and Wood (1970) examined the activities of older persons with a median age of 71 in four retirement communities. These writers point out that retirement communities are attractive because they provide opportunities for an active social life in a facilitative setting. The residents stated they did not particularly desire "productive" activities and were more interested in recreational and leisure activities. While some residents (over a fourth) said that retired persons should take part in public service or community activities, over half (53%) said that older persons had earned their leisure and should not feel obligated to become involved in such groups. The researchers pointed out that retirement communities facilitate the transition to a retirement role because of the presence of age peers with a compatible orientation toward leisure.

Activities and Social Class

Retirement communities provide some unique reflections on the class structure of the larger society. There is considerable variation in the economic levels, the value of homes, and the facilities and amenities offered by retirement communities. The communities may vary from small manufactured homes (the small "trailer parks" are an example) to luxury communities with homes valued at many hundreds of thousands of dollars. The affluence of the residents is also reflected in the kinds of recreational facilities that are available. A community designed for those with modest resources typically will have a small recreation hall for community meetings, dances, shared meals, and opportunities for playing cards and bingo. Holidays, birthdays, and other special occasions are held in the community hall, the center of social life for the residents. When I asked the manager of a small manufactured homes community (about 150 homes) what the residents enjoyed most, he answered, "The residents like to eat. We have a lot of potluck suppers."

On the high-income end of the economic scale, one may observe expensive facilities that include a large clubhouse, one or more golf courses, tennis courts, and one or more large swimming pools. The presence of a swimming pool is one indicator of the difference between modest retirement communities and their more luxurious counterparts. The lowest income communities will not have a pool. As one ascends the economic scale, the pools become larger and fancier with more elaborate support facilities such as extensive lounging space to sit and enjoy the sunshine, a whirlpool bath, exercise machines, and changing facilities. It is interesting that the percentage of swimmers in a retirement community tends to be quite small. There may be exercise groups and ballet swimmers, but they involve only a small number of persons.

Members like having a pool available, however, even if they don't use it often. A pool may be a mark of the social status of the community—an example of Veblen's conspicuous consumption as well as a recreational or exercise locale. Some retirement communities have great interest in shuffleboard activities with leagues, competitions, and elaborate play-off scheduling.

Class manifests itself in relation to activities in interesting ways. In smaller and lower income communities, the streets and yards are quite busy, particularly in the morning, as members meet, talk, and exchange greetings, discussing the activities of the community and events in the larger world. As one ascends the community class hierarchy, the amount of visible street activity tends to decline. Part of the street-level social activity relates to the sheer size of a community, the size of the lots, and the distance between the dwelling units. In smaller communities the residents live closer together and the opportunity for friendly, neighborly relations is enhanced in comparison with those where residents live farther apart. In higher income communities there is perhaps a greater amount of travel throughout the United States or abroad, which also reduces the amount of neighborly contact. People are away from home for longer periods of time.

While there may be a considerable range of income and affluence within a higher income community, activities do not appear to be class related. Two aspects of the paradox of class are at work here. Generally speaking, the residents of retirement communities are not primarily interested in who one *was* or what one earned. The community tends to have some leveling effect. This results in people not revealing their class position. Class is not relevant in the realm of activities, for when people play golf or bridge, the important factor is the person's ability as a golfer or a bridge player.

Case Study of a Retirement Community

Over a period of years social scientists at the University of Florida have studied retirement communities in various parts of the United States (Streib et al., 1985). The communities encompassed a variety of residential environments, including small "trailer parks" with a minimum of amenities and luxurious villages with expensive homes and a variety of services and facilities. Among the communities studied was Pine Woods in central Florida. This community has been selected for analysis here because it has been studied over the longest period of time, and observations are available permitting us to explore changes and adaptations of both the community and the residents over a time period of approximately 13 years.

Pine Woods is an adult manufactured home community located on 300 acres. The land was purchased by a large insurance company in 1972 and construction was begun in that year. The location was selected because of the mild climate, rolling hills, woodlands and waterways, and isolation from the congested coastal areas of Florida. The president of the company that developed Pine Woods had studied many retirement communities in the United States and, as a result, placed special emphasis on recreational facilities and activities programs. It was planned that the community would remain relatively small to maximize a friendly, village atmosphere. Hence the current size of 1,147 dwelling units was reached in 1981 and the number has remained stable. By 1981 there were about 2,000 residents, and in the past decade there has been a slight decline in population due to the death of some residents and relocation by others. In February 1992 there were 47 vacant dwelling units for sale.

When the community was started in 1972, a $2 million multipurpose clubhouse was built. The clubhouse has a 1,600-seat auditorium and is the hub of social and recreational life. There are covered shuffleboard courts, a swimming pool, saunas and whirlpools, and a marina with access to a lake for boating and fishing. There are also a number of small meeting rooms for various kinds of activities. Pine Woods has a closed circuit television system, cable television, paved and lighted streets, 24-hour security, a security gate that is manned, and a call-button system linking the residence with the security system, enabling the residents to summon emergency assistance.

There is a Pine Woods Residents Cooperative Association whose board of directors is responsible for overall policy and financial arrangements. A general manager has day-to-day responsibility for the community and for the paid staff. The rich array of activities includes a paid recreation director who helps organize activities, recruit leaders for the various clubs, print a newsletter, and respond to residents' suggestions.

One important source of information about the community is the detailed research conducted by Hall in 1988. In this study the report of residents' activities was based upon 24-hour diaries in which residents recorded what they were doing each hour for a randomly selected day of the week chosen by the researcher.

The randomly selected study population was divided between those residents classified as "early settlers" and "newcomers." Early settlers had lived in the village for 9 or more years, and the newcomers for 4 years or less. The population was also subdivided into those who were currently married and those who were not. The married newcomers category consisted of 12 males and 16 females and the early settlers consisted of 17 males and 13 females. The median age of the newcomers was 68 years and the early settlers 75. The age difference is of substantive significance in relation to participation in activities.

Activities were classified into four categories: (a) at home, (b) non-club related within the village, (c) club related within the village, and (d) outside the village. Each of the above locational categories had as many as 10 additional specific categories. For example, non-club related within the village included visiting unrelated residents, walking/biking, attending weekly scheduled clubhouse activities, playing cards in other residents' homes, and providing help to sick residents. Types of activities outside the village included visiting/shopping for consumer goods, attending religious services, obtaining medical care for self/spouse, and community volunteer work.

Comparing married newcomers and married early settlers in terms of how 24 hours were spent, the two categories reported similar time budgets. When the two types of residents are compared for the four locational categories stated above, there are no significant differences. The amount of time reported for the activities was surprisingly similar as was the rank order of activities. The only significant difference among the 35 coded categories was "obtaining medical care for self/spouse," which was the most commonly reported activity for married early settlers. These findings indicate that people in a retirement community continue to participate in activities even when their health declines.

Interpretive Conclusion

In this chapter we have shown how the life course of individuals in retirement communities is associated with the stages in the life course of the community itself. Retirement communities pass through similar stages as they are established, marketed, and mature. Full maturity in retirement communities, like the maturity of the individuals who live in them, is complex and variegated.

For an analysis of individuals, there is the continuing and growing issue of how the residents adapt to their changes in health status and to life-style changes that may result from decline in functional ability (sight, hearing, energy levels, and so on).

At the community level, the decline in activity levels of substantial numbers of residents is associated with change in the mature community. The mature community faces three emergent issues: The first is the aging of the residents and a gradual shift in their needs and interests. The second is the possible decline in the physical appearance and functioning of the community itself. Finally, the emergent issue is the change in the social structure as a result of the aging of the residents and the decreasing numbers of persons who exercise leadership roles in the great variety of programs and activities.

Closely related to changes in the residents and in the community is change in the activities. The pattern described cross-sectionally over the life course by Gordon and Gaitz (1976) is found in retirement communities. Although the stage of the life course involves only older ages, there is a gradual shift from active to more sedentary activities. The case study discussed here shows that, as a community and its residents age in place, there is an increase in the need for health care and more time is spent in obtaining health and medical care outside the community. As health-related activities increase, residents become spectators rather than participants in leisure activities requiring physical ability. Put simply, the swimming pool may be empty but persons will continue to enjoy bingo, potluck suppers, or performances.

One of the more interesting questions is this: What "causes" the decline in activities requiring physical abilities? Some social scientists (McPherson, 1992) argue that the withdrawal from social activities results from changes in the social environment and not from declining capacities. A social environmental explanation for the decline in activities is inadequate, however, because the changes in the social environment have their origin in the declining capacities of the residents (Lawton, 1980).

Once the retirement community reaches the mature stage of development, there is a kind of balance attained. Residents, leaders, managers, and developers all hope (and often expect) that the mature equilibrium will somehow maintain itself over long periods of time. As residents age in place and as their functional ability and interests change, however, the retirement community must necessarily change with them. One mitigating factor is, of course, that some older or sicker residents leave and are replaced by younger retirees. (It should be emphasized that this discussion concerns leisure-oriented, residential retirement communities and does not apply to continuing care retirement communities, which have a built-in set of residential accommodations to handle the aging in place phenomenon by providing increasing levels of support and nursing care.)

In conclusion, retirement communities and their residents exhibit parallel processes that can be described in terms of stages and that relate to both the life course of the individual and that of the community. As the aging individual generally declines in functional ability, there is an accompanying differential disengagement in activities, especially those requiring a large expenditure of energy. The differential disengagement of the individual is associated with changes and adaptations in the social organization of the community. As the older cohorts gradually withdraw, replacement residents must be recruited to maintain the community's social viability and also assume leadership positions in the clubs and activities. Because a retirement community has clearly delimited boundaries, the physical appearance of both public and private buildings and spaces must be maintained for the community to remain attractive for replacement cohorts. Thus, by simultaneously focusing on both the community and the residents, we gain a deeper understanding of the social psychology of individuals and the structure of the community where they live. A sociological analysis of this kind enables us to explore the activities and roles of individuals in an environmental context.

References

Bultena, G., & Wood, V. (1969). The American retirement community: Bane or blessing? *Journal of Gerontology, 24,* 209-217.

Bultena, G., & Wood, V. (1970). Leisure orientation and recreational activities of retirement community residents. *Journal of Leisure Research, 2,* 3-15.

Cumming, E., & Henry, W. (1961). *Growing old: The process of disengagement.* New York: Basic Books.

Cutler, S. J., & Hendricks, J. (1990). Leisure and time use across the life course. In R. H. Binstock & L. K. George (Eds.), *Handbook of aging and the social sciences* (pp. 169-185). San Diego, CA: Academic Press.

Dannefer, D., & Sell, R. R. (1988). Age structure, the life course and "aged heterogeneity": Prospects for research and theory. *Comprehensive Gerontology, 2,* 1-10.

Folts, W. E., Streib, G. F., & Logan, K. M. (1993). Leisure oriented retirement communities. In W. E. Folts & D. E. Yeatts (Eds.), *Housing and the aging population: Options for the new century.* New York: Garland.

Gordon, C., & Gaitz, C. M. (1976). Leisure and lives: Personal expressivity across the life span. In R. H. Binstock & E. Shanas (Eds.), *Handbook of aging and the social sciences* (pp. 310-341). New York: Van Nostrand Reinhold.

Hall, S. R. (1988). *The graying and transformation of a retirement village.* Unpublished doctoral dissertation, University of Florida, Graduate School, Gainesville.

Hunt, M. E., Feldt, A. G., Marans, R. W., Pastalan, L. A., & Vakolo, K. L. (1984). *Retirement communities: An American original.* New York: Haworth.

Kelly, J. R. (1974). Socialization toward leisure: A developmental approach. *Journal of Leisure Research, 6,* 181-193.

Kelly, J. R. (1977). Leisure socialization: Replication and extension. *Journal of Leisure Research, 9,* 121-132.

Kelly, J. R. (1982). Leisure in later life: Roles and identities. In N. J. Osgood (Ed.), *Life after work: Retirement, leisure, recreation and the elderly* (pp. 268-292). New York: Praeger.

Kelly, J. R. (1983). *Leisure identities and interactions.* London: George Allen & Unwin.

Kelly, J. R., Steinkamp, M. W., & Kelly, J. R. (1986). Later life leisure: How they play in Peoria. *The Gerontologist, 26,* 531-537.

La Greca, A. J., Streib, G. F., & Folts, W. E. (1985). Retirement communities and their life stages. *Journal of Gerontology, 40,* 211-218.

Lawton, M. P. (1980). Environmental change: The older person as initiator and responder. In N. Datan & N. Lohmann (Eds.), *Transitions of aging* (pp. 171-193). New York: Academic Press.

Longino, C. F., Jr. (1982). American retirement communities and residential relocation. In A. M. Warnes (Ed.), *Geographical perspective on the elderly* (pp. 239-262). London: John Wiley.

Longino, C. F., Jr. (1990). Geographical distribution and migration. In R. H. Binstock & L. K. George (Eds.), *Handbook of aging and the social sciences* (pp. 45-63). San Diego, CA: Academic Press.

McPherson, M. (1992, April 10). *Age segregation in voluntary associations: Some considerations.* Paper presented at the annual meeting of the Southern Sociological Society, New Orleans.

Moen, P., Dempster-McClain, D., & Williams, R. M., Jr. (1992). Successful aging: A life-course perspective on women's multiple roles and health. *American Journal of Sociology, 97,* 1612-1638.

Osgood, N. J. (1982). *Senior settlers: Social integration in retirement communities.* New York: Praeger.

Osgood, N. J. (1983). Patterns of aging in retirement communities: Typology of residents. *Journal of Applied Gerontology, 2,* 28-43.

Palmore, E. (1979). Predictors of successful aging. *The Gerontologist, 16,* 441-446.

Streib, G. F., Folts, W. E., & La Greca, A. J. (1985). Autonomy, power, and decision-making in thirty-six retirement communities. *The Gerontologist, 25,* 403-409.

Streib, G. F., & Schneider, C. J. (1971). *Retirement in American society.* Ithaca, NY: Cornell University Press.

Problems and Prospects: Looking to the Future

Every chapter in this edited volume suggests voids and inadequacies in our knowledge as well as a developing basis of understanding of activity and aging. Some of the chapters focused on the viability of later life and the potential of activity engagement to enhance quality of life significantly. Others pointed more to limitations experienced by older persons as well as the potential remaining for them. As in all of current social gerontology, there is an implicit or explicit demarcation of the "active old" from the "frail." It is not surprising that with a focus on activity the predominant focus is on the vast majority with the ability to be active.

That does not mean that there are no problems. Individuals have problems of both decremental and traumatic loss related to health, primary relationships, and economic resources. The life course tends to be more of a zigzag than linear for most persons. All such losses affect the personal and social resources for meaningful activity. There are also policy problems related to housing, health care, retirement incomes, and all the other elements of life that are made available or denied through some combination of market and public provisions. All such resources are differentially allocated not only by age but also according to a number of factors that may coalesce for some into severe deprivation.

Yet, in some ways, age seems to be becoming increasingly irrelevant. We no longer find age to be a valid index of personal abilities or resources. More and more, we are discovering that the diversity of older lives is really no less than for those earlier in the life course. Activity is one focus that demonstrates the variety. Older people do all kinds of things in all kinds of ways. Further, some kinds of activity with the right associates may provide just what we may have thought was lacking—excitement, involvement, challenge, a sense of competence and worth, and profound satisfaction.

Of course, we need to know more about such activity and how it fits into the overall life patterns of older adults. We need to know more about contexts, provisions, barriers, facilitating factors, access, adaptation, and organization. We need to know more about continuities and discontinuities in identities, values, risk, relationships, and inhibitions. We need to know more about what actually occurs in the process of activity, both in the discrete experience and in the longer term line of action. We need to know about contexts and resources as well as about attitudes and emotions. And we need to know more about the isolated, the withdrawn, and those who have been denied access and opportunity. There is no shortage of researchable issues to be addressed by a variety of approaches, strategies, and methods.

If this volume serves no other purpose well, it is my hope that it will demonstrate the importance of the topic. Activity is not peripheral to older lives. It is central to the quality of later life. It is central to the lives of older persons who continue to make their way along the journey of life seeking to find satisfaction and create meaning.

Index*

*Does not include references to their own work by authors within the chapter they have written

About the Authors

Rebecca G. Adams is Associate Professor in the Department of Sociology at the University of North Carolina at Greensboro. She received the Ph.D. from the University of Chicago, with an emphasis on the sociology of aging. Her major research interest is friendship patterns, especially as they are affected by geographic separation and by cultural and structural context. She is coeditor of *Older Adult Friendship: Structure and Process* (Sage, 1989), coauthor of *Adult Friendship* (Sage, 1992), and author of numerous articles. She is currently conducting two friendships studies: One is an examination of the cultural conventions and structural conditions affecting the development of friendships among members of a nonterritorial music subculture. The other, funded by the AARP Andrus Foundation, is a study of older adult friendship patterns and mental health.

Robert C. Atchley is Director of the Scripps Gerontology Center and Distinguished Professor of Gerontology at Miami University, Oxford, Ohio. He has published more than 50 articles and book chapters and 15 books on various aspects of aging. His recent research is on the impact of retirement on marital satisfaction, the flow of economic resources to support long-term care, the impact of aging and frailty on self-concept, and the relation between wisdom and spiritual development. His text *Social Forces and Aging* is in its sixth edition.

Rosangela K. Boyd is Assistant Professor in the Temple University Department of Sport and Leisure Studies, where she teaches in the undergraduate and graduate programs in therapeutic recreation and leisure behavior. She holds a Ph.D. from Clemson University, where she acted as the program director of several research studies focusing on older adults. One such study was the Humor Project, conducted with nursing homes throughout South and North Carolina. At Temple University, she has continued to expand her research agenda with projects in the areas of minority aging and older adults with developmental disabilities. She has conducted workshops, presented at conferences, and contributed to the professional literature regularly in the areas of aging, humor, and cultural diversity.

David A. Chiriboga is Professor and Chair of the Department of Graduate Studies, School of Allied Health Sciences, University of Texas Medical Branch, Galveston. He holds joint appointments with the Department of Preventive Medicine and Community Health and the Department of Internal Medicine at the same campus. In 1972 he obtained a Ph.D. in human development from the University of Chicago. With the Department of Psychiatry, University of California, San Francisco, from 1969 to 1983, he served on the faculty of doctoral programs in human development and health psychology. From 1984 through 1886 he was Visiting Professor at the UC Davis Department of Community Health and from 1985 to 1986 also served as Director, Gerontology Education and Training Center, San Jose State University. A member of the editorial boards of *Generations*, the *Journal of Aging and Health*, and the *Journal of Allied Health*, in 1988-1989 he also served as president of Division 20 (Adulthood and Aging), the American Psychological Association. He currently is Associate Director of the Center on Aging for his campus and is Co-Director with the federally funded Texas Consortium of Geriatric Education Centers.

Stephen J. Cutler is Professor of Sociology, the Bishop Robert F. Joyce Distinguished University Professor of Gerontology, and Director of the Center for the Study of Aging at the University of Vermont. He received his Ph.D. in sociology from the University of Michigan. He is currently editor of the *Journal of Gerontology: Social Sciences*. His principal gerontological research interests include transportation, voluntary association participation, sociopolitical attitude change, caregiving, everyday cognitive problems, and ethical issues. He is coauthor of *Middle Start: An Experiment in the Educational Enrichment of Young Adolescents* (Cambridge University Press) and coeditor of *Major Social Problems: A Multidisciplinary View* (Free Press).

Nicholas L. Danigelis is Professor of Sociology at the University of Vermont. He received his Ph.D. in sociology from Indiana University. His principal gerontological research interests include voluntary association participation, the meaning and consequences of productive activity, sociopolitical attitude change, alternative housing arrangements, and social theory. He is coauthor of the recently published *No Place Like Home: Intergenerational Homesharing Through Social Exchange* (Columbia University Press).

Valeria J. Freysinger is currently Assistant Professor at Miami University, Oxford, Ohio, in the Department of Physical Education, Health and Sport Studies. She received her master's and doctoral degrees from the University of Wisconsin—Madison. Her graduate work was in the areas of leisure studies and life span development/gerontology. Her research and teaching interests include leisure as a context of psychosocial development, leisure and well-being, and gender, race, and class as mediators of the experience of development and leisure. She has coauthored a book titled *A Leisure of One's Own: A Feminist Perspective on Women's Leisure* and is the author of a number of journal articles and presentations on women and leisure and leisure, development, and well-being. Currently she is working with several existing longitudinal data bases to examine continuity and change in the meaning and role of leisure across the life course.

Sharon R. Kaufman (Ph.D.) is a medical anthropologist whose areas of expertise include development in late life, adaption to illness, changing values in health care, and the culture of medicine. She has conducted research with well and chronically ill elderly populations and with physicians. She is committed to both theoretical and applied aspects of research in the areas of health care delivery, gerontology, and anthropology. She is affiliated with the Institute for Health and Aging, the

Department of Social and Behavioral Sciences, and the Medical Anthropology Program at the University of California, San Francisco.

John R. Kelly is Professor in the Department of Leisure Studies of the University of Illinois at Urbana-Champaign. He has also been Professor in the Institute for Research on Human Development and Director of the Office of Gerontology. His Ph.D. in sociology is from the University of Oregon, and he holds master's degrees from Yale University, the University of Southern California, and the University of Oregon. Among his eight published books are *Peoria Winter: Styles and Resources in Later Life* (Lexington), *Freedom to Be: A New Sociology of Leisure* (Macmillan), *The Sociology of Leisure* with G. Godbey (Venture), and *Leisure* (2nd edition, Prentice-Hall). His research has focused on the changing role contexts and meanings of leisure through the life course and has been supported by the National Institute on Aging and other agencies.

Douglas A. Kleiber is Professor and Department Head of Recreation and Leisure Studies and a member of the Gerontology Faculty at the University of Georgia. He received a Ph.D. in educational psychology from the University of Texas at Austin in 1972 and has held academic positions at Cornell University, St. Cloud State University, and the University of Illinois before moving to Georgia in 1989. His research has dealt with motivation and expressive behavior over the life span and the impact of leisure behavior on developmental processes, particularly identity formation. He was a coeditor of two volumes in the JAI Advances in Motivation and Achievement series, one titled *Motivation and Adulthood*, and is Associate Editor for the *Journal of Leisure Research*. He was recently elected President of the Academy of Leisure Sciences.

M. Powell Lawton has been Director of Research at the Philadelphia Geriatric Center for the past 29 years as well as an Adjunct Professor of Human Development at the Pennsylvania State University and Professor of Psychiatry, Medical College of Pennsylvania. His doctorate, in clinical psychology, is from Columbia University. He has done research in the environmental psychology of later life, in assessment of the aged, the psychological well-being of older people, caregiving stress, affect and aging, and evaluative studies of programs for the aged and for the mentally ill. He is the author of *Environment and Aging* and

Planning and Managing Housing for the Elderly as well as being editor of other books. He is past President of the Gerontological Society of America, was the first editor of the American Psychological Association's journal *Psychology and Aging*, and is Editor-in-Chief of the *Annual Review of Gerontology and Geriatrics*.

Helena Znaniecka Lopata was born in Poland and came to the United States during World War II. She obtained her Ph.D. from the University of Chicago in 1956 and is Professor of Sociology and Director of the Center for the Comparative Study of Social Roles at Loyola University of Chicago. Her research focuses on social roles of American women, the Polish American community, friendship, and occupations and professions, using a symbolic interactionist perspective. Publications focused on widowhood include *Widowhood in an American City, Women as Widows: Support Systems, Widows and Dependent Wives: From Social Problem to Federal Policy*, and a forthcoming *Widowhood: Myths and Realities*. She has also edited *Widows: The Middle East, Asia and the Pacific* (Volume 1) and *Widows: North America* (Volume 2).

Roger C. Mannell is a psychologist and Professor of Recreation and Leisure Studies. He was Director of the Centre of Leisure Studies at Acadia University in Nova Scotia before joining the University of Waterloo, where he now serves as Chair of the Department of Recreation and Leisure Studies. He has been a regular contributor to the social psychological study of leisure. In particular, he has been interested in social and personality factors that influence the nature of optimal experiences and in turn how these experiences affect the quality of life. Currently his research includes studying the impact of the changing relationship between work and leisure on the life-styles of Canadian workers. He was the 1989 recipient of the Allen V. Sapora Research Award and in 1991 was awarded the Theodore and Franklin Roosevelt Research Excellence Award by the National Recreation and Parks Association.

Edward McAuley is a Professor in the Department of Kinesiology, University of Illinois at Urbana-Champaign. He received his Ph.D. from the University of Iowa and has held faculty positions at the University of Oregon, Kansas State University, and the University of Iowa College of Medicine. His research area of interest is exercise and health psychology with particular emphasis on physical activity as it relates to self-referent thought, affect, and aging. This focus has been approached from a primarily social cognitive perspective employing attributional and self-efficacy models of behavior and emotion. He has published over 50 scholarly articles in refereed journals in psychology, exercise science, and medicine. He is associate editor of the *Journal of Sport and Exercise Psychology* and a member of the editorial board of the *Journal of Aging and Physical Activity*. A recipient of the Early Career Distinguished Scholar Award from the North American Society for the Psychology of Sport and Physical Activity (NASPSPA) and a 5-year First Independent and Transition Award (FIRST) from the National Institute on Aging, he is currently engaged in a multidisciplinary line of research that focuses on biopsychological processes in the maintenance of exercise behavior in aging populations.

Francis A. McGuire is Professor of Therapeutic Recreation in the Department of Parks, Recreation and Tourism Management at Clemson University. He received his doctorate in leisure studies at the University of Illinois. He is the author of numerous book chapters and journal articles in the gerontology field. His current research interest is the role of humor in improving the quality of life of residents of long-term care facilities. He is also pursuing research topics related to leisure behavior across the life span and intergenerational programming.

Nancy J. Osgood is Associate Professor of Gerontology and Sociology at Virginia Commonwealth University/Medical College of Virginia in Richmond, Virginia. She obtained her Ph.D. in Sociology and Certificate in Gerontology in 1979 from Syracuse University. She has authored and coauthored numerous articles, book chapters, and books on the topics of recreation, leisure, and aging, creative arts and aging, elderly suicide, and geriatric alcoholism. Her most recent book is titled *Suicide in Later Life: Heeding the Warning Signs* (Lexington). In 1990 she was the guest editor for a special edition of the *Journal of Applied Gerontology* devoted to creative arts and aging. She is the editor of *Life After Work: Retirement, Leisure, Recreation, and the Elderly* (Praeger, 1982), coauthor with M. Jean Keller of *Dynamic Leisure Programming with Older Adults* (NRPA, 1987), and coauthor with Patch Clark of *Seniors on Stage: Applied Theatre Techniques with the Elderly* (Praeger, 1985).

Robert C. Pierce attended Stanford University, the University of Illinois, and the University of Hawaii. He has done research in intellectual functioning in geriatric mental illness, human development, ethnic identity among immigrants and their children and grandchildren, and the dimensionality of satisfactions in leisure and work. He has recently retired from the Center for AIDS Prevention Studies, Prevention Sciences Group, University of California, San Francisco.

Robert O. Ray is currently Professor and Chair of Recreation Resources Management in the Department of Continuing and Vocational Education at the University of Wisconsin—Madison. He received his Ph.D. from the University of Maryland, College Park, in 1975 and joined the University of Wisconsin faculty in 1976. His research and teaching focus on the development of leisure behaviors across the life span and, in particular, how leisure life-styles develop, change, and are maintained throughout life's many phases. He is further interested in how human service providers can be better informed on issues of human development through continuing professional education. His publications have appeared in the *Journal of Leisure Research, Therapeutic Recreation Journal, Gerontology and Geriatrics Education*, and *Adult Education Quarterly*, among others. He has served as consultant and adviser to agencies such as nursing homes, senior centers, the Veteran's Administration, and other human service-oriented organizations.

Carol Cutler Riddick is Associate Professor in the School of Education and Human Services at Gallaudet University. She received a Ph.D. from Pennsylvania State University majoring in recreation with an emphasis in gerontology and health planning, an M.S. from Florida State in health planning, and a B.A. from Florida State in sociology. She has held a postdoctorate in Applied Gerontology (funded by the Gerontological Society of America and the Administration on Aging) and is an elected Fellow of the Behavioral and Social Sciences section of the GSA. Topics for her scholarly writings have included older women's mental health, evaluative research of leisure interventions designed to improve the health of older persons, caregiving, and gerontological education.

Gordon F. Streib served as Graduate Research Professor in the Department of Sociology at the University of Florida, Gainesville, for 14 years. He is Professor Emeritus and is also Joint Professor, Department of Community Health and Family Medicine, College of Medicine, University of Florida. He is Professor Emeritus of Cornell University, where he taught for 26 years. He received his Ph.D. from Columbia University and has been a Fulbright Professor to Denmark and to Ireland. He has published on many topics in sociology and gerontology: housing, retirement, social stratification, intergenerational relations, and cross-cultural studies of aging. In 1989 he received the Robert W. Kleemeier Award from the Gerontological Society of America for outstanding research in gerontology. In 1991 he received the Doctor of Letters, *honoris causa*, from the University of Waterloo, Ontario, Canada.

Walter Tokarski is University Professor for Leisure Studies at the German Sports University, Director of the Institute for Leisure Studies, and Director of the Institute for European Sports Studies. He is also Honorary Professor for Leisure Studies of the University of Ghent/Belgium, member of a variety of leisure and recreation organizations, a board member of the European Leisure and Recreation Association (ELRA), as well as Director of the Board of the World Leisure and Recreation Association (WLRA) and member of the Research Board "Sociology of Leisure" of the International Sociological Association (ISA). He is the author of numerous articles and books on leisure, sports, life-styles, and aging.

Judith E. Voelkl is the Associate Director for Education and Evaluation of the Geriatric Research, Education and Clinical Center in the VA Medical Center, Ann Arbor, Michigan. Previously she has held faculty positions at the University of Illinois and the University of Utah. She received her Ph.D. from the Pennsylvania State University. Her research interests include the daily experiences of older adults residing in nursing homes, optimal experiences among older adults, and the maintenance of one's leisure identity through the transitions of later life.